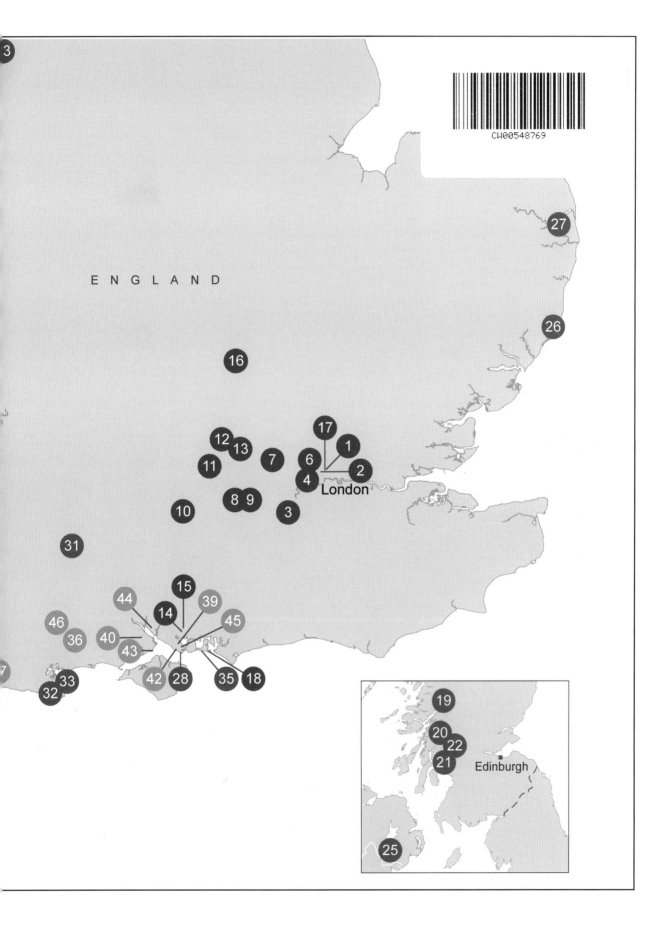

# D-Day UK

100 Locations in Britain

# D-Day UK
## 100 Locations in Britain

Simon Forty

Historic England

Published by Historic England, The Engine House, Fire Fly Avenue, Swindon SN2 2EH
www.HistoricEngland.org.uk

Historic England is a Government service championing England's heritage and giving expert,
constructive advice.

First published 2019

ISBN 978 1 84802 540 0

*British Library Cataloguing in Publication data*
A CIP catalogue record for this book is available from the British Library.

For more information about images from the Archive, contact Archives Services Team, Historic
England, The Engine House, Fire Fly Avenue, Swindon SN2 2EH; telephone (01793) 414600.

Brought to publication by Rachel Howard, Publishing, Historic England.

Typeset in Georgia Pro Light 9/11

Edited by Kathryn Glendenning
Indexed by Caroline Jones
Page layout by Eleanor Forty
Printed in the UK by Gomer Press

FRONT COVER: *see* p 159.
FRONTISPIECE: **Ready to cross the Channel,
these soldiers were part of an invasion that
put more than 150,000 men into Normandy
on 6 June.**
RIGHT: **Major warships at anchor in
Portsmouth Harbour – a key port for the
invasion. This aerial photograph was taken in
April 1946.**

# Contents

# Preface

In June 1944 Allied forces invaded France to liberate Europe and destroy Nazism. Immortalised in film and book, D-Day is, rightly, seen as a turning point in 20th-century history and opened a land campaign that finished less than a year later in the unconditional surrender of the enemy.

The speed, means and method of this victory have been discussed and debated ever since. Most of the discussion has concentrated on the landings and the battles that followed: the bravery of the soldiers, sailors and airmen; the effectiveness and personality of the commanders; the efficiency and abilities of the respective tactics, weapons and armies.

The locations are written indelibly in our memories: Omaha and Juno, Pegasus Bridge, Arromanches, Pointe du Hoc, Sainte-Mère-Église. Understandably, much of the military remembrance – the cemeteries and memorials – are on the French side of the Channel, as are most of the remnants of war – bunkers, vehicles, scarred buildings.

However, like the tip of an iceberg, the D-Day landings and the battle of Normandy – about two months' fighting from 6 June until the end of August – were the result of years of preparation that took place to a great extent in Britain. It was in Britain that the plans were developed, the logistics organised and the weapons prepared. It was in Britain that the soldiers boarded the ships to take them to France, from Britain that the air forces provided aerial cover and the armada set sail. It was in Britain that large numbers of young American, Canadian, Polish and French men and women spent so much time that they became part of the everyday life of the country. And it wasn't all work: the influx of that many young men and women – including more than 100,000 black troops – had a striking affect on Britain's social scene. After the war, 60,000 war brides left Britain for a future in North America. British and American culture hadn't become one entity, but it had certainly joined at the hip.

The first Americans arrived in Northern Ireland in January 1942 – although 'Special Observers' had been there since spring 1941. By May 1944 their ranks had swelled to around 750,000, a figure that doubled before 1944 was out. Some of these soldiers spent a short time in Britain before heading to the Mediterranean theatre; others spent as much as 20 months training for action.

This invasion – often dubbed the 'friendly invasion' – affected most people in Britain in one way or another. The Americans had to be housed and fed; they had to have places to train and trainers to tell them what to do. They had to have equipment and places to practise using it. The supplies for the battles to come had to be stored somewhere. The details of the invasion had to include secure locations for final preparation, places to board ships and receive final orders. And then there were the naval facilities, and those needed for the US Air Forces: airfields, runways, hangars. This was no mere temporary posting. This was the creation of an American infrastructure in a way that hadn't been done before. The rulebook had to be created.

Over the next two years the preparations for the invasion of France took form. It wasn't a linear progression: political considerations, fighting in Africa and the Mediterranean, the strength of the opposition – all these things interrupted progress until late 1943. From then on the countdown had begun and while the actual end date changed slightly, it wasn't a question of if, but when.

*D-Day UK*, published to mark the 75th anniversary of D-Day, chooses 100 locations in Britain to tell the story of how the invasion of France came about. It covers

During the Second World War, Liverpool was a significant port, to which many convoys headed – as is remembered by this stone. It was also the location of the Commander-in-Chief, Western Approaches, and No 15 Group, RAF – two of the major elements fighting the critical convoy battles in the Atlantic.

the practicalities of the planning process, the main people and the major organisations involved. It looks at the specialist training the troops needed and the major exercises; gives an insight into some of the logistical issues, covers the movement of troops from marshalling camp to embarkation – for delivery to France by landing craft or aircraft; examines the range of air assets over the battlefield, from fighters through medium bombers to the heavies; and touches on the naval side of the landings, particularly the minesweepers and landing craft.

Choosing 100 locations proved to be a difficult job and I'm sure that many would disagree with my choices: too much air and not enough naval; too much in Hampshire and not enough in Essex; too much American and not enough British or Canadian; too much that can't be seen today. In the end it's impossible to please everyone.

Finally, I decided early on not to include museums in the listings: there could have been 100 of them alone, including the Imperial War Museum, National Army Museum, RAC Tank Museum, D-Day Museum, Royal Signals Museum, Fleet Air Arm Museum, the excellent Portsmouth naval museums (the Submarine Museum, Naval Museum and Explosion Museum of Naval Firepower), Bletchley Park, Cobbaton Combat Collection, museums at airfields (Tangmere, Shoreham, Dunkeswell), up to and including the Commando display in the Fort William Museum. All these and many more have material related to D-Day and are worth a visit.

### Acknowledgements

This book is a team effort. It wouldn't have happened without the help of four people: Dr Patrick Hook, my brother Jonathan, my wife Sandra, who all contributed materially, writing entries, helping with illustrations and providing information; and Leo Marriott for his wonderful aerial photography and continued help with photographs and advice.

I'd also like to thank the following for their help: Michelle Barratt and Casey Wheeler at Gosport Council; Glenn Booker; Hilary Cummings at St Paul's School; Richard T Drew (check out his marvellous website www.Atlantikwall.co.uk); Bob Hunt (www.portsdown-tunnels.org.uk); Dr C S Knighton, Principal Assistant Keeper of Archives at Clifton College; Robert Liddiard;  David Moore (www.friendsofstokesbay. co.uk and www.victorianforts.co.uk); Geoff Slee (www.combinedops.com); David Sims; and David Thurlow (www.pillboxes-suffolk.webeden.co.uk).

I would also like to thank Wayne Cocroft, Rachel Howard, John Hudson, Sharon Soutar and Lucinda Walker from Historic England, Kathryn Glendenning and Caroline Jones, and my daughter Eleanor for the design.

Finally, thanks to Richard Wood for companionship on various visits to military locations, in particular one excellent weekend around the Portsmouth area: seeing it all by bike is the best way!

General George C Marshall, Army Chief of Staff 1939–45, oversaw a massive expansion of the US Army and Army Air Forces. He oversaw fighting on two fronts, in the Pacific and Europe, and played a great part not only in the ultimate victory but also in the rebuilding of Europe after the war. The Marshall Plan saw the United States assist European countries – in particular Great Britain – financially, primarily to bolster the defence against communism. Winston Churchill dubbed Marshall the 'architect of victory'; Harry S Truman said he was 'the greatest military man that this country has ever produced'; Franklin D Roosevelt wouldn't let him take on the command of the invasion of Normandy, telling him, 'I didn't feel I could sleep at ease if you were out of Washington.'

# Glossary and abbreviations

| | |
|---|---|
| 2TAF | Second Tactical Air Force |
| XIX TAC | XIX Tactical Air Command |
| AAA | anti-aircraft artillery |
| ACIU | Allied Central Interpretation Unit |
| ADGB | Air Defence of Great Britain |
| AEAF | Allied Expeditionary Air Force |
| AFHQ | Allied Force Headquarters |
| ALG | Advanced Landing Ground |
| ANCXF | Allied Naval Commander, Expeditionary Force = Admiral Bertram Ramsay |
| ASW | antisubmarine warfare |
| ATS | Auxiliary Territorial Service |
| AVRE | Armoured Vehicle Royal Engineers |
| Bn | Battalion |
| | 2/401st = 2nd Battalion 401st Regiment |
| | Bracketed numbers/letters after unit number eg 91st (L4) = tail codes of aircraft in that unit |
| Bty | Battery |
| C-i-C | Commander-in-Chief |
| CBTC | Commando Basic Training Centre |
| Cdo | Commando (a unit of commandos) |
| Co/Coy | Company (US/BR) |
| | C/326th = C Company, 326th Battalion/Regiment |
| COPP | Combined Operations Pilotage Parties, whose personnel were termed COPPists |
| COSSAC | Chief of Staff to the Supreme Allied Commander |
| CSS | Combined Signals School |
| CTC | Combined Training Centre, so No 1 = 1CTC; No 2 = 2CTC etc |
| D+1 | D-Day (6 June) + 1 = 7 June; D+2 = 8 June etc |
| DD | Duplex Drive; DD tanks were amphibious |
| DUC | Distinguished Unit Citation, an honour awarded by the US Army to units |
| DUKW | manufacturer's (GMC) code: D – Designed in 1942; U – Utility; K – All-wheel drive; W – Dual-tandem rear axles |
| DZ/LZ | Drop Zone/Landing Zone |
| Enlisted man | US term; British would use Other Rank |
| ETOUSA | European Theater of Operations US Army |
| FAA | Fleet Air Arm |
| FG | Fighter Group |
| Force O | The units attacking Omaha Beach; U = Utah, G = Gold, J = Juno, S = Sword Beaches |
| FUSAG | First US Army Group |
| GC&CS | Government Code and Cypher School |
| GIR | glider infantry regiment |
| GWR | Great Western Railway |
| H-Hour | The planned landing time on the Normandy beaches (H+20 = 20 minutes after the planned landing time) |

**General Eisenhower's letter to the troops before D-Day.**

| | |
|---|---|
| hard | A prepared (usually concrete) ramp allowing vehicles and personnel to embark a vessel with a ramp |
| Kriegsmarine | German Navy |
| LC/LS | Landing Craft/Landing Ships (for further LC/LS abbreviations and definitions *see* p 49) |
| Luftwaffe | German Air Force |
| Mulberry Harbours | Two artificial harbours taken to France (*see* pp 96–7) |
| NATUSA | North African Theater of Operations US Army |
| *Neptune* | The assault phase of Operation *Overlord* defined in the First (US) Army plan as 'to secure a lodgment area on the Continent from which further offensive operations can be developed'. Officially, *Neptune* finished on 3 July 1944 when the last of the Assault Force commanders withdrew from the assault area. |
| OTU | operational training unit |
| *Overlord* | Codename for the battle of Normandy, initiated by Operation *Neptune* |
| PATSU | patrol aircraft service unit |
| PIR | parachute infantry regiment |
| PLUTO | Pipe Line Under the Ocean |
| PoW | prisoner of war |
| QM | Quartermaster |
| RAAF | Royal Australian Air Force |
| RAF | Royal Air Force |
| RASC | Royal Army Service Corps |
| RCAF | Royal Canadian Air Force |
| RCEME | Royal Canadian Electrical and Mechanical Engineers |
| RCT | Regimental Combat Team |
| RE | Royal Engineers |
| Recon/Recce | Reconnaissance (US/BR) |
| REME | Royal Electrical and Mechanical Engineers |
| RN | Royal Navy |
| RNAS | Royal Naval Air Service – forerunner of the FAA |
| RNPS | Royal Naval Patrol Service |
| RNVR | Royal Naval Volunteer Reserve |
| RNZAF | Royal New Zealand Air Force |
| RSB | Railway Shop Battalion |
| RTR | Royal Tank Regiment |
| sea echelon | Airborne unit delivered by sea |
| SHAEF | Supreme Headquarters, Allied Expeditionary Force |
| Sqn | Squadron |
| TCC | Troop Carrier Command (US) |
| TCG | Troop Carrier Group |
| TCW | Troop Carrier Wing (US) |
| USAAF | United States Army Air Forces |
| USATC | US Army Transportation Corps |
| USN | US Navy |
| USSTAF | United States Strategic Air Forces |
| VADs | Voluntary Aid Detachments |
| VCS-7 | Navy observation squadron; *see* HMS *Daedalus* pp 182–3 |
| WAAF | Women's Auxiliary Air Force |
| WRNS | Women's Royal Naval Service |

# D-Day: An Introduction

This book assumes a certain level of knowledge about the invasion of Normandy. As a reminder, here is a brief chronology and some facts and figures that will help contextualise the events and locations discussed in this book.

**1939: 1 September** Germany invades Poland; this leads to the declaration of war on Germany by Britain and France two days later.
**30 December** The first Canadian troops arrive in Greenock, Scotland: more than 330,000 will train in England – most at Aldershot – and, as the largest Empire contingent ever to serve in Britain, Canadians are to defend Sussex and the south coast against attack.

**1940: 3 April** German invasion of Norway begins as German ships leave harbour.
**9 April** Germany invades Denmark.
**9/10 May** German troops enter Luxembourg, the Netherlands, Belgium and France.
**26 May–4 June** Rescue of nearly 340,000 Allied troops from Dunkirk.
**25 June** Fall of France (Armistice is signed on 22 June and takes effect on 25 June; Battle of Britain starts soon after).

**1941: 22 June** Start of Operation *Barbarossa* – Hitler's invasion of Russia.
**7 December** Japanese attack on Pearl Harbor.

Preparation for the invasion of Normandy saw US forces stationed in Britain's West Country, and British and Canadians in the east. Follow-up forces were similarly located: the Americans in Wales and the British in Essex. Both had to rendezvous off the Isle of Wight, negotiate channels swept free of mines and land on five sectors of Normandy.

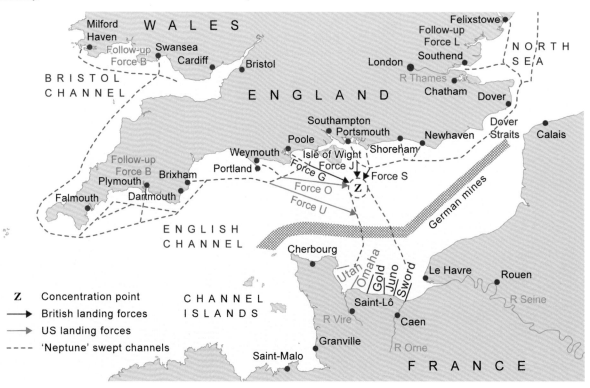

**11 December** Germany declares war on the United States.

**22 December** First Washington Conference – codenamed *Arcadia* – leads to 'Germany first' (the decision to give the battle against Hitler priority over that against Japan; this led to US bombers being sited on British airfields).

**1942: 26 January** The first US troops arrive in Britain as part of Operation *Bolero* – the build-up of US forces in Britain to strike against Germany, although that date is the subject of some controversy. The Americans want to invade as quickly as possible; the British are more concerned about the weight of the attack. The invasion was originally codenamed *Sledgehammer* and then *Roundup*; it became *Overlord*.

**19 August** The failure of Operation *Jubilee*, the mainly Canadian attack on Dieppe, strongly militated against an early invasion of Europe.

**23 October–11 November** The second battle of El Alamein sees the German/Italian army defeated by General Bernard Montgomery, commander of the Eighth (BR) Army; the Axis forces retreat back towards Tunisia.

**8–16 November** Operation *Torch* – the invasion of North Africa by British and American forces – hastens the end of the desert war. (Final surrender 13 May 1943.)

**1943: 12–25 May** Third Washington Conference, codenamed *Trident*, sets the date for the invasion of Normandy as May 1944.

**9 July** First moves in Operation *Husky*, the assault on Sicily.

**3–17 September** Allied invasion of Italy.

**December** Dwight D Eisenhower is nominated Supreme Commander of SHAEF (the Supreme Headquarters, Allied Expeditionary Force).

**1944: January** D-Day is put back to June to allow more time for landing craft construction.

Exercise *Duck*,* the first major US exercise, takes place. It is followed by *Duck II* and *III* in February, then *Fox* in March.

**22 April** Exercise *Tiger*, a major US D-Day rehearsal, starts. During this exercise German E-boats attack a convoy of eight LSTs (landing ships), sinking two.

**23 April–7 May** The major D-Day rehearsal, Exercise *Fabius*, takes place.

**15 May** Final briefing for D-Day landings held at St Paul's School, London.

**4 June** D-Day is postponed for a day by General Eisenhower because of the weather.

**6 June** 00:10 Pathfinders drop.

00:35 Capture of the bridges over the Canal de Caen and River Orne.

02:00 Bombers leave the UK to soften up the defences.

03:30 The assault units board their landing craft.

04:40 12th SS-Panzer Hitlerjugend and Panzer Lehr divisions ordered to the coast; order is rescinded pending Hitler's OK.

06:30 H-Hour for Utah and Omaha.

07:10 Rangers land on Pointe du Hoc.

07:25 H-Hour for Sword Beach.

07:25 H-Hour for Gold Beach.

07:35 H-Hour for Juno Beach Mike sector; 07:45 Nan sector.

* The dates for exercises are complicated. The decision to undertake an exercise leads to a period of planning. After this, there is movement to the exercise area, which, when it comes to amphibious operations, involves embarkation and a boat trip. After the exercise has taken place, there follows a return to camp, then a period of reporting, discussion and critiques. The dates given in this book for exercises generally refer to the main days of the exercise.

# 1 | Command and control

LEFT

**There's no doubt that Allied air superiority played a significant role in the success of D-Day and in the days that followed. From airfields in Britain, Allied medium bombers were able to pulverise the French transport infrastructure.**

The Allied invasion of Normandy was one of the largest and most complicated military operations ever seen. An assault on an enemy shore whose defenders had had four years to prepare against attack was never going to be easy. It required detailed planning and organisation of all three services and a comprehensive timetable that ensured the delivery of men and equipment to their designated locations on time, in the correct order and with suitable support. To make things more difficult the participants were multinational, all with slightly different agendas and motives. Quite simply, it was a recipe for disaster.

That it wasn't a disaster pays tribute not only to the prowess of the Allies' fighting forces but also to the planning, command decisions and control exerted by the Supreme Commander, Allied Forces Europe – General Dwight D Eisenhower – and his staff. They had to put up with bickering at national level – the debate as to when the invasion should take place raged for many months – and between the commanders in-theatre, particularly the air commanders. They had to bypass overtly nationalistic tendencies on both sides, achieve strategic and tactical consensus and then plan the attack in minute detail.

The United Kingdom is small and even in 1944 was relatively congested. This meant that the arrival of well over a million Americans, as well as large numbers of Canadians and other nationalities, led to housing difficulties and sparked social issues – but it also meant that lines of communication and supply were short. After

RIGHT

**General Eisenhower (Ike) takes up his position in Norfolk House, the location of Allied Force Headquarters (AFHQ), in January 1944.**

five years of war Britain was close to exhaustion, with service manpower issues, all the infrastructure problems caused by bombing and the adoption of a total war economy, and the shortages of raw materials and other commodities caused by German attacks on ship-borne imports – but it was still committed, unwaveringly, to the fight. The Allied planners were both helped and hindered by the proximity of Britain to the Continent, which meant shorter distances but also that the enemy was nearby, allowing opportunities for German aerial reconnaissance and attack which had to be taken into account at every step. Finally, Britain's size meant that it was harder for the Germans to infiltrate spies and agents: British intelligence had turned or compromised all such attempts and had won the intelligence war. They were able to supply the enemy with disinformation and mislead its High Command to so great an extent that Germans' belief in an invasion through the Pas de Calais continued on into July.

There's no doubt that the Allies had stolen a march on the Germans in the intelligence war. The Axis intelligence services had had their successes: the Italians' P Section of the Servizio Informazioni Militare, the military intelligence service, had been able to provide Generalfeldmarschall Erwin Rommel, when he was commanding the forces in North Africa, with detailed information of his enemy's plans thanks to their acquisition of the US *Black Code*, which was used to encode highly detailed reports about the state of the war, troop movements and equipment prepared by Colonel Fellers, military attaché to the US embassy in Egypt between January and

Stores, fuel and ammunition were
stockpiled around Britain ready for
D-Day. This is Newbury racecourse,
photographed on 6 July 1943.

June 1942. German radio intercept companies were able to pick up a great deal of information from the Allies' lax radio usage. German cryptanalysts were able to read British Naval codes up to 1943, but this pales into insignificance when compared to the *Ultra* and *Magic* decrypts (American breaking of Japanese diplomatic cypher) and the Double-Cross system (*see* p 36).

Information is all very well: it must also be used effectively. The key decision made by the Allies was the appointment of a man who could make the important decisions: General Eisenhower, who proved himself an able diplomat and leader – and would, of course, go on to show the same abilities as President of the United States. Eisenhower was not necessarily everybody's first choice: General George Marshall, President Roosevelt's Chief of Staff, was many people's suggestion. Roosevelt wanted Marshall in Washington and so Eisenhower got the job. The results speak for themselves. While his military strategies may not have pleased all of his subordinates, he got the job done, despite the personalities of his generals.

The decision to have General Bernard Montgomery, Admiral Bertram Ramsay and Air Chief Marshal Trafford Leigh-Mallory as the primary commanders of land, sea and air forces is, perhaps, more contentious – particularly when seen from a 21st-century perspective. It's easy to fall into the trap of looking at the wartime period with today's view. At that time, the United States was not the dominant political force it is today. It was on the way to becoming the world's dominant power, and certainly no one could match it economically and it didn't play second fiddle to anyone – but in the alliance between the United States and Britain, both sides had to compromise and remember who the real enemy was. Britain, with the power of its empire behind it, was still a force to be reckoned with.

The entries in this section examine the main organs of command: Eisenhower's HQ, those of his main subordinates and the HQs of the main air assets whose bombing in spring 1944 did so much to soften up the German defenders. It covers intelligence (both photographic and through deciphering German codes), the deception operation (*Fortitude*) and ends by looking at the clandestine COPPs (Combined Operations Pilotage Parties) who gathered so much physical intelligence on the target beaches and then marked the way for the opening assault.

General Charles de Gaulle made a nuisance of himself in London, pushing to ensure that his country's voice was heard. Grudgingly, it was, and de Gaulle became head of the Provisional Government of the French Republic in June 1944.

# 1 Eisenhower's office, 20 Grosvenor Square, London

**Grosvenor Square, in the affluent district of Mayfair, London, had a distinctly American accent during the Second World War, with the US embassy at No 1 and No 20 housing General Dwight D Eisenhower's office and the US Navy HQ. According to the American Ambassador John Gilbert Winant, other buildings on the square housed 'further military installations and offices occupied by the overflow from the Embassy itself' – to the extent that the square was dubbed 'Little America'.[2]**

On 24 June 1942 Eisenhower, as commanding general, took up the reins of the recently formed ETOUSA – European Theater of Operations US Army. His office was a single room in the corner of the first floor of No 20 Grosvenor Square and his eye was firmly set on an invasion of Europe – at that stage still known as *Roundup*. However, Rommel's successes in the North African desert led to the adoption of Operation *Torch* – the Allied landings in North Africa – and Eisenhower was chosen to be the Allied Commander-in-Chief. In February 1943 he took charge of the new North African Theater of Operations, which included Italy, and Lieutenant General Frank M Andrews took over ETOUSA.

　　In December 1944 Eisenhower was appointed Supreme Commander, Allied Expeditionary Forces and his mission was to oversee the invasion of France – Operation *Overlord*. The Combined Chiefs of Staff ordered him: 'You will enter the continent of Europe and in conjunction with other Allied Nations, undertake operations aimed at the heart of Germany and the destruction of her Armed Forces.'[3] Unsurprisingly, when Eisenhower arrived back in London from the Mediterranean in

Eisenhower in his office at No 20 Grosvenor Square, London.

The statue of Eisenhower (by Robert Lee Dean) in front of the second US embassy building, No 38 Grosvenor Square. The US embassy moved in 1960 from No 1 Grosvenor Square to No 38, a building designed by Eero Saarinen. This photograph shows the gilded aluminium eagle, sculpted by Theodore Roszak and with a 35ft wingspan, sitting on top of the embassy. Today, the US embassy is in Nine Elms, south of the Thames.

No 20 Grosvenor Square has been renovated to become apartments, since this wartime photograph was taken.

January 1944, he returned to his office in Grosvenor Square and to the command of ETOUSA, swapping jobs with General Jacob L Devers who took over Eisenhower's role as head of NATUSA (the North African Theater).

Eisenhower did not stay in Grosvenor Square for long, however. Convenient though the location was, Eisenhower found Mayfair too crowded and his staff too tempted by the nightlife. He quickly decided to leave central London, which led to the move to Camp Griffiss in Bushy Park, Teddington (*see* pp 8–10).

There are two memorials to Eisenhower in Grosvenor Square: a bronze statue sculpted by Robert Lee Dean and a plaque on the wall of the building that signifies the location of his headquarters. It reads: 'In this building were located the headquarters of General of the Army Dwight D Eisenhower, Commander in Chief Allied Force June–November 1942, Supreme Commander Allied Expeditionary Force January–March 1944.'

# 2 SHAEF, Norfolk House, 31 St James's Square, London

**The early planning for *Overlord* took place in Norfolk House – the location of Allied Force Headquarters (AFHQ), where Operation *Torch* had been planned – under the aegis of Lieutenant General Frederick Morgan, who was Chief of Staff to the Supreme Allied Commander (COSSAC).**

Appointed after the Casablanca Conference in January 1943, Morgan and his combined American and British staff had developed a plan that had been constrained both by the availability of equipment – such as landing craft, a very significant factor – and the logistical need to bring sufficient men and materiel together in Britain. They had to work, Morgan said, with 'a map which starts at one end with San Francisco and ends at the other end in Berlin'.[4]

When Eisenhower arrived at Norfolk House to take up his post as Supreme Allied Commander, the Supreme Headquarters, Allied Expeditionary Force (SHAEF) was established using many of the key personnel from AFHQ and COSSAC. Eisenhower brought in his own man – Lieutenant General Walter Bedell Smith – as Chief of Staff and Morgan became Smith's deputy.

There was, Stephen Ambrose notes in his biography of Eisenhower, 'a single-mindedness not present in *Torch*'.[5] Helped by the experience of three major amphibious landings, the COSSAC plan was dissected by Eisenhower's main lieutenants – including General Bernard Montgomery, who was appointed Allied land forces commander, and Allied air commander Air Chief Marshal Trafford Leigh-Mallory – and discussed at a meeting on 21 January 1944.

**Another view of the key *Overlord* planners, at Norfolk House: L–R back row, General Omar Bradley, Admiral Bertram Ramsay, Air Chief Marshal Trafford Leigh-Mallory, Lieutenant General Walter Bedell Smith; front row, Air Marshal Arthur Tedder, General Eisenhower, General Montgomery.**

A plaque outside Norfolk House reads: 'Norfolk House In this building 24 June 1942 – 8 November 1942 General of the Army Dwight D Eisenhower, Supreme Allied Commander, formed the first Allied Force Headquarters and in conjunction with the commanders of the fighting services of the Allied nations and the authorities in Washington and London planned and launched Operation "Torch" for the liberation of North Africa and later 16 January 1944 – 6 June 1944 as Supreme Allied Commander Allied Expeditionary Force in conjunction with the commanders of the fighting services of the Allied nations and the authorities in Washington and London he planned and launched Operation "Overlord" for the liberation of North West Europe.'

Two plaques are visible on the left of Norfolk House in this photograph – the one pictured above and another which reads: 'The United States of America recognizes the selfless service and manifold contributions of General Dwight David Eisenhower, Supreme Allied Commander, 1944–1945. At this site, General Eisenhower, on behalf of freedom loving peoples throughout the World, directed the Allied Expeditionary Forces against Fortress Europe, 6 June 1944. This plaque was dedicated by a United States Department of Defense delegation and the Eisenhower family on 4 June 1990 during the Centennial year of his birth and the 46th Anniversary of Operation Overlord.'

Eisenhower and Montgomery had already seen and discussed the plan with Winston Churchill at Marrakech in Morocco. They insisted that the forces specified were insufficient, and that much bigger landings would be needed if they were to stand a reasonable chance of success.

Eisenhower stayed at Norfolk House for only a few weeks before moving the main part of his headquarters to a new site at Bushy Park, on the western fringes of London, on the weekend of 4–5 March 1944 (*see* pp 8–10); the London building was kept as a rear HQ. (Eisenhower had previously been based at Norfolk House in 1942, before moving to the Mediterranean theatre.)

# 3 Camp Griffiss, Bushy Park, London

**Set up on the Teddington side of Bushy Park (today in the London Borough of Richmond upon Thames), little remains of Camp Griffiss. Originally built as US Eighth Air Force's headquarters, codenamed *Widewing*, from March 1944 it also housed the Supreme Headquarters, Allied Expeditionary Force (SHAEF).**

The 60-acre site of Camp Griffiss was located on requisitioned ground in a royal park, opposite Henry VIII's Tudor palace at Hampton Court. Named after Lieutenant Colonel Townsend Griffiss – the first American airman killed in Europe after the US entered the war – it was built for the US Eighth Air Force, whose commander, General Carl Spaatz, moved in on 15 June 1942. By 1944 Spaatz was the major USAAF figure in the UK, commanding from 22 February 1944 the newly formed USSTAF – the US Strategic Air Forces. Eighth Air Force HQ moved to Wycombe Abbey and Spaatz moved into *Widewing* Block A.

Eisenhower chose it for SHAEF as it was away from the fleshpots of central London, which also minimised the risk of German bombing. However, Winston Ramsey also suggests (in his book *D-Day Then and Now*) that the decision was a mistake: Air Chief Marshal Trafford Leigh-Mallory had suggested Bushey Hall, to the northwest of London – home to Eighth Air Force's VIII Fighter Command. The proximity to Spaatz may, however, have been well judged when there were arguments about control of the strategic air assets in relation to *Overlord*.

To reduce further the threat from air attacks, anti-aircraft batteries were set up nearby and several ponds – such as the Diana Fountain – that could have been used as aerial markers were drained and covered in camouflage netting. The base was also provided with a small airstrip so that senior officers could come and go as they needed to.

General Carl Spaatz (centre) commanded US Strategic Air Forces and, like Air Chief Marshal Arthur 'Bomber' Harris, was loath to release 'his' units from their strategic duties. However, both complied with Eisenhower's requests and the Transportation Plan bombings ensured German reinforcements after D-Day struggled to reach the battle zone. This photograph shows: L–R Major General William E Kepner (head of VIII Fighter Command), Spaatz (at the time, commander of the US Eighth Air Force) and Major General Barney Giles, Chief of the Air Staff and deputy commander of the US Army Air Forces. They are pictured in the control room at *Widewing* in January 1944.

A post-war aerial view of the
Teddington side of Bushy Park,
showing the *Widewing* buildings
stretching alongside the road that
forms the boundary of Bushy Park
(diagonally across the centre of
the photograph) – Eisenhower's
biographer Carlo D'Este called
them 'little more than a collection
of Quonset huts, tents, and hastily
erected temporary buildings in
an ancient royal forest'.[6] Today
nothing remains except a number of
memorials, including those pictured
below.

**BELOW**

Today very little remains of
*Widewing* in Bushy Park. This tablet
(BELOW) marks the site of the HQ of
the US Army Air Forces, July 1942–
December 1944. (Its position is
shown by 'A' on the aerial view.) This
memorial (BELOW RIGHT) marks the
site of Eisenhower's HQ in Bushy
Park. (Its position is shown by 'B' on
the aerial view.)

For three months Camp Griffiss was home to nearly 3,000 personnel – 1,600 US and 1,299 British – and was used as the base to refine existing ideas for Operation *Overlord* into a practicable set of plans. SHAEF was housed in blocks C, D, E and part of F; Eisenhower, Air Marshal Arthur Tedder, Lieutenant General Walter Bedell Smith and Lieutenant General Frederick Morgan all had offices in Block C. Their stay in Bushy Park wasn't long. By June they had moved nearer to the action in Portsmouth (*see* pp 30–3).

### Telegraph Cottage

General Eisenhower found that living in a hotel in Grosvenor Square was far too public, so he moved to a five-bedroom mock-Tudor building in Kingston upon Thames, in south west London. Telegraph Cottage was a 40-minute drive from Grosvenor Square, but only 10 minutes away from Bushy Park. The cottage adjoined a golf course and had a long driveway with a large garden and 10 acres of woodland to relax in.

It wasn't as far out of central London as Eisenhower would have liked and in spite of its more remote location, he still had as many as 20 visitors a day. However, he enjoyed the atmosphere he found there, sharing the building with close colleagues: Commander Harry C Butcher (his naval aide), Major 'Tex' Lee (his army aide), Warrant Officer Walter Marshall (his stenographer) and Sergeant Mickey McKeogh (his orderly). His secretaries and his driver, Lieutenant Kay Summersby, were also billeted close by. They used to come to see him at the cottage in the evenings to watch a movie, play cards or simply pass the time with him. The only thing missing was a dog. After checking that military regulations allowed him to have one, Eisenhower acquired a Scottie he named Telek.

Telegraph Cottage, in Warren Road on Kingston Hill, was Eisenhower's home-from-home from autumn 1942 until 1944. Among his personal assistants at the cottage was his valet, Master Sergeant John A Moaney, Jr, who served him from August 1942 until Eisenhower's death in 1969. The cottage has now been demolished.

# 4  21st (BR) Army Group, St Paul's School, 153 Hammersmith Road, London

**In the lead-up to D-Day, General Montgomery commanded the 21st (BR) Army Group, headquartered at St Paul's School in southwest London. Here he scrutinised the COSSAC plan for Operation *Overlord* and suggested fundamental changes to the size and scope of the landings.**

The premises of St Paul's School, which had been evacuated to Berkshire, had been requisitioned in July 1940 as the headquarters of the Home Forces, then under the command of Montgomery's advocate Lieutenant General Alan Brooke. From July 1943 they became the headquarters of the 21st Army Group, commanded by General Bernard Paget, who chaired a committee looking at the invasion of France. Those plans started off under the codename *Sledgehammer*, became *Roundup* in 1943 and finally evolved into *Overlord*.

Montgomery was informed of his promotion to command 21st Army Group on 24 December 1943. He left Eighth (BR) Army and returned from Italy on 2 January 1944 to take over command of the army group, which would consist of two armies for the invasion: British Second (under Lieutenant General Miles Dempsey) and Canadian First (under General 'Harry' Crerar). Montgomery was happy to settle into offices in his old school.

After spending some time on the plans – and discussing them with Naval Commander-in-Chief Admiral Bertram Ramsay and Air Chief Marshal Trafford Leigh-Mallory – a number of significant changes were proposed at a meeting with Eisenhower on 21 January 1944. The key changes were that the invasion should be broadened and the number of assaulting divisions involved should be increased from three to five, with two or three airborne divisions to secure the flanks. On top of this, the next problem would be the race to build up the forces in the bridgehead so there should be sufficient follow-up forces available – at least two divisions immediately to be able to shore up the bridgehead defences against the anticipated inevitable armoured counter-attacks of some five or six German divisions.

Britain's top soldier, Field Marshal Bernard Montgomery, inspects the Combined Cadet Force (CCF) of St Paul's School after the war. (Montgomery was promoted to Field Marshal in September 1944.) 'Monty' could be a difficult man to deal with, but both Walter Bedell Smith (Eisenhower's chief of staff) and Eisenhower said: 'There wasn't anyone else who could have got us across the Channel and ashore in Normandy; it was his sort of battle.'[7]

Alfred Waterhouse's 1884 building was used by the British military throughout the war. Returned to St Paul's School in 1945, it was demolished in the 1960s. This view shows the north front.

The school still has the map Monty used and the plaque celebrating the building's use in its new site on the other side of the river, in Barnes. This view shows the Board Room.

The problem with the changes to the plan was that they couldn't be achieved with the naval forces available at the time. To reach the necessary level of landing craft and other vessels, the date of the invasion would have to be pushed back from May to June and ships would have to be acquired from other theatres – in particular the Mediterranean. This, in turn, meant that the projected *Anvil* invasion of southern France – what became Operation *Dragoon* – would have to be delayed.

Eisenhower agreed completely and the changes to the COSSAC plan were set before the Combined Chiefs-of-Staff in Washington. Their approval meant that Operation *Overlord* was slated for the end of May/beginning of June.

On 15 May SHAEF's presentation of the final plan was unveiled at St Paul's in front of King George VI and the chief Allied commanders. It was a tour de force by Eisenhower and Montgomery: those who attended left the school convinced of the likely success of the enterprise.

# 5  First (US) Army, Clifton College, Bristol

**Clifton College was the temporary home of the headquarters of the First (US) Army, commanded by General Omar Bradley, who was slated to take over the 12th (US) Army Group after the battle of Normandy was won. The site saw extensive planning for the D-Day landings.**

While the COSSAC plan was prepared, the British headquarters of the 21st (BR) Army Group and Second (BR) Army were increasingly involved. Lieutenant General Frederick Morgan, Chief of Staff to the Supreme Allied Commander, and ETOUSA commander General Jacob L Devers pushed for the appointment of a senior American Army commander in Britain to parallel the British activities. On 25 August 1943 General George C Marshall, Army Chief of Staff, contacted Eisenhower and asked for General Omar Bradley. Eisenhower acquiesced and Bradley took with him experienced men who had fought under him in North Africa and the Mediterranean. As Bradley said in his autobiography, *A Soldier's Story*, 'It may have been unfair of me to strip II Corps of so many of its best officers, I could not in good conscience abandon an experienced staff and risk the Channel invasion to an inexperienced one.'[9]

Bradley brought a number of men with him from the Mediterranean theatre, all with significant combat time behind them. 'Of the four principal general staff posts,' he wrote, 'two were slated for these Mediterranean veterans ... And of the 18 special staff section chiefs, nine were to be filled from II Corps.'[10] There were other experienced men available, such as Brigadier General Henry B Sayler, Chief Ordnance Officer of ETOUSA 1943–45. He was not only a former classmate of Eisenhower's in the US Military Academy Class of 1915, but had also undertaken a large part of the planning for the US landings in North Africa. Consequently, he had vital first-hand experience of the requirements of moving vast numbers of men onto a narrow stretch of coastline.

Bradley established his headquarters in the Gothic buildings of Clifton College in Bristol, which became operational in October 1943. The school had been evacuated to Bude in Cornwall. Bradley himself used the School House Housemaster's drawing room as his office, while the top floor was converted into a listening post for messages from GCHQ. The floor below this was turned into a map room where the American

Eisenhower chose General Omar Bradley to command First (US) Army in Normandy. This photograph shows Bradley at Clifton College (at 'A') with First Army staff. Bradley took over Clifton College from Major General Leonard T Gerow, commander of US V Corps. Unlike Gerow, however, Bradley didn't sleep in the building, explaining: 'The bed's too damned close to your desk.' He told Gerow: 'I've been sleeping under a situation map for almost nine months. Now I want to get away from it at night.'[8]

In 1953 Clifton College was presented with an American flag to acknowledge its role from 1942 to 1944. A plaque at the school reads

'The flag of the United States was flown from the Wilson Tower when the forces
V Corps – General Hartle
1st Army – General Omar Bradley
and 9th Army – General Simpson
were stationed at Clifton
from October 1942 to
September 1944 and was
presented to the school by
the United States Army.'

This flag is on permanent display within the college. It has 48 stars because Alaska and Hawaii were not admitted to the union until 1959. The current US flag of 50 stars is flown from the Wilson Tower on 4 July and other appropriate occasions. General Bradley returned to Clifton as guest of honour at the college's annual Commemoration festival in 1953, while he was in England as Eisenhower's personal representative at the Queen's coronation.

component of the D-Day landings was planned in detail, and the library was used to compile the ordnance logistics.

Bradley and his senior staff moved into The Holmes, which belonged to Bristol University. They commuted from there to Clifton College every day. They had a daunting task before them: they had to organise everything needed by the around 600,000 men who were either in or attached to the First Army and who would be involved in the assault. Bradley also had to prepare for the day that the 12th Army Group became operational. He had a lot on his plate.

After First Army's tenure, Clifton College was taken over by Lieutenant General 'Texas Bill' Simpson, commander of what became Ninth (US) Army. He arrived in the UK on 6 May 1944, attended the D-Day briefing on 15 May and then took up residence in Bristol. He is pictured here addressing the troops. Ninth Army HQ moved to France in September 1944.

# 6 RAF Fighter Command, RAF Bentley Priory, Stanmore, London

**Throughout the Second World War, RAF Fighter Command's headquarters was located at RAF Bentley Priory, a non-flying station that played a significant role during the Battle of Britain as Air Chief Marshal Hugh Dowding's command centre.**

RAF Bentley Priory had been upgraded just before the war started, and among the modifications was the provision of an underground operations block. The excavations, which started in 1939, reached down 42 feet. The facility was completed the following year and it started functioning on 9 March 1940. It became the hub of RAF Fighter Command's response to the Luftwaffe attacks, synthesising information from many different sources – radar, wireless intercept stations, human observers – to ensure an immediate and effective response to attacks.

As the war progressed, it became obvious that provision for aircraft to land was imperative in order to allow important meetings to be held. Air Ministry War Department opinion said that it would take at least six months to construct two short landing strips, but Air Commodore Richard 'Batchy' Atcherley pulled some strings and managed to get the Americans to lay two 300-yard-long cinder strips in just four days. A Bellman hangar (a steel prefabricated building) was erected to go with them.

Air Chief Marshal Trafford Leigh-Mallory, commander of the Allied Expeditionary Air Force (AEAF), had his office in Bentley Priory. The communication facilities for the control of air operations were the best Britain could offer. A large amount of the planning for the air component of the invasion of Normandy was undertaken at Kestrel Grove, just a few hundred yards to the west of Bentley Priory. On D-Day itself, the progress of the landings were monitored from the AEAF War Room in the secure bunker at Bentley Priory, and several VIP visitors arrived to see things for themselves. These included King George VI, Winston Churchill, Field Marshal Jan Smuts – a South African who advised Churchill throughout the war – and the Supreme Commander himself, Eisenhower.

RAF Bentley Priory was Air Chief Marshal Hugh Dowding's HQ during the Battle of Britain, housing Fighter Command from 1936 until 1968. It also housed the Royal Observer Corps. General Omar Bradley, commander of the First (US) Army, remembered in his autobiography, *A Soldier's Story*, 'Leigh-Mallory's CP [Command Post] was located in Stanmore, in a neglected mansion that overlooked an equally neglected garden and beyond it the spires of Harrow.'[11] Today a museum, outside the entrance is a replica Hurricane.

# 7 Allied Expeditionary Air Force, Hillingdon House, RAF Uxbridge, London

**The Allied Expeditionary Air Force (AEAF) was designed to control the air operations for D-Day. It was commanded by Air Chief Marshal Trafford Leigh-Mallory, Eisenhower's Allied Air Commander-in-Chief, from headquarters set up in Uxbridge, London.**

Air Chief Marshal Trafford Leigh-Mallory has had a bad press, mainly because of the arguments about who controlled the air assets over the Normandy battlefield. However, he had also made enemies because of his attitude during the Battle of Britain, as he was seen to have plotted to replace Air Chief Marshal Hugh Dowding. He was also accused of politics while lobbying to become commander of the AEAC. In the end he was sidelined by the politics, and overall control of the air would be Eisenhower's through his deputy, Air Marshal Arthur Tedder. L–R Coningham, Montgomery, Leigh-Mallory.

The seeds of the failure of the joint command of the Allied air forces had been sown in Sicily. The development of tactical air operations in North Africa – where the US Army Air Forces (USAAF) learned from the more experienced British – led to a flexible and versatile air force with an integrated approach to missions. It had harried the enemy without mercy, but had already started to divide along nationalistic lines. By the time D-Day came along, the tactical air forces had split into those serving the British units and those serving the American units. While the twain did meet – the joint response to the Mortain counter-attack is a case in point – the view that General George Patton expressed to Eisenhower in Sicily ('the US is getting gypped',[12] suggesting there was too much British control of things) had taken hold and Eisenhower talked about the 'absolute continuity of American command of all American units from top to bottom'.[13]

To this national split must be added the differences between the behemoths of the strategic bombing campaign: the so-called 'Bomber Barons' General Carl Spaatz and Air Chief Marshal Arthur 'Bomber' Harris. Their involvement in the battle of Normandy was always going to be grudging, and while there is little evidence to show that they cavilled at any specific requests for operations, it took Eisenhower's threat to resign his position to ensure that command of the strategic bombing forces during the battle of Normandy was placed under his control – through his deputy, Arthur Tedder and not Leigh-Mallory, who was a man with a fighter background. Spaatz pushed his plan to hit oil. Harris raised the problem of civilian casualties. This brought Churchill and the politicians into the argument: understandably, they were worried about French casualties and Eisenhower had another battle to fight. In the end, Eisenhower's combination of subtle diplomacy and strength of argument won the day both for his control of the strategic bombers and also the Transportation Plan proposed by Professor Solly Zuckerman, Scientific Director of the British Bombing Survey Unit: stopping German reinforcement of their forces in Normandy by destruction of bridges, railways and transport nodes.

In truth, the arguments about who was in charge didn't really matter. The Luftwaffe's front line forces had been so eroded in Operation *Pointblank*, whose primary missions were the reduction of Luftwaffe fighter forces and the general reduction in the war potential of Germany, that Allied air supremacy was de facto from the start of *Overlord*: 'The German Air Force was more impotent than I expected,' Leigh-Mallory said.[14] He might not have had control of the strategic bombers, but what he did do was direct the tactical air support of the Allied forces throughout Operation *Overlord* by means of the RAF Second Tactical Air Force (2TAF) and the USAAF Ninth Air Force.

The commander of the AEAF, Air Marshal Arthur Coningham, was the architect of tactical air operations in the North African desert and his methods were adopted by the Americans when they entered the war. According to a dispatch by Leigh-Mallory, he 'was the one air commander with whom ... [Montgomery] dealt in his capacity as Commander-in-Chief, Land Forces, during the initial phases of the operation'[15] and he had the authority to act on requests made for support by the army. Control of the tactical air forces during the preparatory and assault phases of the operation was exercised through the Combined Operations Room at Hillingdon House, RAF

Uxbridge, which was staffed by US Ninth Air Force and 2TAF. Coningham also employed the Combined Control Centre, operated by a British and American staff from No 11 Group, RAF, and US IX Fighter Command (with representation from VIII Fighter Command). It used the existing static signals system augmented by additional communication facilities. Here all fighter operations in the initial phases of *Overlord* were planned, coordinated and controlled. Coningham also commanded the Combined Reconnaissance Centre which, according to Leigh-Mallory's dispatch, 'coordinated and directed visual and photographic reconnaissance by British and US forces'.

Montgomery thought Leigh-Mallory did an excellent job of supporting the troops in the front line and spoke out strongly on his behalf, saying to the War Office: 'We must definitely keep Leigh-Mallory as Air Commander-in-Chief. He is the only airman who is out to win the land battle and has no jealous reactions.'[16] Montgomery's praise further antagonised Tedder and other airmen.

The AEAF had other significant functions during the battle of Normandy: delivery of airborne forces, protection of the Allied naval armada, strikes against enemy naval forces and protection of the airspace around the beaches. It is a matter of record that these functions were performed in exemplary fashion. No Allied ships were sunk by German U-boats or naval forces; the reconnaissance photography was delivered as required; and the airborne troops were delivered – albeit in a less concentrated fashion than was hoped – without the casualty levels that Leigh-Mallory feared.

On 9 August AEAF headquarters moved to Normandy.

The Transportation Plan, proposed by Professor Solly Zuckerman, was violently opposed by the 'Bomber Barons', who believed that round-the-clock strategic bombing of Germany was more important than the invasion. The fact that they wildly overestimated the accuracy of their bombing and the effect on Germany's production (which increased in 1944) makes the vehemence of their opposition to the plan understandable but no less incorrect. However, once the plan had been pushed through, Spaatz and Harris proved 'surprisingly cooperative', according to Eisenhower's biographer, Carlo D'Este.

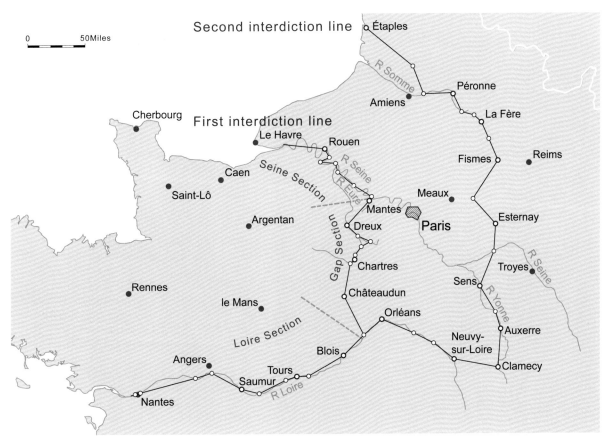

# 8  RAF 2TAF, Ramslade House, Bracknell, Berkshire

**The RAF's Second Tactical Air Force (2TAF; the Desert Air Force was 1TAF) was constituted on 1 June 1943 with its headquarters at Ramslade House, the future home of part of the RAF Staff College. Composed of units from both Fighter Command and Bomber Command, 2TAF was the British arm of the Allied Expeditionary Air Force (AEAF).**

2TAF's original commander was Air Marshal John d'Albiac. Its primary roles were identified as:

- air defence for the ground forces, their lines of communication and base areas
- close support for the ground forces by fighter-bombers
- tactical use of medium bombers
- tactical reconnaissance, both photographic and visual.

Tactical air support, developed by the British in North Africa, proved extremely effective in Normandy. Although perhaps not as overwhelming as initial reports suggested, the Allied 'Jabos' (fighter-bombers) always harried the Germans – in particular in the killing fields around Mortain and Falaise.

Bomber Command provided light bombers – No 2 Group – while the Fighter Command element was made up of Nos 83, 84 and 85 Groups. There was also No 38 Group that towed assault gliders and No 140 Squadron was a strategic photo-reconnaissance unit.

On 21 January 1944 Albiac was succeeded by Air Marshal Arthur Coningham, who, having fought through the campaigns of North Africa and Italy, had far more experience of supporting fast-moving ground troops – although in Normandy he had to wait a bit for the fast-moving part. After the landings had taken place, 2TAF was used to support the British and Canadian forces and on 4 August the headquarters moved to Normandy.

How well did it perform? If that question had been asked at the time – of friend or foe – the answer would have been: to great effect. More recently, analysis has downplayed the accuracy and, therefore, the effectiveness of the RAF's rocket-armed Typhoons and USAAF's P-47 Thunderbolts and suggested that artillery was the main threat to German tanks and vehicles. That's as may be, but at the time this was certainly not the view expressed by the Germans. The time and care they took to camouflage their vehicles and provide flak defences, and their fear of moving by day, certainly curtailed their aggression. Three events show the sort of contributions 2TAF made:

- On 7 June, as Panzer Lehr division moved to the front, it lost more than five tanks, 84 SP guns, prime movers and halftracks, and 130 trucks and tankers, much of it to air attack.
- On 10 June, after receiving *Ultra* intelligence (*see* pp 34–5), 2TAF attacked the HQ of Panzer Group West, killing 18 staff officers and injuring the commander, General Geyr von Schweppenburg. The armoured counter-

Air Marshal Arthur Coningham was an effective leader of 2TAF, although Eisenhower's biographer Carlo D'Este called him one of 'the war's foremost prima donnas'.[17]

attack that he was planning didn't happen and the Panzers were thrown in piecemeal to be ground down against the British and Canadian forces.

- On 17 July the Desert Fox himself, Generalfeldmarschall Erwin Rommel, was strafed by a 2TAF pilot and hospitalised.

Ramslade House became the RAF Staff College in 1945 but was sold off for regeneration in 2004.

# 9 USAAF Ninth Air Force, Sunninghill Park, Ascot, Berkshire

**Adjoining Windsor Great Park, Sunninghill Park was the headquarters of the American Ninth Air Force from November 1943 to September 1944. In the run-up to the invasion of Normandy, its primary role was the establishment of air supremacy and the targeting of Nazi military infrastructure.**

The US arm of the Allied Expeditionary Air Force (AEAF), the Ninth Air Force was commanded by Brigadier General (promoted to Lieutenant General in April 1944) Lewis H Brereton, who had been commander of the US Middle East Air Forces. Moving to Britain when the Ninth Air Force in North Africa was amalgamated with the Twelfth, Brereton was tasked with building up the new Ninth Air Force's strength and making it fully operational. Starting out with the medium bomber component from the VIII Air Support Command, by May 1944 he had expanded Ninth Air Force to include around 5,000 aircraft, spread through 45 flying groups made up of 160 squadrons. These were divided into three commands that covered the major aspects of combat airpower – namely, bomber, fighter and troop carrier capabilities. The number of personnel he was responsible for ran to over 220,000 when the ground support elements were included.

In order to control all these groups efficiently, Brereton built up a robust team to lead the various commands, including

**The Douglas A-20 Havoc was used by the Ninth Air Force until the end of 1944. Note the 'invasion stripes', which were applied on most Allied aircraft, other than heavy bombers, to assist identification and reduce the likelihood of friendly fire incidents. The order to add the stripes reached units on 3 June 1944.**

- Brigadier General Samuel E Anderson, who led IX Bomber Command. This was made up of the medium bombers from the VIII Air Support Command and two elements from the headquarters of the original Ninth Air Force.
- Brigadier General Elwood R Quesada, who led IX Fighter Command, and later, after the Ninth Air Force moved to mainland Europe, also commanded IX Tactical Air Command. IX Fighter Command was based at RAF Middle Wallop, in Hampshire, and was tasked with attacking German forces in Normandy and flying air cover over the beachhead. The first units deployed to France on 16 June were from IX Fighter Command.

- Brigadier General Otto P Weyland, who took over XIX Air Support Command from Quesada when he moved to IX Fighter Command.
- Brigadier General Paul L Williams, who took on IX Troop Carrier Command. This was established in order to take new units and get them organised and trained for battle. He was chosen as he had a lot of experience directing airborne operations in North Africa and Italy and his command would have to deliver the US airborne forces to the Cotentin Peninsula on the night of 5/6 June in Waco and Horsa gliders.

The Ninth Air Force had a prodigious throughput – by the time Operation *Overlord* was launched it had trained 11 medium bomb groups, 19 fighter groups, 14 troop carrier groups and a photo-reconnaissance group. Well before this, at the beginning of April, it had begun *Pointblank* operations against German military installations, including airfields, railway yards and bridges. These attacks were undertaken to help the invasion. However, as the actual landing zone was still secret, they had to be made over the whole of northern France in order to keep Hitler and his generals guessing. Flying around 35,000 sorties in May 1944, Ninth Air Force did much to help pave the way for D-Day success.

The B-26 Marauder was an excellent tactical bomber. This Ninth Air Force B-26 is seen over Sword Beach's Queen sector on D-Day.

# 10  USAAF XIX Tactical Air Command, Aldermaston Court, Berkshire

**Aldermaston Court or Manor is a Victorian rebuild of a Stuart house that had been severely damaged by fire in 1843. An airfield was built in its parkland, RAF Aldermaston, used by Ninth Air Force from 1943 (*see* p 117). This is the rear facade of the building.**

**Aldermaston Court, located between Newbury and Reading, was the headquarters of the USAAF's XIX Tactical Air Command. Activated on 4 January 1944 as US Ninth Air Force's XIX Air Support Command, it was redesignated in April 1944. It is best remembered for the tactical air support it provided General Patton's Third (US) Army.**

There were two USAAF Tactical Air Commands – the larger IX, commanded by Brigadier General Elwood R Quesada, who had made his name in the Mediterranean theatre, and XIX TAC. Under the command of Brigadier General Otto P ('Opie') Weyland, XIX Tactical Air Command gained eternal fame playing its part in the gallop across France by Patton's Third Army. After the First (US) Army achieved the breakthrough with Operation *Cobra*, Patton's forces exploited the gap and the paucity of German forces that could organise an effective defence and advanced 400 miles deep into France. This left a long, exposed flank and it was XIX TAC that helped to keep it protected. Patton is said to have called Weyland 'the best damned general in the Air Corps'.

**'Opie' Weyland commanded XIX TAC and provided General Patton with superb air support throughout the European campaign.**

Weyland, who had been in command of 84th Fighter Wing, set up headquarters about half a mile to the north of RAF Aldermaston in Aldermaston Court, a large country house. XIX TAC's offensive aircraft were contained in two fighter wings, both based in Kent: 100th, at Lashenden (Station 410), and 303rd, at Ashford (Station 417). (These were two of the advanced landing fields built in the south of England to cater for the massive increase in air forces needed to sustain Allied air supremacy over the Normandy battlefield.) Between them these two wings could field 21 squadrons of P-47 Thunderbolt and P-51 Mustang aircraft which were used for a wide variety of operations, including close-air support, attacking battlefield supply routes, dive bombing, air defence and reconnaissance.

The close-air support role was particularly successful due to the tight working relationship that was established between the army and the USAAF. For instance, when tank crews spotted enemy units, they passed the information on to their embedded air liaison officers, who then called in air strikes by radio. When necessary, the artillery assisted by marking the relevant areas with smoke shells.

# 11 Allied Central Interpretation Unit, RAF Medmenham, Buckinghamshire

**The Allied Central Interpretation Unit (ACIU) was responsible for analysing aerial photography taken by American and British reconnaissance aircraft to produce a daily intelligence report. It was at the ACIU that Flight Officer Constance Babington Smith's team discovered the V1 flying bomb sites that would be attacked in Operation *Crossbow*.**

Constance Babington Smith was a PI – a photo interpreter – taking the results of photo-reconnaissance missions (often flown at low level in unarmed aircraft) and teasing out the secrets, using stereoscopic imagery to ensure accuracy of measurements.

The Central Interpretation Unit was set up on 1 April 1941, bringing together a number of units into one location. It gained the 'Allied' part of its name on 1 May 1944 after American personnel first became involved and lost it in 1945 after the Americans returned home. The Bomber Command Damage Assessment Section was incorporated in 1942; so too was the Night Photographic Interpretation Section of No 3 PRU (Photo-Reconnaissance Unit), Oakington, Cambridgeshire.

Photo-reconnaissance had been raised to great levels during the First World War but this had not been sustained in the interwar years and initially, in 1939, the intelligence community had to run to catch up. The aircraft were too slow to evade enemy fighters; the cameras were prone to condensation at high altitudes; and when the photos reached interpreters, the techniques learned from experience in 1914–18 had to be relearned.

There's no doubt they did exactly that. While most coverage of the intelligence war centres, understandably, on Bletchley Park and the codebreakers (*see* pp 34–5), most practical intelligence came from photo interpretation, so much so that pretty much every operation would require photo-reconnaissance at an early stage.

All this photography led to a massive archive, increasing daily by 25,000 negatives and 60,000 prints to create around 36 million photographs by the end of the war. To cater for this there were more than 1,700 personnel.

Photographic intelligence was hugely important in the Second World War, providing planners and commanders with detailed information. The development of photo-reconnaissance involved improvements to aircraft (Spitfires, Mosquitoes, Mustangs and Lightnings were the best wartime platforms), cameras and tactics, but provided information on everything from the weather to troop movements and bomb damage assessment.

# 12 RAF Bomber Command, RAF High Wycombe, Buckinghamshire

**RAF High Wycombe, in the village of Walters Ash, was set up as the headquarters of RAF Bomber Command in the late 1930s. In 1944 it was the province of Air Chief Marshal Arthur 'Bomber' Harris, whose mission was the strategic bombing of German industry – and who felt any involvement in D-Day was a diminution of effort.**

Controversial, pugnacious and with the ear of the prime minister, Air Chief Marshal Arthur Harris's methods and the results of area bombing have led to much post-war criticism. The substantial casualty list – civilians and bomber crew – has left a difficult legacy.

In fact, 'Bomber' Harris accepted that his command – along with the equivalent US strategic bomber arm, the Eighth Air Force – would have to be involved in the invasion. Once the internal politics had been sorted out and it had been agreed that they would not come under the command of Air Chief Marshal Trafford Leigh-Mallory (*see* p 16), both played a significant role before and after D-Day.

In the early part of the war Bomber Command had been hampered by a lack of heavy bombers, but this changed with the arrival of the Lancaster in February 1942. This coincided with the appointment of Harris as Commander-in-Chief with a remit to attack German industrial capacity – his belief was that in doing so it would cause a collapse in civilian morale, and bring an end to the war. Famously, he said: 'The Nazis entered this war under the rather childish delusion that they were going to bomb everyone else, and nobody was going to bomb them. At Rotterdam, London, Warsaw, and half a hundred other places, they put their rather naive theory into operation. They sowed the wind, and now they are going to reap the whirlwind.'[19] He pushed hard for better navigational aids and instituted more rigorous training to improve bombing results.

Harris shocked the German population when he launched his first 1,000-bomber raid on Cologne in May 1942. He followed it up with other large-scale attacks – they didn't stop the war, but they did have a serious effect on the Nazi war economy. Early in 1944, Bomber Command began targeting infrastructure in northern France in order to reduce the German's ability to hold the country after the invasion. That this was successful can be seen in the words of Rommel, who is said to have demanded: 'Stop the bombers or we can't win!' As an example of the sorties made in the run-up to D-Day, the Bomber Command Museum of Canada identifies:

- attacks on railways and marshalling yards as part of the Transportation Plan (37 rail targets saw 22 'sufficiently damaged to require no more attention' and 15 'severely damaged')
- 2,198 mine-laying sorties to protect the flanks of the seaborne invasion, supplementing the operations of Coastal Command
- enemy airfields put out of action
- military locations (camps, depots, factories) attacked, including 30 coastal batteries (10 overlooking the invasion beaches – Fontenay, Houlgate, La Pernelle,

More than 7,000 Lancaster bombers were built and they saw service with Bomber Command from 1942. A total of 3,249 were lost in action during 156,000 sorties.

Longues, Maisy, Merville, Mont Fleury, Pointe du Hoc, Ouistreham and St Martin de Varreville – were hit by a 1,000-bomber raid on the night of 5/6 June)

• deception operations, including dropping dummy paratroopers and operations *Taxable* and *Glimmer*, which created the impression that the invasion was taking place towards the Pas de Calais.

It's sobering to realise that before the invading army even reached the beaches, Bomber Command had lost 300 aircraft with 2,500 crew killed attacking invasion targets. Eight aircraft from 1,211 sorties were lost on the night of 5/6 June alone; a further 11 aircraft from 1,160 sorties were lost the next night.

RAF High Wycombe – codenamed *Southdown* – was the nerve centre of Bomber Command, hidden in a heavily wooded area that was hard to spot from the air. All the station's buildings were disguised as innocent civilian structures – the fire station, for instance, was constructed to resemble a village church. Tunnels were dug to connect all the various parts of the station, and an Operations Block was excavated 55ft below ground. To further hide the station's existence, it was given the postal address 'GPO High Wycombe'.

RAF High Wycombe's buildings were designed to look like civilian structures, to disguise the site's military purpose.

# 13  USAAF Eighth Air Force, RAF Daws Hill, Buckinghamshire

**RAF Daws Hill became the headquarters of the USAAF's 'Mighty Eighth' Air Force when General Carl Spaatz set up the US Strategic Air Forces (USSTAF) in *Widewing* (Bushy Park, *see* pp 8–10). The Eighth Air Force bombing conducted in the run-up to the invasion of Normandy was organised and coordinated from Daws Hill, just down the road from 'Bomber' Harris in High Wycombe.**

Codenamed *Pinetree* and with the designation USAAF Station 1101, the Eighth Air Force headquarters was located at the top of a large ridge called Daws Hill, just outside the town of High Wycombe, on land that belonged to Wycombe Abbey School.

The Eighth Air Force was commanded by James Harold Doolittle, who made his name in the long-range raid on Japan following Pearl Harbor, a mission that earned him the Congressional Medal of Honor. Doolittle was promoted to lieutenant general on 13 March 1944. The Eighth Air Force's main role was the strategic planning and control of the bombing of Germany's industrial and domestic infrastructure. While the RAF chose to operate at night, the Eighth Air Force did so by day. This was made less dangerous by Doolittle's innovative use of fighter cover. When the Americans first undertook bombing runs over mainland Europe, the fighters protecting the bombers had to stay with them at all times. However, Doolittle allowed them to fly ahead to seek out and destroy any enemy aircraft they could find, which proved to be far more effective. Once the bombing had been completed, the fighters were then permitted to attack airfields and other targets of opportunity, such as transport links, as they returned home.

One of the Eighth Air Force's first major missions was codenamed Operation *Argument*. This was a series of attacks on German aircraft manufacturing that was jointly undertaken with the RAF. It quickly became known as 'Big Week' by the men involved. The RAF started by bombing Leipzig on the night of 19 February 1944. This was followed by the Eighth Air Force, who put over 1,000 B-17s and B-24s, together with more than 800 fighters, into an attack on 12 aircraft factories. The RAF also provided 16 squadrons of Mustangs and Spitfires as additional cover. Over the next few days other similar massive raids took place, causing huge disruption to the German aircraft industry.

Throughout the spring of 1944, the Eighth Air Force divided its priorities between attacking targets along the French coast as a prelude to Operation *Overlord*

When General Spaatz became commander of US Strategic Air Forces his position as head of Eighth Air Force was filled by James Doolittle. They had been close associates for some time. Here they are seen in North Africa during a handover ceremony of former USAAF Curtiss P-40 Warhawk fighters to a Free French combat fighter group. L–R General Carl Spaatz, French Major General Bergeret and then Major General James Doolittle, who made the presentation. At the time, General Spaatz was in command of Allied air forces in the North African theatre.

Eighth Air Force Operations Room, RAF Daws Hill.

and bombing Germany. This was particularly true in Berlin, where radar-equipped bombers caused enormous damage to both industrial and civilian infrastructure.

On D-Day itself the Eighth Air Force was extremely busy. Its P-51 and P-47 fighters were given the task of providing high cover for bombers and troop carriers and to ensure the Luftwaffe did not get close to the beachhead. Nine of its groups patrolled from Dungeness to Jersey – with the P-47s in the east and the P-51s in the west. They had very little to do. In his book *The Mighty Eighth*, Roger Freeman identifies '1,873 sorties [by VIII Fighter Command] between dawn and dusk in 73 patrols and 34 fighter-bomber missions'. By the end of the day, 'total claims by VIII FC … amounted to 26 in the air, the same figure as Command fighters missing'.[20] The Eighth's heavy bombers flew more than 2,300 sorties on D-Day, attacking both coastal defences and troop formations.

Eighth Air Force's VIII Fighter Command was headquartered at USAAF Station 341, Bushey Hall (often confused with Bushy Park, where SHAEF and USSTAF had their HQs), near RAF Uxbridge (*see* pp 16–17). From September 1943 it was commanded by Major General William Kepner. It had 15 fighter groups, many of which were involved during the run-up to D-Day and after, although its primary focus was protection of Eighth Air Force's VIII Bomber Command.

Formation of four P-51 Mustangs belonging to 375th Fighter Squadron, 361st Fighter Group (a unit of the Eighth Air Force). Based at Bottisham, in Norfolk, the squadron usually flew bomber escort missions but also flew in support of ground forces in Normandy.

# 14 Fort Southwick Underground Headquarters, Portsdown, Hampshire

**Fort Southwick, which overlooks the naval base of Portsmouth, Hampshire, was the secret communications centre for Operation *Overlord*. Sited in a network of tunnels buried 100ft below ground, it coordinated both naval and army operations before, during and after the invasion of Normandy.**

During the Second World War the operational part of Fort Southwick was a large and secret underground headquarters that was originally built in 1942 by 172 Tunnelling Company of the Royal Engineers as a naval command centre. It is located on Portsdown Hill, underneath a large Victorian Palmerston Fort built 1861–70. Its protection against enemy action meant it was the ideal site for the communications centre for Operation *Overlord*. Using the call sign 'MIN', it had more than a hundred rooms in its tunnel complex, including all the facilities needed for such an operation. Among these were offices, dormitories, toilets, cypher rooms, information rooms, message-decoding rooms, telecommunications rooms (including the

**ABOVE**
Fort Southwick Underground Headquarters gathered information on the naval forces from a variety of sources, including radar, to plot an accurate image of what was happening in the Channel.

**RIGHT**
Modern aerial view of Fort Southwick, taken from the west. The Grade I-listed building is due to be converted into flats.

The Main Operations Plotting Room. Note the coat of arms above the plotting table. Bob Hunt's excellent Portsdown Tunnels website identifies WRNS C Ward as the designer. It depicts a member of the WRNS and a WAAF with the motto 'This blessed plot'.

Naval Signals Distribution Office) and teleprinter rooms (one each for the Royal Navy and RAF).

The Royal Navy used the headquarters to follow the progress of the invasion of Normandy on D-Day (and thereafter), and to forward command and control instructions from General Eisenhower's HQ at nearby Southwick Park (*see* pp 30–3). The movements of all the ships were plotted on large table maps in the Main Operations Plotting Room, largely by a team of Wrens (a corruption of WRNS – Women's Royal Naval Service) and WAAFs (from the Women's Auxiliary Air Force). This work continued right up until VE Day. The map plots were not only essential for the coordination of all the Allied shipping in the channel during this period, but also for ensuring their protection. While there were few enemy aircraft still in the area, German E-boats were still operating.

The telephone exchange used women from the WRNS and WAAF, as well as staff from the Auxiliary Territorial Service (ATS). On D-Day itself, 5,000 signals were sent out via the various channels and more than 450 young women were on duty night and day. Fort Southwick had a back-up: HMS *Forward* at South Heighton, Newhaven, in Sussex. Also excavated by 172 Tunnelling Company, Royal Engineers, the tunnels here would have taken over had Fort Southwick been put out of action.

## 15  SHAEF Advanced Command Post, Southwick House, Portsdown, Hampshire

**Built in 1800, Southwick House was requisitioned by the Royal Navy in 1941 to become the home of HMS _Dryad_ – the RN Navigation and Fighter Direction School – bombed out of its offices in Portsmouth. Few could have foreseen what a critical role the house would play in the run-up to D-Day, when it and its grounds housed the Advance Command Post and Forward HQ of the Supreme Headquarters, Allied Expeditionary Force (SHAEF).**

Following a reconnaissance by Monty's Chief of Staff, Major General 'Freddie' de Guingand, HMS _Dryad_ was moved out of Southwick House in 1944 and the groundwork was laid for its use by Allied Supreme Commander General Eisenhower, Naval Commander-in-Chief Admiral Bertram Ramsay and Army Commander-in-Chief General Montgomery. It was chosen for two main reasons: first, because it was much closer to the ports from which Operation _Overlord_ was to be launched than the previous sites in London; second, because of its close proximity to the underground communications centre at Fort Southwick (*see* pp 28–9).

On 26 April 1944 Admiral Ramsay and his staff moved in: as his was the first headquarters to do so, the navy occupied the main house. (When he left on 7 September he wrote to _Dryad_'s captain (later Vice-Admiral) B B Schofield: 'You turned out of your comfortable quarters to make room for us ... All this enabled us to concentrate unhindered on the final planning and execution of the assault on the coast

Admiral Ramsay, the architect of the naval plan for Operation _Neptune_, was based at Southwick House (RIGHT), photographed here in 2018. He is remembered in a stained-glass window in Portsmouth Cathedral (BELOW).

In the drawing room at Southwick House the Chad Valley toy company's large map is still in evidence. (There's a replica in Portsmouth's D-Day museum, 'The D-Day Story.')

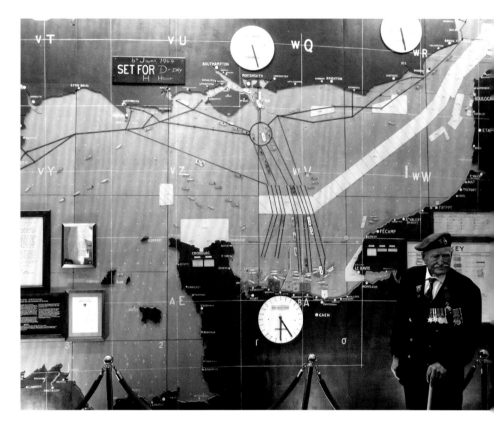

of France.'[21]) Eisenhower, Montgomery and the 21st (BR) Army Group staff were accommodated in the grounds, under the trees for camouflage. (Eisenhower moved in on 2 June, according to his biographer Carlo D'Este.) The large number of personnel needed to keep the headquarters functional were mostly housed in Nissen huts that were sited in the grounds wherever was convenient. The entire nearby village of Southwick was taken over, with the local pub – the Golden Lion – being designated as the Officers' Mess.

Although the main thrust of the invasion had already been planned at SHAEF's sites in London, refinements were going on until the last minute. To this end, according to B B Schofield in his book *Operation Neptune*, the old drawing room in Southwick House, 'panelled with mirrors, had been converted into an operations room and covering the east wall was a huge relief map of the invasion area and the English Channel.'[22] The Chad Valley toy company, based in the Midlands, was asked to make a plywood map of the whole European coastline from Norway right down to the Pyrenees. The two company members who brought the map – and installed only the Normandy sector – were detained for security reasons until the invasion had started. For command meetings – the first of the senior ones was held on 1 June – symbols were attached by Wrens using wheeled ladders in the relevant places, based on the near-constant stream of information which came in throughout the operation. Only they, the commanders-in-chief and their staff were allowed in the room, whose windows were blacked out.

The rough date of the invasion had already been set at a meeting on 1 May. According to Schofield, Ramsay 'insisted that [the enemy's beach obstacles] must be dealt with when they stood in not more than two feet of water'.[23] This meant that, due to tide times, the day had to be either 5 or 6 June, with 7 June if absolutely necessary. This provisional date was important because some of the naval assets – for example the blockships off Oban, Scotland, destined for use in the 'gooseberries' (lines of ships deliberately sunk to act as breakwaters off the beaches; *see* p 97) – would need to weigh anchor eight days before D-Day.

The final decision as to when the invasion should take place was made by Eisenhower in Southwick House, mostly based on up-to-the-minute meteorological advice provided by Group Captain J M Stagg. Having already postponed the landings for a day due to bad weather, and after pondering the many factors involved – from the risks of the enemy discovering the plans if he delayed to the rawness of his troops – it was in this room that Eisenhower finally issued the immortal words 'OK. Let's go' or something along those lines: there has been considerable debate about what he actually said, and who was present, ever since. Shortly afterwards, the commanders then each issued stirring addresses to their troops, urging them on to do their best on such a momentous day.

### *Sharpener* and *Shipmate*

With all the frantic preparations for Operation *Overlord* becoming more urgent by the day, Eisenhower had to be close to where it was all happening, hence his moving the SHAEF headquarters from London to Southwick. His own command post – codenamed *Sharpener* – was not in the same place though, but hidden away in nearby woodland. He kept the establishment small – it was only 200 yards long and less than 70 yards wide. A few hundred yards south of *Sharpener* was Eisenhower's much larger – more than 1,000 staff – D-Day 'forward' headquarters, codenamed *Shipmate*. These locations were in use from 1 June to 1 September 1944, when the forward headquarters moved to France.

Eisenhower's personal office was made up of a tented structure built over a concrete base and his accommodation was provided by a trailer. These were

**BELOW**

Eisenhower's advanced command post – *Sharpener* – was in the trees east of Southwick House, as was identified by Winston Ramsey's *After the Battle*.

**BELOW RIGHT**

Photograph taken at *Sharpener* of Eisenhower with some of the journalists that were accredited with SHAEF. L–R Major W R Carr, Stanley Birch (Reuters), Captain Victor J Meluskey (SHAEF censor), Robert Barr (BBC), Eisenhower, Commander Harry C Butcher, Merrill Mueller (NBC), Edward Roberts (UP), Lieutenant Colonel Thor Smith (SHAEF Press Officer).

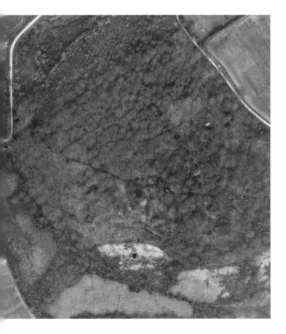

Aerial view looking east – taken on 21 April 1944 – showing Montgomery's 21st (BR) Army Group Tactical HQ and main HQ (in the trees at 'A'), Southwick House ('B') and Southwick Village ('C'). The white road at the top heads towards *Sharpener*.

surrounded by tents that housed such things as a mobile office, a telephone switchboard, accommodation for senior aides and meteorologists, as well as guards and cooks. There were also numerous trailers that contained maps, teleprinters and other relevant equipment.

Many important meetings and decisions were undertaken at *Sharpener*, including discussions about the invasion plans that were held with General de Gaulle and Winston Churchill. Consequently, good communications were an absolutely vital part of the site and regular contact was maintained with both Washington and 10 Downing Street, and after the landings had taken place, with Eisenhower's commanders.

## 21st (BR) Army Group HQ

When SHAEF's advanced headquarters were moved to Southwick House, General Montgomery established a temporary site for his own headquarters in woodland on the estate. He had a mobile home set up as an office, and the various elements of his command were pitched in tents in the grounds north of Southwick House. Montgomery's accommodation was close by at Broomfield House, where he entertained, among others, such illustrious guests as George VI and Churchill, as well as more regular visitors like Eisenhower.

Montgomery stayed at Southwick House until he was satisfied that the landings had gone to plan and that he had done all he could, whereupon he left for the beaches in order to be closer to where he was needed.

# 16 Government Code and Cypher School, Bletchley Park, Buckinghamshire

A brilliant, influential mathematician and scientist, Alan Turing's name is almost synonymous with Bletchley Park. He was involved in many areas, leading the German naval cryptanalysis in Hut 8, working on the 'bombes' that were used to find the settings for the German Enigma machines and other techniques, although he wasn't directly involved with the creation of Colossus, the world's first programmable digital computer. This photograph shows a 2007 statue of Turing made by Stephen Kettle from pieces of Welsh slate.

Bletchley House itself dates from 1883.

**Bletchley Park, also known as Station X, has gained immortality as the location at which the Allies broke the German codes, providing them with vital decrypts, codenamed *Ultra*. It was home to the top secret Government Code and Cypher School (GC&CS), a specialist facility for breaking encrypted communications.**

The work at Bletchley Park was one of the most significant Allied achievements of the Second World War. It allowed commanders to see right into the heart of the enemy's actions, and undoubtedly shortened the duration of hostilities considerably. Its success is summed up pithily by Andrew Roberts in *The Storm of War: A New History of the Second World War*. Talking of Montgomery in North Africa, Roberts says: 'When he put Rommel's picture up in his caravan he wanted to be seen to be almost reading his opponent's mind. In fact he was reading his mail.'[24] This is why the existence of Station X and its activities remained one of the Allies' most closely guarded secrets.

Initially established in 1938, the GC&CS was not only conveniently located near to central road and rail links, but it was also close to the telegraph and telephone repeater station in nearby Fenny Stratford. This was vital as the facility could handle high-volume communications, a critical factor when processing large numbers of radio messages.

The site also went under other codenames, including the 'London Signals Intelligence Centre', and the 'Government Communications Headquarters'. Members of the staff – it rose from about 120 in 1939 to about 7,000 at the beginning of 1944 – had to use the address Room 47, Foreign Office. About three-quarters of the staff were women; some came from non-military backgrounds, but a large number were from the WRNS. The Wrens were nominally posted to HMS *Pembroke V*. Many of the cryptanalysts involved were drawn from all manner of obscure backgrounds, including chess champions, crossword puzzle specialists and, of course, academics such as mathematicians and physicists.

In essence, Bletchley Park took coded enemy radio transmissions and found ways of decrypting them. In the early days everything was done by hand, but as the war progressed, the world's first computers were built to do the job in a fraction of the time.

From May 1943 onwards, US intelligence became closely involved, and several American codebreakers joined the staff. The output of the operation was so highly classified – above 'Most Secret', normally the highest level – that outside the staff themselves, very few people knew about it. Considered to be 'Ultra Secret', those

involved soon shortened it to 'Ultra'. Even Stalin was never officially told that Bletchley Park existed. In order to explain how the information was obtained, a fictional series of spies was invented as the source.

The last word on the subject should be from a man who benefited materially from the intelligence. Eisenhower, in a letter to General Stewart Menzies, head of the British SIS, said the information had been of 'priceless value to me. It has simplified my task as a commander enormously. It has saved thousands of British and American lives and, in no small way, contributed to the speed with which the enemy was routed and eventually forced to surrender.'[25]

**Bletchley Park housed a number of elements in brick-built blocks and temporary huts – eventually 8 blocks and 23 huts. Here the Axis signals were examined and, where possible, decoded through various means. The registration room in Hut 6 (pictured here) housed German army (Heer) and air force (Luftwaffe) decrypts of Enigma messages – the messages moved from registry room to machine room and decoding room.**

**Huts 3 (pictured here) and 4 handled analysis of the Enigma messages.**

# 17 First US Army Group, 20 Bryanston Square, London

**There can be few more successful deceptions in the history of warfare than the suggestion that the Allies' main effort in June 1944 wasn't going to be in Normandy but was coming on the beaches around Calais. For week after crucial week, the Germans kept significant forces tied up awaiting an attack that was a chimera.**

There are few more difficult military operations than an opposed landing on a hostile, defended coast. Right from the start of planning for the invasion of France, Chief of Staff to the Supreme Allied Commander (COSSAC) had thought about deception and measures that would contribute to the Allies achieving tactical surprise in Normandy.

There were many plans – and an earlier deception, Operation *Cockade*, was unsuccessful – but in December 1943 the overall strategy, Operation *Bodyguard*, was accepted. There were many elements to this, but two were particularly successful: *Fortitude North* and *Fortitude South*. The former, as the name suggests, attempted to convince the Germans there would be an invasion of either Denmark or Norway by the fictitious British Fourth Army. *Fortitude South* contrived to keep German eyes focused on the Pas de Calais.

Utilising decoy communications – leaking wireless communications, because the British knew that wireless interception was a strong area of German expertise – they created a role for First US Army Group (FUSAG), a real organisation that had been commanded by General Omar Bradley. For the purposes of the deception, the commanding officer was identified as General George Patton and the headquarters was in Bryanston Square. While the cult of personality created post war, particularly by George C Scott's movie portrayal of the general, was some years away, Patton was certainly a convincing name to use: he had come up against – and bested – German forces in North Africa and Sicily. To add to the subterfuge, Montgomery went to the southeast to meet Patton. Real units were involved as well as phantoms, for example the US 28th Infantry Division. So well did this work that by late 1943, the Germans assessed 34 divisions in southern England; of these, 11 were imaginary.

For all the clever planning, radio traffic management by No 5 Wireless Group, Royal Signals, and deception, the Allies had a number of other advantages in the run-up to D-Day.

First, the British counter-espionage services had identified and apprehended all the German agents sent to Britain and a number of them had been turned. Two others were double agents, the Spaniard Juan Pujol García (Garbo) and the Pole Roman Czerniawski (Brutus). They were run by the XX Committee – the Double-Cross system – chaired by an Oxford don and future vice-chancellor, John Masterman, who fed the Germans false information or true information too late. These agents were so successful that Garbo was awarded the Iron Cross by the Germans (he also received an MBE).

**Dummy landing craft in southern ports added believability to the deception that the Pas de Calais was the Allies' main target.**

Calais itself was heavily defended – as the Canadians found out when they attacked it in Operation *Undergo* in September 1944. Additionally, the French coast between Dunkirk and Dieppe was heavily defended with numerous German army batteries (*Heeres-Küsten-Artillerie-Abteilung/ Regiment:* HKAA/HKAR) and navy batteries (*Marine-Artillerie-Abteilung:* MAA):

**MAA 204 Ostende–Dunkirk**
4 batteries (4 × 105mm, 4 × 150mm, 4 × 165mm, 4 × 210mm)

**HKAA 1244 Dunkirk**
6 batteries (12 × 88mm, 18 × 155mm)

**MAA 244 Calais**
6 batteries (4 × 150mm, 4 × 165mm, 3 × 194mm, 2 × 240mm, 2 × 280mm, 3 × 406mm)

**MAA 242 Gris-Nez**
5 batteries (3 × 150mm, 4 × 155mm, 3 × 170mm, 4 × 280mm, 4 × 380mm)

**MAA 240 Boulogne**
8 batteries (4 × 75mm, 4 × 94mm, 3 × 138mm, 4 × 105mm, 5 × 150mm, 4 × 194mm, 3 × 305mm)

**HKAR 1245 Dieppe**
7 batteries (12 × 88mm, 4 × 105mm, 6 × 170mm, 4 × 220mm)

**Railway guns**
Coquelles, Fréthun, Hydrequent, Nieulay, Pointe aux Oies, Saint-Pol
(1 × 210mm, 13 × 280mm)

Source: Zaloga 2007, 16–17

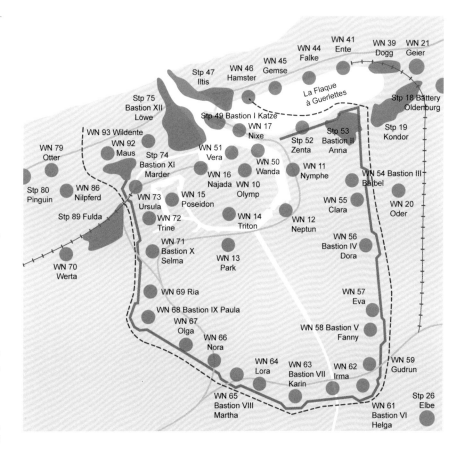

Second, British airspace, if not a no-go area, was difficult for German photo-reconnaissance aircraft. The Allied fighters and night-fighters, in conjunction with integrated radar and wireless intercept systems, provided a coordinated defence that didn't allow the Germans to acquire much hard information – and what they did acquire was often photos of plywood aircraft and rubber dummy tanks and landing craft. The latter at Folkestone, Newhaven and other locations on the south coast were codenamed *Wetbobs* and *Bigbobs* (*see* p 134).

Third, *Ultra* decrypts were able to corroborate the effectiveness of the false information – for example, a decrypt of 10 January 1944 showed that the Germans had discovered the existence of FUSAG and the First (US) Army.

Fourth, the Germans were predisposed to believe what they were being told. Hitler – who had always trusted his intuitive handling of politics and warfare – thought that the Pas de Calais was the main target and Normandy a feint. So did many of his generals, including Rommel. When all the intelligence pointed to this, it simply confirmed what they believed.

In the end, the results speak for themselves. It was well into July before the Germans realised that there was no attack coming across the Strait of Dover and by that time the battle of Normandy was all but lost. As Bradley said in his memoir, 'There for seven decisive weeks, the [German] Fifteenth Army waited for an invasion that never came, convinced beyond all reasonable doubt that Patton would lead the *main* Allied assault.'[26]

# 18  Combined Operations Pilotage Parties HQ, Hayling Island, Hampshire

**In 1940 a small organisation was created to organise raiding parties onto the Continent. From this evolved the Combined Operations Headquarters, commanded from 1943 by Major General Robert Laycock. It played a key role in offensive operations – mainly clandestine – against the enemy and particularly in the preparations and planning for the Normandy landings.**

Best known for its commando actions and the attack on Dieppe, the Combined Operations Command performed many roles in the Normandy landings, but none more important than the work of the Combined Operations Pilotage Parties.

The landings at Dieppe in 1942 had been a disaster: almost 60 per cent of the attacking force that reached the shore were killed, wounded or captured. The tanks – Churchills – found the shingle beach difficult to negotiate, with 12 of the 27 that landed bogging down. The only success had been Lord Lovat's mission which saw No 4 Commando (which included 50 US Rangers) knock out a coastal battery. But as Hitler said to his Western Front commanders: 'We must realise that we are not alone in learning a lesson from Dieppe. The British have also learned. We must reckon with a totally different mode of attack and at quite a different place.' He added: 'If nothing happens in the next year, we have won the war.'[27] Three months later the Allies landed on the North African coast; under a year later it was Sicily and shortly after, mainland Italy. The Allies had learnt their lessons well.

One of the things the Allies had learnt was that they had to know more about the beaches on which they intended to land. What was the beach texture like? How did it shelve? What were the hidden obstacles? What defences were there? Where were the openings to exit the beach? Photo-reconnaissance provided information, as did spies and watchers in situ, but nothing was better than a considered, professional assessment made as a result of information gathered on the spot. Pilotage directions, the ability to pinpoint locations, navigational fixes: all these things required first-hand experience.

The people to do that were the COPPists – men of an organisation set up as a result of the efforts of Lieutenant Commander Nigel Clogstoun Willmott of the Royal Navy. He had worked on secret surveys for a possible attack on Rhodes and could see the benefits of a specialist unit. The Combined Operations Pilotage Parties (COPP) Depot was set up in 1943 at the Hayling Island Sailing Club on Sandy Point, on the orders of Lord Mountbatten, then in charge of Combined Operations. This small unit – around 10 COPPs were formed between 1943 and 1945 and their complement never rose above 200 men – went on to win more than 90 medals and commendations.

The COPPists showed their worth many times during the war, but on New Year's Eve 1943, when Major (later Major General) Logan Scott-Bowden and Sergeant Bruce Ogden-Smith surveyed Gold Beach, they had a major impact on the D-Day landings. The Americans certainly thought so, because they asked the COPPists to do the same thing on their beaches. And so they did. In Neillands and de Normann's *D-Day 1944: Voices from Normandy*, Sub-Lieutenant Jim Booth, of the Royal Naval Volunteer Reserve, remembers other pre-invasion reconnaissance using midget submarines *X20* and *X23*. The trouble with the X-craft was that the COPP canoes didn't fit in them, which meant they had to be towed into the area by a larger sub before using the midget subs to get closer, then swimming in. Booth says: 'My CO, Lt Jeff Lyne, surveyed a lot of the beach obstacles, and we did the gradients, while the REs [Royal Engineers] took sand and beach samples, finding mud and quicksand and so on.'[28] The information was used to help combat-loading for the 79th Armoured

Memorial to the COPP on Hayling Island beach.

The COPPists trained with canoes – wooden framed, folding to fit better into submarines. Note the COPP swimsuits and floatation bags.

Division Funnies (specialised armoured vehicles; *see* p 43) to ensure that the right vehicle was there to overcome the obstacles.

On the day itself, COPPist navigators led units onto the beaches using X-craft (*X20*, commanded by Lieutenant K R Hudspeth, and *X23*, commanded by Lieutenant G B Honour) to provide navigational markers. After the 5 June postponement, the five men in each craft had to undergo the discomfort of an extra day in the foetid air of the small cabin while the midget submarine was precariously placed offshore. By the time the assault craft arrived on 6 June, the crews had been submerged for 64 of the 76 hours they had been at sea.

The COPPists' use of miniature submarines on D-Day helped guide British and Canadian troops to their beaches.

# 2 | Practice makes perfect

All armies need to train – the Greek phalanx of spearmen was no haphazard grouping. Vegetius's *Epitoma rei militaris* of the 4th century CE shows the level of sophistication the Romans brought to military training. Some 1,500 years after Vegetius, Allied armed forces had to fulfil the same requirement to train their soldiers in a much more complicated world. The opposed landings by air and sea on the coast of Europe in 1944 by Allied forces of many nationalities required a range of skills, some involving new weapons and technology that had not been covered during basic training.

The rescue of around 215,000 men of the British Army from Dunkirk (among the 340,000 rescued troops in total) maintained a cadre of trained men in the UK, supported by the first Canadians who arrived around the same time. These troops – albeit short of the equipment left in Belgium and France – formed the basis of the defence of Britain against invasion while new recruits were readied. The infantrymen received six weeks of basic training at a regimental depot, with another six weeks of infantry-specific instruction at an infantry training centre. Thereafter, the training continued at every level – battalion, brigade and division – this training improving as the war continued and lessons from the battlefield filtered through to the instructors.

Italy declared war on Britain on 10 June 1940 and soon there was fighting in North Africa. The success of the Allies' Operation *Compass*, led by General Archibald Wavell, saw the first German troops enter the theatre on 11 February 1941. The protracted war in the desert involved a number of divisions that would see action on D-Day – both British and, after the Allied invasion of northwest Africa by Operation *Torch* in July 1942, American. Fighting in North Africa and, after Japan's invasion of Malaya, Hong Kong and Singapore at the end of 1941, in the Far East and, soon, India meant that there was a constant demand for trained troops, but this still left a significant number sitting in England from June 1940 until June 1944.

These troops – and the increasing number of Americans who started to arrive in Britain from January 1942 – should have constituted the best-trained army ever to have left British shores, but there have been numerous post-war criticisms of its effectiveness. Some of this lack of punch may well have been down to an absence of battlefield experience as contrasted against the many veterans in German ranks. In his book *Military Training in the British Army, 1940–1944*, Timothy Harrison Place suggests the causes for the British Army's perceived tactical weakness in Normandy were a failure to pass on lessons from battles in the Mediterranean theatres to troops training at home, and disagreements between General Bernard Montgomery and the War Office over basic armour doctrine.

'Monty' is a favourite target on both sides of the Atlantic for most issues concerning the efficacy of Allied forces in 1944, surprisingly so when one considers his success in the Mediterranean theatre and complete victory in the battle of Normandy. Some historians of the 1970s and 1980s promoted the idea of German tactical prowess, a condemnation of Allied equipment as against that of their enemies and a perception that the battle of Normandy took too long (fostered by a concentration on the time it took D-Day objective Caen to fall). However, these criticisms do not take sufficient account of the differences between the two sides – a citizen army on the one hand whose 12

Commando training took place from February 1942 at the Commando Depot – later the Commando Basic Training Centre – at Achnacarry Castle near Fort William.

weeks of training should be set against the army of a totalitarian regime, many of whose indoctrination and training had started in the *Hitlerjugend* while they were at school. While there may be some truth in the idea that Allied troops were trained under faulty doctrine, there can be no denying that they came to terms with their deficiencies, and by the end of July 1944, when the Allies broke through the German defensive lines, it was the Germans who were having to solve the problems of brilliant artillery direction, air superiority and a lack of mobility and mechanisation.

The training for combat in the bocage terrain over which much of the battle of Normandy was fought is also often cited as an issue: insufficiently prepared, the US Army's slog through the hedgerows from Carentan to Saint-Lô was prolonged by the lack of suitable tactics. Again, there may be some truth in this, but the proposal on the face of it discounts the similarities between the countryside in Dorset and Devon, where many of the US troops were based and trained, and Normandy. The fact is that the bocage was a much easier environment for the defender, whatever the attackers' doctrine, and US forces did come to terms with the environment to beat a stubborn enemy. Before the fighting in Normandy could take place, the Allies had to assemble four armies (British Second, Canadian First and US First and Third), transport them across the Channel, land on a coastline whose defences had been prepared over four years and included integrated artillery and infantry units in hardened positions, punch through this defensive crust, weather the inevitable counter-attacks and build up sufficient force to liberate western Europe. Infantrymen, artillerymen and tankers constitute only the tip of the training iceberg. Scouting and reconnaissance of beaches was essential; specialised equipment to combat antitank walls and bunkers was vital; waterproof transportation, logistics, POL (petrol, oil and lubricants), food and ammunition had to be catered for; providing signals and communications was a prerequisite. All of these factors had to be examined, planned and the personnel trained – if possible in secret.

A memorial (ABOVE) recognises US 2nd Ranger Battalion, commanded by Lieutenant Colonel James E Rudder, which practised on the cliffs around Bude in north Cornwall (BELOW) for the attack on Pointe du Hoc.

To do this, specialised training camps were set up all over the British Isles, from Achnacarry in Inverness, where the commandos trained, to the US naval base at Loch Erne, Northern Ireland; Slapton Sands in Devon to Burnham-on-Crouch in Essex. Most important for the seaborne landings were techniques using purpose-built craft – from the smallest LCA (landing craft assault) or LCVP (landing craft, vehicle personnel), which could each carry 30–36 men, to the larger LSTs (landing ship tank) – the waterproofing of all vehicles, and the use of DD (Duplex Drive) amphibious tanks that could be launched from ships out to sea and 'swim' into shore (if the sea conditions allowed). Other specialist training included that for army glider pilots, drop training for paratroopers and training on a whole range of specialist vehicles, such as 'Hobart's Funnies' of the 79th Amoured Division: flail tanks (Crabs), ARKs (armoured ramp carriers), bridgelayers, flamethrowers (Crocodiles), AVREs (Armoured Vehicles Royal Engineers) and Bobbins (path layers).

To put all this training into practice, a series of exercises was held in 1944, starting at unit level and getting progressively larger. These gave practical experience to the training regimes on land, allowing issues to be raised and operational processes to be altered. Finally, there were two dress rehearsals for the invasion itself: Exercise *Tiger* (22–30 April) for Force U (destined for Utah Beach) and *Fabius* (23 April–7 May) for the other four beaches. These employed the troops who would take part in the invasion in as close to battle conditions as could be duplicated – indeed, Exercise *Tiger* saw practice become reality when German E-boats became involved to deadly effect (*see* pp 72–4).

With so many training bases in the UK – over 50 in Scotland alone – the locations covered in this chapter can only give a flavour of the training given to the Allied forces in Britain before D-Day.

**Many specialised landing craft were developed during the Second World War, the most numerous being the British LCA and its US equivalent, the LCVP – the Higgins boat. The photograph shows a US landing craft involved in training in north Devon.**

# 19 Commando Basic Training Centre, Achnacarry, Scotland

**The Royal Marine Commandos played a vital role on 6 June in two Special Service Brigades. All these D-Day commandos had trained at Achnacarry, a small private estate in the Lochaber region of the Highlands, which was used as a commando training depot throughout the Second World War.**

The Commando Basic Training Centre (CBTC) was set up in March 1942. It was ideally located for the purpose, surrounded by desolate and challenging mountain terrain on the banks of the River Arkaig on a peninsula between Loch Lochy and Loch Arkaig. Temporary Nissen huts were erected near to the castle as accommodation, eating halls, washing areas and as a NAAFI (Navy, Army and Air Force Institutes) canteen. There was also a large general-purpose building and a hard drill square. When extra accommodation was needed, bell tents were used.

In overall charge was Lieutenant Colonel Charles Vaughan, a hardened First World War veteran who rose from the ranks and who accepted nothing but the best, from fitness to fieldcraft. He established three separate training commandos – Keyes, Haydon and Sturges – named after famous former commandos. These were divided into four training troops, under a captain with the assistance of a command sergeant major, a clerk and a storeman. Each troop was led by an instructor-officer, aided by a troop sergeant. There was also a demonstration troop to help the instructors with the training regime. Much of the training focused on building personal strength as well as teamwork – there was an enormous amount of physical training, as well as tuition in ways to cross obstacles.

During its wartime existence, some 25,000 commandos completed their training here. These included men from Britain, the US Rangers, France, the Netherlands, Norway, Czechoslovakia, Poland, Belgium and even some 'free Germans', among whom were many Jews. The course itself – usually six weeks, sometimes shortened (48 Commando had but 18 days) – was harsh and culminated in a live-firing exercise where the participants had to make an opposed landing around the nearby village of Bunarkaig on Loch Lochy. Casualties were not uncommon.

**ABOVE**

**The Commando Memorial near Spean Bridge and Achnacarry was unveiled in 1952 by HM the Queen Mother.**

**RIGHT**

**The Achnacarry commando training course was rigorous and effective. The American Rangers went through it, too, as did Dutch, French, Belgian and Norwegian special forces.**

On D-Day, the 1st Special Service Brigade (Nos 3, 4, 6 and 45 Commandos plus men of No 10 Inter-Allied Commando), commanded by Lord Lovat, fought its way into Ouistreham and to Pegasus Bridge, where it relieved 6th Airborne Division. The Royal Marines of the 4th Special Service Brigade fought on all three British and Canadian beaches, sustaining heavy casualties in the assault. No 47 Commando arrived at Asnelles and fought through to take Port en Bessin the next day in a significant feat of arms. No 48 Commando took Langrune-sur-Mer with heavy casualties and – with the rest of the brigade – fought on until relieved on 18 August.

## Commandos

There were four different types of commando during the Second World War; some 17,000 men were involved on D-Day.

- Army commandos: the most numerous of the commandos, 15 units were raised in the UK and 4 in the Middle East. These included No 10 Inter-Allied Commando, which was formed from French and other volunteers from German-occupied territories; No 14 – an Arctic commando; No 30 Commando, which specialised in intelligence gathering; and No 62 Commando, the Small Scale Raiding Force.
- Royal Marine commandos: in total 9 battalions – named Commandos – were raised during the war. Numbered 40 to 48, they were gathered into 4 Special Service Brigades, 2 of which (Nos 1 and 4) were involved in the Normandy landings.
- Royal Navy commandos: raised in 1942, these were beach commandos who were responsible for ensuring the efficient movement of men and equipment through the beach area. There were 8 Royal Navy commando units involved on D-Day.
- Royal Air Force commandos: there were 12 'Servicing' commandos totalling some 2,400 men, whose task was to make German airfields secure once they had been taken or to work on the new airstrips built in France.

# 20 No 1 Combined Training Centre, Inveraray, Scotland

**Established on the shores of Loch Fyne, No 1 Combined Training Centre (1CTC) was used for training army and navy service personnel in handling smaller landing craft for beach assaults. Because of the shortage of Royal Navy personnel, 60 officers and 200 men of the Royal Canadian Navy also trained for the work.**

One of the many urgent requirements identified in the planning stages of Operation *Overlord* was for crews and troops to be trained in the use of the many different landing craft – particularly the smaller ones that would be used in quantity. (The main assault craft was the LCA, which could carry 30–36 men.) Training on larger craft took place at CTC Castle Toward, near Dunoon (*see* pp 48–9).

As a result, 1CTC was set up in October 1940. It was in a remote location that some 250,000 Allied service personnel passed through in the course of being trained. The critical aspect about this was that until that point, none of the men involved had ever undertaken beach assaults from a landing craft. Without the necessary knowledge they would have stood little chance of surviving under combat conditions.

The training was not just about getting men off landing craft and onto the beaches, but also all the commensurate weaponry, ammunition and supplies they needed. Since RAF fighter cover was an essential part of the equation, it also gave the pilots and their support crews valuable experience of what was needed. Ground elements of the RAF also received training there, including the RAF Regiment and the RAF Servicing Commandos. Up to 15,000 men were billeted in the area at any stage, and they were taught how to operate in true combined operations style – including

### Combined operations establishments

| | |
|---|---|
| 1 Achnacarry | 26 HMS *Newt* |
| 2 HMS *Lochailort* | 27 HMS *Lizard* |
| 3 HMS *Dorlin* | 28 HMS *Sea Serpent* |
| 4 HMS *Quebec* | 29 HMS *Northney I–IV* |
| 5 HMS *Pasco* | 30 HMS *Warnford* |
| 6 HMS *Armadillo* | 31 HMS *Tormentor* |
| 7 HMS *James Cook* | 32 HMS *Squid* |
| 8 HMS *Brontosaurus* | 33 Calshot (moved to HMS *St* |
| 9 HMS *Roseneath* | *Barbara*, Bognor Regis) |
| 10 HMS *Port Glasgow* | 34 HMS *Mastodon* |
| 11 HMS *Monck* | 35 HMS *Medina* |
| 12 HMS *Warren* | 36 HMS *Vectis* |
| 13 HMS *Dundonald* | 37 HMS *Manatee* |
| 14 Dundonald Air Station | 38 HMS *Turtle* |
| 15 HMS *Dinosaur* | 39 HMS *Dartmouth II* |
| 16 HMS *Stopford* | 40 Salcombe (moved to |
| 17 HMS *Arbella* | Exmouth) |
| 18 HMS *Mylodon* | 41 HMS *Foliot I, II and III* |
| 19 HMS *Woolverstone* | 42 HMS *Appledore* |
| 20 HMS *Helder* | 43 Staines |
| 21 HMS *Westcliff* | 44 Amersham (30 Assault Unit |
| 22 HMS *Wildfire III* | base) |
| 23 HMS *Robertson* | 45 Combined Operations HQ |
| 24 HMS *Allenby* | (the War Office, Whitehall, |
| 25 HMS *Haig* | London) |

Inveraray lies on the banks of Loch Fyne, some two hours south of Achnacarry. This 1941 photograph shows the commando training camp in the left foreground and Inverary Castle at top left. There were a number of camps in the area and more than 250,000 men passed through 1CTC.

live firing and the consequent deaths and injuries this caused – with the army, Royal Navy and Royal Air Force all working together in a cohesive manner.

Alongside the combined activities, the army and navy also ran their own separate regimes. The army schools were divided into four parts: the Brigade Group, Army Tank, Royal Engineers and Royal Electrical and Mechanical Engineers; these undertook specialist training. The Royal Navy ran its own base, HMS *Quebec*, to provide and maintain the craft used in 1CTC's training operations and to accommodate the personnel while they were being trained. A smaller component of the base – *Quebec II* in Largs – also trained staff officers in how to conduct combined operations. More than 1,000 officers (153 Royal Navy and Royal Marines, 379 British Army, 122 Canadian Army, 351 RAF and 153 Allied) passed through its doors.

Lord Mountbatten, Chief of Combined Operations, suggested that the Combined Signals School (CSS) be set up to train RN Beach Signals: this happened on 1 November 1941. The Beach Signals – an advance party consisting of three signallers with a portable radio – were the important link between the front line and headquarters before it was safe for the HQ to come ashore.

Although training at 1CTC was of huge importance to D-Day, the men who trained there also undertook operations in Norway, North Africa, Sicily, Italy, the east Mediterranean, France, Holland and Madagascar.

Loch Fyne provided facilities for training troops in amphibious warfare prior to the D-Day landings. This is an LCT Mk 2, one of 70 built (20 were lost 1941–44), which could carry 250 tons of cargo or four 40-ton tanks.

# 21 HMS *Brontosaurus*, Castle Toward, Dunoon, Scotland

**Gothic Revival Castle Toward dates back to 1820, when it replaced a medieval castle. Little remains of HMS *Brontosaurus*, CTC2, which played a valuable role in preparations for D-Day.**

**HMS *Brontosaurus* was 2CTC and provided a vital part of the D-Day training for officers and crews on how to operate larger landing craft as part of amphibious landings.**

Castle Toward was built in the first quarter of the 19th century and commissioned as a Royal Navy shore establishment in 1942. 1CTC (*see* pp 46–7) concentrated on the use of smaller landing craft. 2CTC – also known as CTC Castle Torward – covered larger vessels. Based on the Firth of Clyde, HMS *Brontosaurus* was initially set up to train Royal Navy personnel, with the army being trained at HMS *Dundonald*. However, it was soon realised that *Brontosaurus*'s remit needed to be expanded to include the relevant officers and men from the army and the RAF Regiment, and this happened in November 1942. The main points taught were the methods of loading and disembarking tanks, vehicles, personnel and supplies in LCTs, LCPs and LSIs (*see* panel, opposite). Mock assaults were made on various beaches in the locality.

**LCTs off Juno Beach, 6 June.**

**Different types of British Landing Craft (LC) and Landing Ships (LS)**

**LCA**  LC Assault – more than 600 used; lightly armoured, they were heavier than their US equivalent, the LCVP – the Landing Craft, Vehicle Personnel (*see below*).

**LCA (Hedgerow)**  LCA armed with 4 × 6 Spigot mortars.

**LCC**  LC Control – two per D-Day beach, equipped with radar to find safe routes to the beaches.

**LCF**  LC Flak (anti-aircraft use) – the only Royal Navy warship class to have a German name! Converted from LCTs, they had eight 20mm cannon or four 2-pounder Pompoms.

**LCG(L)**  LC Gun (large) – armed with two 4.7-inch naval guns; 25 LCGs were produced.

**LCG(M)**  LC Gun (medium) – armed with two 25-pounders.

**LCH**  LC Headquarters – this was a British conversion of an LCI(L), carrying communications equipment.

**LCI**  LC Infantry – the early large version could carry 6 officers and 182 men; later versions increased this to 9 officers and 200 men.

**LCM**  LC Mechanised – early LC capable of carrying vehicles up to 16 tons; the LCM(4) was most numerous.

**LCN**  LC Navigation – used by the Royal Marines and Special Boat Service for surveying landing sites.

**LCOCU**  LC Obstacle Clearance Unit.

**LCP(L)/(M)/(R)**  LC Personnel (large)/(medium)/(ramped) – the US Higgins boat. It had to be loaded by scramble net from larger ships. Before the ramped version, infantry (25 carried by RN version/36 by US) had to jump off the bow.

**LCRU**  LC Recovery Unit – recovered ailing craft.

**LCS(L)**  LC Support (large) – Mk I armed with a QF 2-pounder Daimler armoured car turret; Mk II had a 6-pounder.

**LCS(M)**  LC Support (medium) – armed with two 0.5-inch MGs and a 4-inch mortar to fire smoke.

**LCT**  LC Tank – some 487 LCTs or derivatives were produced. (Currently *LCT-7074*, the only such LCT in the UK, is under restoration for display at Southsea's D-Day Story museum from 2020.) Heavier than the US version, they could carry more tanks. The Mk I was designed on Churchill's orders to take three 36-ton tanks. The US developed the idea and took over design and construction. There were also:

**LCT(A)**  LC Tank (armoured) – planned to provide fire support for the landings, with two Centaur tanks (without engines) on board. Montgomery insisted they be able to drive onto the beach. They were too heavy and only 20 of 80 landed in the first hour – and only 28 over the rest of the day.

**LCT(R)**  LC Tank (rocket) – armed with 1,000 RP-3 rockets, first used during Operation *Husky*. Around 20,000 were fired on 6 June. Some 36 LCT(R)s were converted from LCTs.

**LCV**  LC Vehicle.

**LCVP**  Landing Craft, Vehicle Personnel – the American LCVP was developed from the earlier LCV and LCP, the most common US small landing craft.

**LSI**  LS Infantry – known to the Americans as Attack transports; took infantry to a lowering position (from 6–10 miles offshore), where they transferred to LCAs. The largest could carry around 1,500 men.

**LSM**  LS Medium – some were developed into LSM(R) (rocket).

**LST**  LS Tank – originally a British design, they were reworked and more than 1,000 were built in the US.

**LVT**  Landing Vehicle Tracked (also known as amphibian) – US-designed, named Alligator, Buffalo, etc. Could carry a jeep and some had gun turrets

## 22 HMS *Armadillo*, Glenfinart House, Ardentinny, Scotland

**Since the invasion of Normandy would see huge numbers of men and equipment passing over the assaulted beaches, those areas required precise command and control. To train for this, HMS *Armadillo* was set up, a specialist training camp for RN Beach Commandos, whose role was to go ashore and set up a protected base for the beach commander to operate from.**

It's not just the enemy defences that cause a problem for an attacker during an amphibious landing. Large-scale beach assaults require precision planning and control: clearing obstacles and marking the beach; command and control of the beach; setting the beachmaster's area; removal of casualties and PoWs; coordination of the arrival of men, equipment, vehicles and stores. A central part of the control element on D-Day was performed by the beach commander, who operated from the shore to coordinate the flow of incoming and outgoing landing craft. In order to make this hazardous role possible, the RN Beach Commandos had to secure the chosen area in advance of the beach commander's landing.

Entirely distinct from both Royal Marine and army commandos, the beach commandos needed to be specially trained for the task in hand, a matter that was highlighted by the heavy casualties they sustained in the Dieppe raid.

**ABOVE**
Little remains today of HMS *Armadillo*, the final corrugated iron hut having been demolished in 2011. The memorial, photographed here in the same year, has since been raised on a plinth.

**RIGHT**
Postcard view of Glenfinart House. It sits on the side of Loch Long, well placed to train RN Beach Commandos. In 1960 the house burnt down, leaving only the tower.

As a result, they were sent to HMS *Armadillo*. This facility could take between 500 and 600 men at a time, and due to the rigorous nature of the work, both officers and ratings were mixed together. They not only practised amphibious landings on the shores of Loch Long – under mock attack by the RAF – but also trained in reconnaissance, as well as various more specialised beach skills. To go alongside this, they undertook advanced infantry training, including weapons handling, tackling assault courses, embarking and disembarking from landing craft under battle conditions, field survival, rock climbing and the ubiquitous route marches. This lasted for an intensive 10 weeks.

Each of the beach commando groups – denoted by letters rather than numbers, from A to W (the latter being all-Canadian) – numbered around 70, with 10 officers and 60 ratings, the officers including the principal beachmaster (usually a lieutenant commander), a deputy and three beachmasters. Each commando had an HQ and three units, one for each landing area. The beach commandos were responsible to the high-water mark of a beach; the army was responsible above that.

As an example of how it worked on D-Day, on Juno Beach three RN Beach Commandos (P, S and U) were involved. The first personnel to arrive recced the beach, identified the locations for the beachmasters and assessed the physical nature of the beach. The advance party arrived at H+20 (20 minutes after the assault landing) and began to relay information back to the Deputy Senior Officer Assault Group – the Advanced Beach Signal stations should have been working by H+30. Those on the beach sectors Mike Green and Nan Green were working by then, and Nan White just a little later. That on Nan Red was not ready until H+120.

The main party arrived and surveyed the beach to choose where the LSTs (landing ships) would come in – all the while assisting with unloading and making good the beach. After the fighting had died down, they cleared the beach obstacles.

**The badge of Combined Operations (BELOW) incorporated the RAF eagle, a Tommy gun and an anchor and is obvious on these RN Commandos (RIGHT) on the beach near Courseulles on 13 June 1944. Note the signalling lamp and nearby tin helmet, in case of air attack.**

## 23 No 1 Parachute Training School, RAF Ringway, Cheshire

**Parachute training for soldiers, airmen and various others was undertaken at RAF Ringway – today's Manchester Airport – with descents being made either from a static balloon or an aircraft onto nearby Tatton Park. Glider training was also undertaken in the area.**

The Germans used paratroopers to great effect in their invasions of Denmark, Holland and Belgium in 1940, but at that stage the Allies had no equivalent assault troops. Shortly after he had become prime minister, Winston Churchill decreed that a force of 5,000 trained paratroopers should be put together as soon as possible. A parachute training school was quickly established at Manchester's Ringway Airport – the site was chosen partly because it was well away from the intense air raids of eastern England, and partly because it already had suitable buildings.

It was soon realised that the airport itself was too busy also to act as the landing ground for the parachutists, so Lord Egerton's nearby Tatton Park estate was chosen for this part of the training. In the early stages all jumping was done from aircraft, but this was too slow, so due to the need to maintain maximum throughput, three static balloons came into use. This was because each one could drop three times as many trainees per hour as a single aircraft. They were modified hydrogen-filled barrage balloons, each of which had an internal capacity of 42,000 cubic feet. A

**BELOW AND BELOW RIGHT**
Static drops were the easiest way to start off the training of potential paratroopers. From 800ft, the descent took around half a minute.

special cage was suspended underneath that either featured a hole in the floor as per the Armstrong Whitworth Whitley bombers, or in the side, simulating those found on Douglas Dakota aircraft. The parachutists would climb in together with an RAF instructor and the balloon – which was secured by a cable to a winch vehicle – would then be raised to 800ft. A positive side effect was that due to the lack of a slipstream, accidents were reduced during the training phase.

Once the trainees had successfully completed two or three balloon jumps, they would move on to doing around five from real aircraft. In January 1944, the old Whitley bombers began to be replaced by Douglas Dakotas. Whereas the former could carry only 10 parachutists, the latter could take 20. They were not only bigger inside, but also featured large side doors, which made jumping much easier, as well as faster. This resulted in the men dropping much closer together, a vital aspect in combat.

In 1941, the German *Fallschirmjäger* (paratroopers) gained their greatest – and final – victory. Dropped in large numbers over Crete, they sustained heavy casualties but captured the island and some 12,000 Commonwealth troops. Ironically, the German High Command felt that the casualties precluded further mass use of paratroopers and they were subsequently used by the Germans to great effect as infantry. The Allies, however, took note of the positives and used massed drops of airborne troops – as well as coup-de-main operations – on D-Day, sealing off the beachhead from attacks to the flanks and showing themselves to be elite fighting men.

# 24 Pegasus Bridge training, Countess Wear, Exeter, Devon

In Devon, at Countess Wear outside Exeter, the River Exe and the 16th-century Exeter Ship Canal (TOP) are in a similar configuration to the River Orne and Canal de Caen at Bénouville, in Normandy (ABOVE). Today, the Normandy bridges are better known as Pegasus and Horsa.

**It was essential for the success of the British landings on Sword Beach that the eastern flank was secured before German counter-attacks were launched. This required the capture and defence of two vital bridges by a coup-de-main glider operation.**

Sword Beach, on the eastern edge of the D-Day beaches, was protected from attack by the parallel waterways of the River Orne and the Canal de Caen. It was essential that the road bridges over these were seized early on to ensure German reinforcements could not use them to penetrate the flank.

However, to complicate matters, it was also vital for the bridges to be kept intact if the British 6th Airborne Division was not to be cut off from the rest of the Allied forces and so that they could be used by the Allies at a later date to push on from the beachhead. Intelligence information was that the bridges had been wired for demolition at short notice. To prevent this, the plan called for a glider-borne assault undertaken by a small group of highly trained men. This mission was codenamed Operation *Deadstick*.

The task was assigned to D Company, 2nd (Airborne) Battalion, Oxfordshire and Buckingham-shire Light Infantry (2nd Ox and Bucks), under the leadership of Major John Howard, with Captain Brian Priday as second in command. Two platoons were later added from B Company, along with 30 Royal Engineers from the 249th (Airborne) Field Company to deal with the removal of the demolition charges.

Howard was an unorthodox taskmaster – among many other details, he got his men acclimatised to working at night by ensuring that they rose at 20:00 every evening before going to bed at 13:00. He also requested that his men could practise the task at a location that provided a canal and a river similar to that which they would be attacking.

In the months before D-Day, training for Operation *Deadstick* saw men of the 2nd Ox and Bucks, as Howard later said, 'attacking bridges all over the south of England'. Howard explained:

Every pair of bridges which in any way resembled those to be captured was attacked in every conceivable way and from every direction. Speed and dash were to be essential during this important operation. They became the foundations of every phase of training, from the taped rehearsals in a large field near Wing Barracks at Bulford right up to the final training on the area between the River Exe and the Exeter Ship Canal, at Countess Wear, on the edge of Exeter.[29]

A plaque at the Countess Wear training site reads: 'In May 1944, these bridges played an important part in the preparations for D-Day. They were used over a period of three days and nights, for rehearsals of the famous and crucial glider borne attack on the bridge over the Canal de Caen (Pegasus Bridge) and the River Orne (Horsa Bridge), by the 2nd Battalion Oxfordshire and Buckinghamshire Light Infantry, on the night 5/6 June 1944.'

RIGHT

Survivors of the raid, including John Howard (centre), at Château St Côme in July 1944.

RIGHT

The proximity of the gliders to the bridge is well shown in this photograph. Note the Café Gondrée across the canal – one of the first houses to be liberated in France on the night of 5/6 June.

Countess Wear featured two bridges that were similar to the Benouville and Ranville bridges, being 50 yards long, and located on the same road.

Howard said of the area: 'The Exeter bridges were only 100 yards apart, whereas those in Normandy were 500 yards, but from the training point of view the shorter distance was an advantage, as the attacks were easier to control ... Every advantage was taken of these past few weeks' training. Nothing was left to chance.'[30]

As a result, the men spent the best part of a week continuously conducting exercises and familiarising themselves with the split-second timing of their assigned roles. In order to minimise the risks of losing key personnel, they were also trained to do each other's tasks. Colonel David Wood, one of the officers who took part in the assault, said that by the end they were utterly sick of the sight of the bridges. All the hard work proved worthwhile, though, as the actual attack – which went in at 02:00 on 6 June – was not just successful but an almost perfect display of airmanship. The downside was the first British casualty of the campaign: Lieutenant Den Brotheridge, who is buried in Ranville Cemetery.

# 25  Armagh, Co Armagh, Northern Ireland

RIGHT
Men of the 2nd Infantry Division listen to General Patton. His inspirational – if profane – speeches motivated the troops.

RIGHT
Men of the 2nd Infantry Division listen to General Patton. His inspirational – if profane – speeches motivated the troops.

BELOW
General Patton flew into Greencastle, Northern Ireland, and visited many sites during his stay, including Derrygally House, where the 654th Tank Destroyer Battalion was based.

**Northern Ireland's rugged terrain, together with its distance from the eyes of the enemy, made it a natural choice as a training ground for pre-invasion troops. General George Patton, commander of the Third (US) Army that was not taking part in the D-Day landings, nevertheless played his part with inspirational speeches.**

The first wave of US troops who trained in Northern Ireland went off to fight in North Africa and Italy, but the second batch was destined for the beaches of Normandy. Consequently, pre-D-Day training was an absolutely vital part of their schedule. The 2nd Infantry Division, who sailed from the New York Port of Embarkation on 8 October 1943, began arriving in Belfast on 17 October. Shortly after them came 12,000–15,000 men of the 82nd Airborne Division, considered to be the elite of the US forces, who arrived in late 1943, having already seen action in Italy. They left Naples in November aboard the USS *Frederick Funston* and disembarked in Belfast in December.

The troops were dispersed wherever suitable accommodation could be found that still gave them access to training areas. For example, the 505th Parachute Infantry Regiment – part of the 82nd Airborne Division, under Lieutenant Colonel Herbert F Batcheller – had their headquarters in the Cookstown and Castledawson areas, together with 2,000–3,000 men. After two months in Northern Ireland, where they undertook extensive manoeuvres and did further battle training, they were then moved on to Leicestershire in England for more intensive pre-invasion training.

While the US troops were still in Northern Ireland, they were visited by General George Patton between 30 March and 4 April 1944. On 1 April, troops from the 2nd Infantry Division were lined up along The Mall in Armagh. After Patton and Major General Walter M Robertson had inspected them, Patton addressed them outside the

Armagh County Museum. His speech was one that he had honed since February and would continue to use. This is an extract:

> Men this stuff that some sources sling around about America wanting out of this war, not wanting to fight, is a crock of bullshit. Americans love to fight. All real Americans love the sting and clash of battle.
> Americans love a winner. Americans will not tolerate a loser. Americans despise cowards. Americans play to win all of the time. I wouldn't give a hoot in hell for a man who lost and laughed. That's why Americans have never lost and will never lose a war; for the very idea of losing is hateful to an American.
> Death must not be feared. Death, in time, comes to all men. Yes, every man is scared in his first battle. If he says he's not, he's a liar. Some men are cowards but they fight the same as the brave men or they get the hell slammed out of them watching other men fight who are just as scared as they are. The real hero is the man who fights even though he is scared ... Remember that the enemy is just as frightened as you are, and probably more so.[31]

General Patton addresses the 2nd Infantry outside Armagh County Museum.

The 2nd Infantry Division went on to land at Omaha Beach on D-Day +1 (7 June) near Saint-Laurent-sur-Mer, Normandy, as part of the First (US) Army. On 18 August 1944 they were transferred to Patton's Third Army.

# 26 Orford Battle training area, Suffolk

**To answer the need for a specialist tank training area to prepare for breaking through German coastal defences (known as the Atlantic Wall), a site was established between Orford and the River Alde. It was primarily used by the 79th Armoured Division to practise assaulting antitank obstacles, scaling craters and attacking simulations of Atlantic Wall strongpoints.**

There were many tank training areas in Britain – such as Castlemartin in Wales, Kirkcudbright in Scotland, Salisbury Plain in Wiltshire and Bovington in Dorset. These were traditional training grounds to train armoured units. However, when the invasion of mainland Europe was being contemplated, it soon became obvious that overcoming the Atlantic Wall obstacles was a primary consideration. Beach antitank walls, antitank ditches, strongpoints integrating wire, bunkers and emplacements, enfilading 88mm guns: to overcome these defences a wide variety of technical solutions were tested. While some were little more than madcap ideas, others, such as 'swimming' tanks and those equipped with flails or flamethrowers, worked very well. In April 1943, the experiments were put under the charge of Major General Percy Hobart, who commanded the 79th Armoured Division.

The unit's job was to sort out the wheat from the chaff among the tanks (which became known as 'Hobart's Funnies') and then to train crews to use them. To do this

*Dieppe had shown how difficult it was for armour to leave a beach constrained by antitank or sea defences. The Churchill Ark – an armoured ramp carrier – was one of the designs that was produced for the 79th Armoured Division to combat this. Some 50 were produced and they saw action on D-Day.*

Today, the antitank training wall at
Orford is overgrown but intact.

required a large area – in the end, three sites in Suffolk were set aside, with the Orford
Battle Training Area being the main one. This covered about 12 square miles and
included the villages of Iken and Sudbourne, which had to be evacuated in advance.
Some of the houses were used for accommodation, and many Nissen huts were also
erected. The headquarters was at Sudbourne Hall. All manner of structures were
created across the training area to simulate the expected situation on landing. This
included antitank ditches and obstacles, a mocked-up section of the Atlantic Wall and
large numbers of shell craters.

The basic unit, known as an AVRE – the Armoured Vehicle Royal Engineers – was
derived from the Churchill tank that was well armoured, but in standard form was
inadequately gunned. Instead, the main armament was removed and replaced with a
wide range of specialist devices. Some were fitted with petard trench mortars – these
were short-range guns that threw 40lb bombs to destroy concrete emplacements;
24 rounds could be carried by each tank. To go alongside these, the crews also had
standard demolition charges that could be laid by hand under cover of the tank and
then remotely detonated. Other 'specials' included mine-clearing snakes that were
either made up of long steel pipes packed with explosives or rocket-powered hoses
that were fired into position and then pumped full of a nitroglycerine-based explosive.

Some AVREs carried small bridges that could span 30ft, while others carried
frame charges, fascines (bundles of brushwood) for filling in ditches, or rolls of
matting to create temporary roadways for following vehicles (Bobbins).

The 79th Armoured Division spearheaded the landings on the British beaches
and proved a huge success.

# 27  Duplex Drive Tank Freshwater Training Wing, Fritton, Norfolk

**The area around Fritton Decoy, a lake on the rural Norfolk/Suffolk border near Great Yarmouth, was taken over by the British 79th Armoured Division in order to develop amphibious tanks and then train the necessary crews in how to operate them.**

The development work that had been carried out at places like Orford (*see* pp 58–9) had shown that amphibious tanks – known as Duplex Drive or DD Tanks – were a practical solution to many of the problems thrown up by beach assaults. As a result, they became a major component in the invasion planning, and the only one of 'Hobart's Funnies' to be used by the US Army.

In order to refine the techniques of using DD tanks and to train the necessary crews, Fritton Decoy and the surrounding land was used as an exercise area. The freshwater lake itself – previously used as a wildfowling area – was just over two miles long, about 300 yards wide and up to 15ft deep. The remoteness of the location was ideal as it helped the authorities to maintain secrecy. The site was equipped with the relevant infrastructure: this included an accommodation area, workshop and maintenance facilities, dummy landing craft slipways, simulated beach obstructions and various roadways. It also included a location where crews were trained in exiting their vehicles and in survival techniques. This involved a DD tank inside a water tank that was filled as if the vehicle had foundered.

By the time of D-Day, a special variant of the M4 Sherman medium tank was used. Often referred to as 'Donald Duck tanks' by the troops, they were fitted with flotation screens made of waterproof canvas that provided sufficient buoyancy for them to stay afloat. They were also equipped with a special propeller powered by the tank's engine to drive them forwards when in the water. Due to the scarcity of these valuable assets, however, most of the training was undertaken using older Valentine tanks.

The DD tanks were used with mixed success. On Omaha, the US forces launched too far out, without consideration of the choppy seas, and all but two foundered (interestingly, the two that didn't were commanded by men with small-boat experience). On the British beaches they worked well and contributed significantly in the assault.

Aerial photograph of Fritton Decoy in 1944, showing the four LC(T) ramps from which the DD tanks were launched (marked 'A' on the photograph) and the tank park (marked 'B'; under the magnifier there are 36 DD Valentines visible). (The 'decoy' part of the lake's name means it was used for the breeding and maintenance of waterfowl.)

# 28  Duplex Drive Tank Saltwater Training Wing, Stokes Bay, Hampshire

Tested on the Tetrarch light tank in 1941, Nicholas Strassler's invention – the DD flotation system – was first used on the Valentine tank: 625 were converted by Metro-Cammell from 1942. The Valentines shown in this photograph are from B Wing, 79th Armoured Division, at Stokes Bay.

**After undertaking freshwater training at Fritton, the crews moved to the Saltwater Training School near Gosport. Here they perfected the vital loading and launch techniques used during the invasion landings.**

The still waters of Fritton Decoy were a good starting point, but crews then moved to the south coast to gain saltwater experience. This was much more demanding as it involved the rigours of coping with the sea – stronger winds, bigger waves and cruel tides. This phase of their training was undertaken at the western end of Stokes Bay, an area that faced onto the Solent to the south of Gosport, near Lee-on-Solent, Hampshire.

The school was run by the B Instructional Wing of the 79th Armoured Division from October 1943, and work on improving the techniques of using the Duplex Drive tanks started at the beginning of 1944 and continued until May. Most of this effort was focused on loading and launch techniques – by the time this phase was over, they had conducted more than 30,000 test and training launches and 1,200 men had passed through. Again, Valentine tanks were used for training, during which the crews under instruction had to 'drive' across the Solent – home to some of the most vicious tides in the world – and land at Osborne Bay on the Isle of Wight.

# 29 DUKW Training Centre, Carlyon Bay, Cornwall

**The DUKW is a six-wheel-drive amphibious vehicle that was first produced in 1942. It was first used in combat conditions during Operation *Husky* – the landings on Sicily. The success of the new amphibian was phenomenal.**

American military historian Roland Ruppenthal states: 'The amphibians were used for many purposes, including some not intended. They carried stores far inland to forward dumps, evacuated casualties and prisoners, and in at least one emergency were used to transfer a Ranger battalion to meet a sudden enemy counterattack. Their versatility was immediately recognized, and heavy demands were made on them.'[32]

The DUKW was developed by the National Defense Research Committee and the Office of Scientific Research and Development in the United States. Although it performed well, the military did not understand its capabilities and initially rejected it. It was only when a DUKW rescued seven men who would otherwise have lost their lives after a coastguard vessel ran aground that orders were placed and the DUKW came into general service.

The DUKW was excellent for the transportation of troops and supplies over both land and water – it was said that it was capable of landing stores in one-third of the time required by any other kind of landing craft, with a 50 per cent saving in manpower. As a result, it was considered ideal for backing up any amphibious military operations. Although it was a little unwieldy on firm terrain, it was very stable when in the water.

As it was so new, improvements were made over time. The Assault Training Center at Woolacombe (*see* pp 64–5), for example, improved the gear needed to unload cargo into DUKWs alongside coasters, following exercises in November 1943. Since the DUKW was so unlike any other vehicle, the crews needed more training than simply – in the case of the British drivers – learning how to deal with left-hand drive. In the UK this was done in several locations, including Towyn in Wales, Slapton in Devon, Carlyon Bay, near St Austell in Cornwall, and Annick Water, in Ayrshire, Scotland. There were a number of exercises specifically for D-Day. In one of these, involving the 536th General Transport Company, Royal Army Service Corps (RASC), DUKWs were reversed onto LSTs (landing ships) and then took part in a mock invasion of Canvey Island.

Some 2,000 DUKWs were supplied to Great Britain under the Lend-Lease programme, and as a result a permanent training base for them was established at Towyn, on the coast to the south of Barmouth, in west Wales – the RASC Amphibious Training Centre. All eleven of the general transport companies that were equipped with DUKWs for the Normandy landings had their crews trained there, and each company had 90 DUKWs.

DUKWs training out of Carlyon Bay. The Cornish Riviera Club, taken over for military use during the war, is visible in the top right of the photograph.

**RIGHT**
DUKWs on the beach at Carlyon Bay. The Riviera Club (top centre) had originally opened in the 1930s – created, it is said, at the instigation of the future Edward VIII. After the war it became a major concert venue.

**BELOW**
DUKWs proved to be extremely efficient ferrying supplies from ship to shore. This is Omaha on 6 June.

# 30  US Assault Training Center, Woolacombe, North Devon

The Woolacombe Memorial is dedicated 'to the thousands of American soldiers whose preparation on the sands of Woolacombe and Saunton in the months preceding D-Day carried them to glorious victory on the sands of Normandy'.

**All the spearhead regiments that would land on Omaha and Utah beaches on D-Day – from the 1st, 4th, 28th and 29th Infantry Divisions – trained along the sandy beaches of north Devon under the capable tuition of the Assault Training Center (ATC).**

Having examined carefully the British No 1 Combined Training Centre at Inveraray in western Scotland (*see* pp 46–7) – where 250,000 men, including six US battalions, trained – the US Army established the ATC in June 1943. There were strong similarities in the range of training but obviously differences, too, accommodating different tactics and equipment.

The ATC was a 16-square-mile area of north Devon, centred on the town of Woolacombe. Most of the surrounding beaches were used: Saunton, Croyde, Braunton Burrows and Woolacombe, the latter believed to be ideal due to its similarity to Omaha Beach in all the major aspects, including its topography, the tides, its size and the sand consistency.

Engineer Colonel Paul W Thompson established his headquarters at the Woolacombe Bay Hotel, the Pandora Hotel became the hospital and the Assault Training Center then set about preparing the beach for exercises. This involved removing all the existing defences and remodelling the area to simulate what the troops would encounter in Normandy. Those destined for the ATC were actually told they were going to Wales, in order to maintain a degree of operational security: had

A 1944 view of Woolacombe, looking north-east. Morte Point – the headland visible on the right – was the northern boundary of the ATC. The Woolacombe Bay Hotel is at 'A'.

The training at the ATC was realistic. In this photograph, an infantry unit training on the beach at Bude, south of Woolacombe, uses a Bangalore torpedo to clear wire.

the Germans known about the site, it's possible they would have been able to work out that Normandy was the chosen invasion point.

When everything was ready, on 1 September 1943 the ATC opened for business. Some 5,000 demonstration troops were involved, along with naval units handling landing craft out of Appledore and Instow. The first regiment to run the gauntlet was the 116th Infantry from 29th Division; they would have a second run-through in March 1944. The troops began undertaking simulated landings under heavy fire, doing so in all possible weather conditions. Once ashore, they would then negotiate barbed wire and deal with booby traps before the demolition teams would advance to take out the pillboxes. It was lifelike training using live firing and demolitions.

And then, as quickly as it had begun, in May 1944 most of the troops vanished overnight and the locals knew that the invasion of Europe was imminent.

Some 10,000 men passed through the ATC in its short existence, progressing from exiting static simulations to live-fire exercises.

## 31  Salisbury Plain training area, Wiltshire

**The open landscape of Salisbury Plain made it a natural choice as a military exercise area and it has been used as such since 1897. Hundreds of thousands of troops were trained there for the invasion of Normandy.**

Salisbury Plain covers some 300 square miles and stretches from Warminster and Westbury on the western boundaries to Ludgershall and Tidworth in the east. Almost half of it is today owned by the Ministry of Defence (MoD), much of it purchased by the War Office, the MoD's predecessor, during the Second World War. Across this area are several major military establishments, such as those at Warminster, Larkhill, Bulford and Tidworth. Today's Royal School of Artillery at Larkhill, for instance, was a substantial centre in 1943; there were well over 2,500 permanent staff. Over the course of the war it provided training for more than a million gunners. There were many live-firing ranges – including those at Bulford, Larkhill and Perham Downs.

Likewise, Tidworth Barracks was home to a wide assortment of troops. From 27 November 1943, the US 2nd Armored Division was resident up until the Normandy invasion. Initially the division was under the leadership of Major General Hugh Gaffey, but he was replaced by Major General Edward H Brooks, a decorated First World War veteran, in April 1944. The division was then shipped over to Normandy on 6 June, landing on Omaha Beach on D+3 (9 June).

The US 5th Infantry Division (Mechanised) – nicknamed the 'Red Diamonds' – was also at Tidworth. Commanded by Major General Stafford LeRoy Irwin, the unit had left Iceland in early August 1943, having been sent to England to prepare and undergo training for the Normandy landings. They were stationed at Tidworth Barracks before moving to Northern Ireland. They landed on Utah Beach in Normandy on 9 July 1944.

**Great Britain doesn't have a large land area, and in 1943–44 what it did have was full of military units, equipment and training areas. Salisbury Plain had been linked to the military for many years; other tank and live-firing training areas included Lulworth in Dorset, Otterburn in Northumberland, Castlemartin in Wales and Kirkcudbright in Scotland. All are still active today. These M3 Mediums are at Perham Downs.**

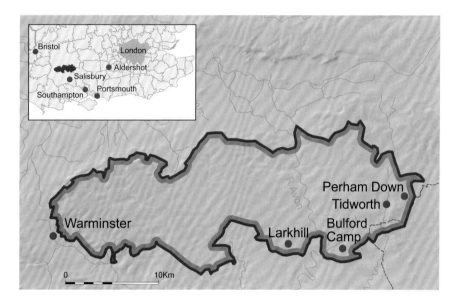

The Salisbury Plain training area is bounded by Warminster in the west and Perham Downs in the east. It's close to the south coast ports and was extensively used by British and American troops.

After the 2nd Armored Division left, Tidworth Barracks became the temporary base of the 9th Armored Division, which, among other achievements, had been part of Operation *Fortitude South* (*see* p 36).

As a postscript, it's interesting to note that one result of the Normandy campaign was a significant increase in the number of German PoWs arriving in the UK. This led to more than 1,000 prison camps in Britain and many of the PoWs were held in camps on Salisbury Plain.

The 29th Infantry Division was one of the two US infantry divisions that attacked Omaha Beach. It had arrived in England in October 1942, having crossed the Atlantic on RMS *Queen Mary*. It's seen here in 1943 training at Tidworth.

# 32 Tyneham evacuated village, Dorset

**The need for exercise areas in the run-up to Operation *Overlord* led to several villages being evacuated to make way for the troops. Two, in particular, have caught the public imagination because they are still in use by the Ministry of Defence – Imber, on Salisbury Plain in Wiltshire, and Tyneham, near Lulworth in south Dorset.**

**In a strange way, Tyneham and its surrounding area have benefited from their military ownership. The area has been spared the developers, is a haven for wildlife and is unspoilt – although that is little compensation for those who were never able to return to their homes.**

Part of the plan drawn up for the invasion of Normandy detailed that American troops who were shipped across the Atlantic would undergo further training before taking part in the landings. In order to provide the appropriate exercise areas, in 1943 the villages of Imber, on Salisbury Plain in Wiltshire, and Tyneham, in south Dorset, were evacuated of all civilians.

This was relatively easy to achieve in the former instance as the War Office owned almost all the land in and around the village, and so the residents were technically just tenants who could be moved out at short notice. At Tyneham, though, the land had to be requisitioned, with this taking place just before Christmas

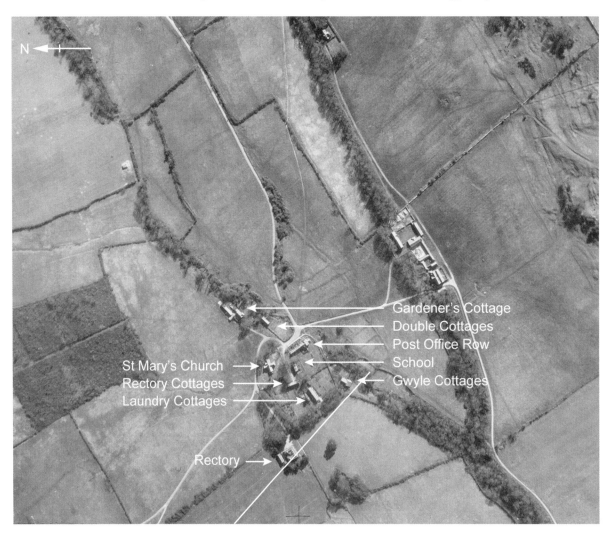

St Mary's Church
Rectory Cottages
Laundry Cottages
Gardener's Cottage
Double Cottages
Post Office Row
School
Gwyle Cottages
Rectory

**ABOVE AND ABOVE RIGHT**
Imber was never returned to the people who left it in 1943 and it is still used by the military to train for fighting in built-up areas.

1943. Although the inhabitants in both places were told that these were temporary measures and that they would be able to return after the war, they were never actually allowed back.

The village of Imber lies to the west of the road between the villages of Tilshead and West Lavington, in a particularly remote part of Salisbury Plain. Since it was scheduled to be used by US forces as a free-fire training area, the inhabitants were given 47 days to leave. Many even left food for the troops in their houses, thinking that it wouldn't be long before they were back home. Imber is still in use today for FIBUA training (fighting in built-up areas). There is little access to the village and little remaining other than the church.

Tyneham is equally haunting. Located just to the northeast of Worbarrow Bay on the south Dorset coast, it lies in a quiet valley between two ridges of the Purbeck Hills, near Lulworth on the Isle of Purbeck.

Military involvement with the village started during the First World War with the nearby presence of Lulworth Ranges and Bovington Camp. In 1941 it became an administrative centre for RAF Brandy Bay radar station. In 1943 Tyneham was requisitioned by the War Office. It was amalgamated into the Lulworth firing range, along with 7,500 acres of the surrounding heath and chalk downland. The US 2nd Armored Division trained here in April 1944.

Requisitioning the village displaced 225 people – the last person to leave left a note on the door of the church saying, 'Please treat the church and houses with care; we have given up our homes, where many of us lived for generations, to help win the war to keep men free. We shall return one day and thank you for treating the village kindly.'

Tyneham can be visited on the days the range isn't open and many people – more than 100,000 per annum at the last count – take the opportunity to do so on the 140 days a year it is open. It is still quiet and tranquil and, thanks (unwittingly) to the army, unspoilt.

# 33  Studland Bay training area, Dorset

**The final weeks before D-Day saw a series of exercises held around Britain to iron out specific operational and tactical issues. Six weeks before D-Day, therefore, Exercise *Smash* was a major rehearsal undertaken on the lengthy sandy beaches of Studland and Shell Bays.**

Studland Bay, looking from Fort Henry bunker (at 'A') towards the Little Sea, a lake in today's Studland and Godlingston Heath National Nature Reserve.

The locations had been chosen because – unlike so many of Britain's south coast beaches, which are pebbly – these were similar to the sandy beaches of Normandy. A further bonus was that most of the civilian population had already been evacuated, so keeping the exercise secret was much easier and there was less risk of accidental injury or death as the result of stray shells landing in unexpected places. Before the practices could take place, however, all of the existing beach defences had to be dismantled and the minefields lifted.

On 18 April 1944, under the watchful eyes of Prime Minister Winston Churchill, Allied Supreme Commander General Eisenhower and King George VI, a live-fire exercise was conducted. The VIPs were kept safe in Fort Henry – a structure that stood on Redend Point overlooking the bay. This was a newly built concrete observation bunker with walls and ceilings that were 3ft thick; overall, it was 90ft long. Using live ordnance, though not usual, was considered vital in order to make the rehearsals as realistic as possible. It wasn't just live artillery shells and small arms ammunition that was used – the RAF also dropped real bombs on the beaches.

The exercise involved the British 50th Infantry Division and also saw the first use of the DD tanks in a large-scale operation – again, as it was training, they had to use the older Valentines instead of the M4 Shermans. These were launched from further out than was usual as the larger landing craft were unable to get close in. The crews involved were terrified that shrapnel would puncture their flotation skirts – they knew that if this happened, the tank would sink immediately. As it was, four or five tanks were lost and six men drowned; two of the tanks are still there under 15 metres of water. This was nothing like as bad as things proved in reality – on D-Day at Omaha Beach alone, 27 of 29 DD Shermans foundered, with many of the crews dying.

The realism of Exercise *Smash* came as a surprise to some of the participants. According to a thesis written by Ethan Rawls Williams, 'Veteran members of the Durham Light Infantry remarked that the training during the *Smash* exercises approached an intensity not seen since combat in North Africa or Sicily.'[33]

## Major US training exercises in 1944

***Duck I*** (3–4 January): 29th Infantry Division, Slapton Sands.
***Duck II*** (9–16 February): 29th Infantry Division, Slapton Sands.
***Duck III*** (23 February–1 March): 29th Infantry Division, Slapton Sands.
***Fox*** (1–10 March): 16th Regimental Combat Team (RCT) (1st Infantry Division) and 116th RCT (29th Infantry Division), Slapton Sands.
***Muskrat I*** (13–23 March): 12th Infantry Regiment (4th Infantry Division), Firth of Clyde, Scotland.
***Otter I*** (15–18 March): 3rd Battalion of the 8th Infantry Regiment (4th Infantry Division), Slapton Sands.
***Mink I*** (15–18 March): 1st Battalion of the 22nd RCT (4th Infantry Division), Slapton Sands.
***Otter II*** (19–22 March): 1st Battalion of the 8th Infantry Regiment (4th Infantry Division), Slapton Sands.
***Mink II*** (19–22 March): 2nd Battalion of the 22nd RCT (4th Infantry Division), Slapton Sands.
***Muskrat II*** (24–26 March): 12th Infantry Regiment (4th Infantry Division), Firth of Clyde.
***Beaver*** (29–31 March): 8th and 22nd Infantry RCTs (4th Infantry Division), Slapton Sands.
***Curveball I*** (27 April): 82nd AB Division, location unknown.
***Curveball II*** (6 May): 82nd AB Division, location unknown.
***Eagle*** (11 May) 82nd and 101st AB Divisions, Hungerford–Newbury.
***Tiger*** (22 April–1 May): US troops assaulting Utah and AB troops, Slapton Sands.
***Fabius*** (23 April–7 May): all British and Canadian beach units, US units assaulting Omaha, various locations.

Grade II-listed, Fort Henry (at 'A' opposite) is on Redend Point and was used to observe live-firing amphibious training exercises such as *Smash*.

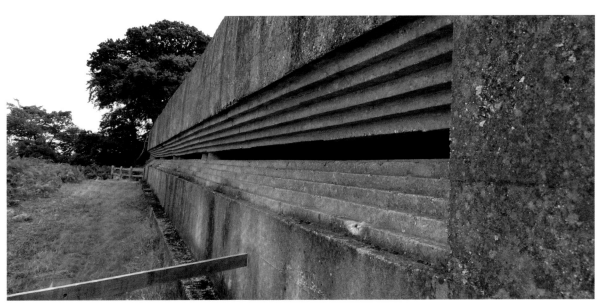

# 34  Slapton Sands training area and evacuated villages, Devon

**Slapton, in south Devon, was requisitioned by the British government in late 1943 for use by US forces destined to land on Utah Beach, which Slapton Sands resembled. The inhabitants were evacuated at short notice and the US personnel moved in.**

On 12 November 1943 a proclamation was posted in the South Hams villages of East Allington, Blackawton, Chillington, Sherford, Slapton, Strete, Stokenham and Torcross: 'Every person should leave the area by December 20th.' Force U – destined to land at Utah Beach – would use the 30,000 acres or so cleared for landing practices. Utah Beach, on the southeast of the Cotentin Peninsula above the River Vire, was composed of gravel, behind which was a strip of land, and behind that a low-lying area of flooded land. Since the topography of Slapton Sands in Devon bore a direct similarity to this layout, it was selected for use for manoeuvres. As the area was still populated with civilians, around 3,000 had to be moved out of harm's way before the exercises could start.

Slapton Sands, the aerial view (ABOVE) taken from the south-east; the map (BELOW) showing some of the surrounding evacuated villages. There are memorials at both ends, one to the dead of Exercise *Tiger* and the other an obelisk remembering the evacuation of the area so it could be used for live firing.

There's a surprising twist to the choice of Slapton. In early July 1938 there was an earlier amphibious exercise there. It was instigated by a certain Brigadier Bernard Montgomery – and it is likely that this is why Slapton was suggested to the Americans in 1943. The first American landing took place there on 16 August 1943, before the area was requisitioned, when elements of the 175th Infantry Regiment, 29th Infantry Division, arrived. Further practice landings took place both before and after the evacuation of the civilians – those after the event using live fire, which damaged many of the properties in the area. But the main reason for the evacuation was a large-scale rehearsal of the assault on Utah Beach less than two months before the invasion: Exercise *Tiger*.

## Exercise *Tiger*

Although there were tragic outcomes when first 'friendly fire' and later an attack by German *Kriegsmarine* E-boats cost many hundreds of lives, *Tiger* was an important part of the D-Day preparations. It opened under the command of Admiral Don P Moon, US Navy, on 22 April 1944, lasting until 30 April. It involved the landing of around 30,000 troops from nine large LSTs (landing ships) under live naval fire.

The first major problem that reared its head was that not all those involved were using the same radio frequencies. This resulted in the Royal Navy escort vessels (two destroyers, three motor torpedo boats and two motor gunboats) being in the wrong place at the wrong time, and when a patrol of nine E-boats was sighted, the warning message wasn't received by the LSTs. Consequently, when the

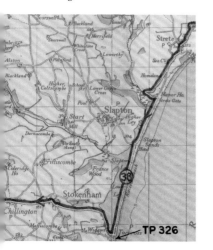

TP 326

**ABOVE**
Slapton Sands was used by Force U destined for Utah Beach, although its configuration from this angle is more like that of Omaha.

**RIGHT AND ABOVE RIGHT**
Blackpool Sands lies to the north-east of Slapton Sands and was part of the same training area. The activities on the beach are the object of interest to some very young spectators in this wartime photograph (ABOVE RIGHT). The modern-day photograph (RIGHT) shows the beach in more peaceful times.

'Bessie', a waterproofed M10 tank destroyer on the beach at Slapton, along with other armoured vehicles and a bulldozer. Note in the foreground the wire netting used to improve beach roadways. In the background are three landing craft: two LCTs – the smaller landing craft tank – and an LST. This one, *325*, saw action in the landings on North Africa, Sicily and at Anzio, before being used to land 59 vehicles and more than 400 troops on Omaha Beach. Today, *LST-325* is preserved at Evansville, Indiana.

Exercise *Tiger* took place 22–30 April 1944, and during the night of 27 April a convoy of poorly protected LSTs was attacked by E-boats, leading to many casualties. This M4 tank was recovered from the sea and placed at Slapton as a memorial to those who died.

German E-boats attacked Convoy T-4 early on 27 April in Lyme Bay, there were many more casualties – at least 749 men died – than would have otherwise been the case.

Radio and command problems also led to many needless friendly fire deaths during the dawn landing practices. This came about because there were unexpected delays in the firing schedule, and because some of the men weren't told, they were directly under the naval bombardment when it came. It is thought that as many as 450 were killed.

Despite the tragic loss of lives, the exercises highlighted a number of deficiencies that were addressed in detail. Consequently, the mistakes encountered gave lessons that played a very important part in the later success of the invasion. These included standardising radio frequencies, giving the troops full training in the use of life vests and the provision of small craft to collect floating survivors. Since Exercise *Tiger* was part of the lead-up to D-Day, the whole affair – including the loss of so many lives – was kept under strict secrecy until much later.

# 35 Hayling Island training area, Hampshire

**Following the Studland rehearsals, a second round of practice landings was undertaken to further refine the planning and control. Known as Exercise *Fabius*, these were dispersed over six different sectors along the south coast of England.**

A number of important lessons were learned during Studland Bay's Exercise *Smash* (*see* p 70). In order to further refine command and control before the D-Day landings took place, a second round of rehearsals was undertaken from 23 April to 7 May 1944, with the assault landing planned for 3 May. These were the biggest amphibious trials conducted during the Second World War and were split into six different exercises:

- Exercise *Fabius 1* involved the US 1st and 29th Infantry Divisions and took place on Slapton Sands, Devon (*see* pp 72–4). This was a rehearsal of the landings on Omaha Beach.
- Exercise *Fabius 2* involved the British 50th (Northumbrian) Infantry Division and took place on the beaches of Hayling Island, Hampshire. This was the rehearsal of the landings on Gold Beach. During this exercise seven men were drowned and this led to a change in the way infantry left LCI(L)s (a type of landing craft; *see* p 49). On D-day they would be transferred to shore by LCMs, which worked more efficiently.
- Exercise *Fabius 3* involved the 3rd Canadian Infantry Division and took place on the beaches of Bracklesham Bay, West Sussex. This was the rehearsal of the landings on Juno Beach.
- Exercise *Fabius 4* involved the British 3rd Infantry Division under Major General Tom Rennie and took place on the beach of Littlehampton, West Sussex. This was the rehearsal of the landings on Sword Beach.

M4 medium tanks land from an LCT during Exercise *Fabius*.

- Exercises *Fabius 5* and *6* involved the Anglo-American supply units who were under training for support missions. Most of their rehearsals were conducted in the Thames Estuary and the East Coast ports, as well as at ports in the Southampton/Portsmouth area.

The commanders did everything they could to simulate the conditions the troops would experience when they landed in Normandy.

As with the Studland Bay rehearsals (*see* p 70), Prime Minister Winston Churchill and Allied Supreme Commander General Eisenhower were onlookers. In this case, they viewed the action from the roof of the nearby Royal Hotel on Hayling Island (at 'A' below). From there, they observed the assault on Beachlands by the 50th (Northumbrian) Infantry Division, who were destined to land at Gold Beach on D-Day.

**2018 view of the seafront at West Town, Hayling Island showing the Royal Hotel.**

There were so many ships and aircraft involved in the six components of Exercise *Fabius* – from Slapton Sands in the west to the East Coast ports – that if the Germans had seen the enormous numbers, they would have been alerted to the imminence of the invasion. To reduce the risk of enemy observation occurring, the planners scheduled non-stop air and sea patrols to cut off the English Channel and prevent the Germans getting anywhere close.

**LCAs – landing craft assault – carried 30–36 men. Those shown in this photograph are landing on Hayling Island.**

**2018 view of Hayling Island's sandy shingle that was a good facsimile of the French coast for 50th Infantry's exercise in May 1944.**

Mulberry B

June
1944

The leaves of the trees are for
the healing of the Nations.

In loving and grateful memory
of Allan Harry Beckett
1914 – 2005
Designer of the roadways
and anchors for the
Mulberry Harbours in
Normandy, which made
possible the liberation of Europe

# 3 | Logistical challenges

**LEFT**

It was hoped that the Mulberry Harbours would play a significant role in solving some of the logistical challenges posed by the Normandy landings. This fine stained-glass window at St Peter's Church, in Oare, Kent, with its mulberry-tree design, remembers Royal Engineer Allan Beckett. Beckett (*see* p 96) designed floating roadways for the harbours and solved problems with anchoring, as is identified at the bottom of the window.

The mission of the US Army's Quartermaster Corps 'was to supply the troops with food, clothing, equipage, fuel, and all sorts of general supplies in the proper quantity and quality at the right time and in the right place.'[34] That nicely sums up one side of the logistics mission: ensuring the troops had the equipment and supplies they needed, when and where they needed them. Easy to say, but it wasn't so straightforward to do.

For the Americans, Canadians and other troops who used Britain as a staging post, the first step was bringing the troops over the Atlantic. In 1942 and 1943 this was a hazardous journey. Although with hindsight U-boat attrition of convoys was overall less damaging than thought at the time, March and April 1943 were critical months. Allied losses in the Atlantic were 82 ships (484,000 tons) in March and 39 (239,000 tons) in April. The Atlantic War had seen a significant attrition of British shipping and the escort vessels that were needed in the Atlantic were also needed in the Mediterranean to support the invasions of first Sicily and then mainland Italy.

In fact, the U-boat threat was not as bad for troopships because they tended to be faster – particularly when the big liners were used. RMS *Queen Elizabeth*, the largest liner in the world, entered service in military employ in 1940 (her first use as a liner was in 1946) and was used from 1942 in the Atlantic, mainly ferrying US troops. During the war she sailed half a million miles and carried more than 750,000 people – on occasion carrying more than 15,000 troops at a time. Her sister ship, RMS *Queen Mary*, was equally active, with very similar mileage and troops-carried figures. Nicknamed the 'Grey Ghost', the *Queen Mary* carried 15,740 soldiers and 943 crew on one trip (on 25–30 July 1943) – a record. During this trip she survived, just, a giant wave that may have reached 92ft. Another time, while carrying men of the 29th Infantry Division, she sank her escort, HMS *Curacao*, in a collision off the Irish coast: 239 died.

**RIGHT**

RMS *Queen Mary*, anchored on the River Clyde after another transatlantic crossing.

**RIGHT AND BELOW RIGHT**
Ashchurch Camp was an important
location for the storage of
munitions, vehicles and equipment.

The build-up of US forces in England for an invasion of France was codenamed Operation *Bolero* and saw 1.6 million US servicemen in England on 6 June 1944; as late as 30 April 1945 there were still more than 400,000, including airmen and those in hospitals. The immense involvement of American forces in Britain is well summed up by Eisenhower in *Crusade in Europe*:

> Major General John C H Lee reported to command our Services of Supply (SOS). He at once began the appalling task of preparing ports and building warehouses, camps, airfields, and repair facilities, all of which would be needed before we could start an offensive from the British base. The work accomplished under his direction was so vital to success and so vast in proportion that its description would require a book in itself. By the time the cross-Channel assault was launched, two years later, the United Kingdom was one gigantic air base, workshop, storage depot, and mobilization camp. It was claimed facetiously at the time that only the great number of barrage balloons floating constantly in British skies kept the islands from sinking under the seas.[35]

The American units included Ordnance and Quartermaster depots, hospitals and an infrastructure that could supply and resource US forces with all their equipment and supplies. Most of the locations were supplied or built by the British. As an example, the first – and largest – supply depot was G-25 Ashchurch, outside Tewkesbury, Gloucestershire. Built in 1938 for the Royal Army Service Corps (RASC), the US Army Ordnance Corps took over Ashchurch and four other depots in June 1942. Included in the personnel was a unit of black American soldiers, a new experience for Tewkesbury, as was the segregation of white and black troops, something that did not sit well in Britain.

## Canadian Army Overseas

The Canadians also moved to Britain in high numbers – starting on 4 November 1939. On 10 December convoy TC1, composed of five liners – the *Aquitania*, *Duchess of Bedford*, *Empress of Australia*, *Empress of Britain* and *Monarch of Bermuda* – carried 7,449 officers and men of the Canadian 1st Division from Halifax, Nova Scotia. Between 1939 and 1945 nearly 370,000 Canadians crossed the Atlantic in more than 300 sailings. Only one was intercepted: the *Nerissa* was hit by three torpedoes on 21 April 1941 and sank.

The Canadians were deployed on the south coast of England to help set up defences against a possible invasion. From autumn 1941 to early 1944 the defence of Britain was largely in the hands of the First Canadian Army; the 1st, 2nd and 3rd Canadian Infantry Divisions and other formations spent many months in Sussex.

It is worth noting that in summer 1940, when Britain was at its lowest ebb, its army struggling on the sands of Dunkirk, Canada stepped up. In May enlistments were 6,909; in June 29,319 and July 29,171. Including officer and nursing sister appointments, 85,102 men and women joined the Canadian Active Service Force between May and August 1940.

With more and more Canadians arriving in England, a number of reorganisations became necessary. The Canadian Military HQ expanded and was set up in the Sun Life Building, next door to Canada House, on Cockspur Street, London. The Canadian Army Overseas had used the British Royal Army Ordnance Corps, but early in 1942 the Canadian Base Ordnance Depot was created (it was later reorganised as Central Ordnance Depot in January 1944). The Royal Canadian Electrical and Mechanical Engineers (RCEME) was set up early in 1944, because the Canadian Army Overseas had found British repair facilities unable to cope with the sheer volume of work to be done. In the end, RCEME had an establishment of 3,547, of all ranks, chiefly in No 1 Base Workshop (originally Base Ordnance Workshop) at Borden in Hampshire.

A little-known but important unit, the Canadian Forestry Corps had been a great success in the First World War. From the start of the Second World War, Britain identified a similar requirement when supplies from Scandinavia and Russia were cut off. As the timber output of each company of the Forestry Corps was 'roughly equivalent to the timber carried by a ship of 6,000 tons plying regularly from Canada under war-time conditions',[36] so the British government kept asking for more companies. The last new company reached Britain in October 1942, giving the corps a peak strength in February 1943 of 220 officers and 6,771 other ranks. Canadian forestry operations in Scotland ended in June 1945, having produced more than 394 million board feet of sawn lumber, and production in other categories was in proportion.

In autumn 1943, the British Army was running short of junior officers – just at a time when Canada had more officers than could be employed in active battalions. The CANLOAN scheme was devised to allow Canadian officers to volunteer to serve in the British Army. A memorial in Ottawa remembers '673 Canadian Officers volunteered for loan to the British Army and took part in the invasion and liberation of Europe 1944–45. CANLOAN total casualties were 465, of which 128 were fatal.' CANLOAN officers were awarded 41 Military Crosses (one with bar), a Silver Star (US), a Distinguished Service Cross, four *Croix de Guerre* (French), one MBE and an Order of Bronze Lion (Dutch).

**A number of CANLOAN officers served in the British Parachute Regiment – as did Lieutenant G P Comper (left), talking here with Canadian Major General E G Weeks at the first CANLOAN annual reunion, on 14 April 1945.**

# 36 US Army Quartermaster Depot Q-328 West Moors, Dorset

**Now once again a petroleum depot, West Moors started life in 1938 as a British ammunition depot and became a US Petroleum Depot in 1944, in time to be important for the D-Day landings.**

West Moors is well sited. It is near a heavily wooded area owned by the Forestry Commission, between the old Southern Railway main rail line from London to Exeter and the line to Weymouth. It is close to the ports of Weymouth, Swanage, Poole, Lymington, Southampton, Gosport and Portsmouth. It's also close to the training areas of Salisbury Plain, south Dorset (Lulworth and Bovington), Bordon and the New Forest, and is near to St Leonard's Military Hospital.

The US Army arrived in the area in 1943 and developed the depot significantly. A large siding – 8.6 miles of lines with 41 sets of hand-operated points and an iconic triple semaphore signal on the main line – became operational on 14 February 1943 and had been worked up by 24 July.

This wartime aerial view of part of West Moors shows the railway link that closed as part of Dr Beeching's cuts to the railways in the 1960s. In wartime, the depot was accessed as sidings from the line, which ran to Poole and Bournemouth.

POL – petrol, oil and lubricants – has always been the main interest of West Moors.

This was one of six depots in the south of England storing the fuel for the landings and was run by the 3877th Quartermaster Gasoline Supply Company, which was attached to the 306th QM Battalion. All became involved in Exercise *Tiger* and are identified on the 1st Engineer Special Brigade Monument in Normandy, having assaulted with 1st Infantry Division. They would have been operating in Normandy by D+8, with a forward POL (petrol, oil and lubricants) dump that would have issued up to 165,000 gallons of gasoline a day to divisional units. All the petrol was delivered in 5-gallon jerrycans; the diesel in 55-gallon drums.

Every day there were regular train deliveries to the depot and convoys of lorries left carrying fuel to the units. The train loads were sizeable: each rail tank car carried 15 tons of fuel, and each train pulled more than 50 cars. They had a speed restriction and a detailed regime of stopping to check brakes etc for safety. The depot at its peak held 75,000 tons of fuel and outflow peaked at 1,700 tons a day.

Luckily the depot was never attacked by the Luftwaffe – perhaps helped by its proximity to woodland. It was handed back to the British in 1946, when it was used to house PoWs.

The Military Railway Service – part of the US Army Transportation Corps – was instrumental in rebuilding the French railway system, shattered by months of careful bombing. It took 1,500 locomotives to France, many of which had been used in Britain beforehand. This photograph shows an S100 class 0-6-0T at West Moors.

## 37  US Army Quartermaster Depot Q-324 Kingston Maurward, Dorset

**As with so many of Britain's country houses, the Palladian Kingston Maurward was requisitioned in 1939. By 1944 its grounds had become a petrol storage depot for the invasion.**

From the great icons such as Winston Churchill's birthplace, Blenheim Palace, which became first a school then an MI5 outstation, to the less well-known Hinton Ampner in Hampshire, which became a girls' school, large houses all over Britain were taken over by establishments pushed out of the cities by the Luftwaffe. Those taken over by the military became hospitals and headquarters, or billets.

Some were badly damaged by their experience, others were left with unexpected treasures – Agatha Christie's house, Greenway, on the River Dart in Devon, has a D-Day frieze painted by a US Coast Guard lieutenant; Harlaxton Manor, in Lincolnshire, became the officers' mess for nearby RAF Harlaxton and later in the war elements of the British 1st Airborne Division left graffiti before they departed for Arnhem.

Kingston Maurward was somewhat damaged by its military usage: it became the headquarters of a depot responsible for POL (petrol, oil and lubricants). Some of the materiel was under cover, often in Quonset huts – a development of the British Nissen hut first made at Quonset Point, Rhode Island, over 150,000 of which were manufactured during the war – but much of it was outdoors.

The British weather wasn't conducive to leaving everything outside and so tentage had to be used and by 1943 there had been significant improvements to packaging and tents so that even such perishables such as sugar and flour could be stored safely.

**Kingston Maurward in 1943. Many Americans found the requisitioned country houses less than congenial, with their poor heating, poor lighting and – to their minds – inadequate sanitation and showering facilities.**

**Kingston Maurward today.**

Kingston Maurward is 2 miles from the D3 Marshalling Area Camp at Yellowham Wood (*see* pp 124–5), 6 miles from the D9 Marshalling Area Camp at Bincombe, 10 miles from Weymouth Quay (*see* pp 142–3) and 16 miles from the Portland hards (*see* pp 145–6), and was therefore ideally suited for troops and vehicles on their way to Normandy.

**Quonset huts were built in their thousands across Britain and used for personnel as well as storage.**

# 38  US Army 756th Railway Shop Battalion, Newport, Wales

**Much of the preparations for D-Day and the campaign on the Continent rested on the movement of men and munitions. Britain's railways – particularly its engines and rolling stock – had endured considerable attrition since 1939: new blood was needed.**

This photograph, taken on 7 April 1944, shows tank and freight cars at Newport (Ebbw Junction), waiting for D-Day. The 40-ton tank wagons could carry 9,000 gallons and were nearly 41ft long. They had been shipped across the Atlantic in pieces and put together in Newport.

First in Britain and then on the Continent of Europe, men of the USATC – the US Army Transportation Corps – struggled with the logistics of bringing some 1,500 locomotives and 20,000 wagons across the Atlantic. Then they had to rebuild them, get them to France and run them on railway infrastructure that had to be rebuilt after being destroyed by Allied bombers during the fighting.

The 756th Railway Shop Battalion was sponsored by the Pennsylvania Railroad Company, activated on 4 January 1942. It trained in Bucyrus and Crestline, Ohio, and

The background may have been deleted by the censor but this is also the 756th Railway Shop Battalion, Ebbw Junction Supply Depot. The locomotives – mainly S160 class 2-8-0s – were designed for heavy freight use.

crossed the Atlantic to the UK in early September 1943. Ultimately, it was divided into two detachments of about 12 officers and 320 men. D, which operated Depot TC-201 at Hainault, Essex, comprised the Battalion HQ, and was 'the location of what was to become the largest and most active railway car assembly plant in the United Kingdom.'[37] As it grew, so did its personnel. Detachment E, under the command of Major Edwin C Hanly, the Battalion Executive Officer, operated Depot TC-203 in Wales with billets at Caerphilly and the works 12 miles away in Ebbw Junction Shed, the old Great Western Railway erecting shed at Newport, Monmouthshire.

Here, Detachment E, between 7 September 1943 and 17 May 1944, assembled 358 S160 class 2-8-0 and 70 0-6-0 steam locomotives and 24 diesels. Assembly time was 260, 170 and 300 hours respectively, after which the locomotives were run-in (the 2-8-0s by a run on the main line, the others by performing shunting duties) and then stored – mainly at Tonteg, Penrhos and Cadoxten – awaiting dispatch to the Continent. In fact, a number of the S160s were run-in on the British rail network, the American locomotives supplementing the creaking inventory of British motive power.

Making engines wasn't Detachment E's only job. They were also employed making fittings for Liberty ships – 272 urinal troughs and 38,000 berths – and installing the equipment on 14 LSTs (landing ships) so they could handle rail traffic.

The second phase of the operation – the release of locomotives from storage and the checking of those that had been working on Britain's rail system preparatory to their shipping to the Continent – started in September 1944.

# 39 Royal Naval Armament Depot, Priddy's Hard, Gosport, Hampshire

**An essential part of warfare, at Priddy's Hard Armament Depot ammunition was safely made and stored by female workers so that it could be dispersed around the 3,000-vessel fleet before D-Day.**

Priddy's Hard (now the Explosion Museum of Naval Firepower) is in the top left ('A') of this 2018 photograph, which looks over the redeveloped Royal Clarence Victualling Yard. The mill ('B') and bakery ('C') are part of a redevelopment that has enhanced the Gosport side of Portsmouth Harbour.

The land on which Priddy's Hard Armament Depot was constructed was purchased from Jane Priddy by the British Crown in 1750. By Nelson's time, the Grand Magazine held some 4,500 100lb (45kg) barrels of gunpowder and supplied Royal Navy warships like *Victory*. By 1944 large quantities of gunpowder were no longer stored there: cordite, torpedoes, depth charges and Royal Naval small arms ammunition were the new armaments made on site. The depot had increased in size considerably as other locations – such as HM *Gunwharf*, in Portsmouth – closed down. Priddy's Hard gained foundries, testing ranges, repair shops – even an 18-mile internal railway system (the Priddy's Hard, Frater and Bedenham Railway) that linked to the Fareham–Gosport main line at Holbrook and, from 1944, employed Hunslet diesel locomotives.

The workforce was largely female. The men were away fighting and so the women took their place. At times numbering more than 4,000, the workers at

Two photographs from a sequence titled 'Life at Royal Navy Armament Depot Priddy's Hard, Gosport, 25–30 July 1944'. The first shows work in the Shell Painting Room. All shells required identification colours and lettering (for example, to distinguish between armour-piercing and high-explosive). The second is captioned: 'Some jobs are so dangerous that they can only be done by remote control. Here a girl is placing a shell and cartridge in a machine which will pull them apart. The machine is surrounded by an 18-inch wall and is operated by remote control.' The operator can be seen in the mirror at the back.

Priddy's Hard tested weapons, repaired naval ordnance including mines, filled shells and other armaments – even made boxes in which to store the ammunition. They worked hard: some of them worked 12-hour shifts, round the clock.

Priddy's Hard was also a dispersal point for munitions made and stored off-site at sub-depots such as Bedenham, Elson (where depth charges or torpedoes were stored) and Frater (mines) or other Royal Naval Armament Depots such as the Dean Hill underground facility. Sent from these locations, they would be issued to ships.

# 40 PLUTO pumping station, Fawley, Hampshire

This Plaque marks the site from which the Pluto oil & pipe line left these shores for France at the time of the Allied Forces Landing at Normandy in June 1944

A plaque on Shanklin Esplanade commemorating the PLUTO pipeline, which ran from Lepe, in Hampshire, across the Solent and the Isle of Wight to France.

The pipeline was wound around large bobbin-shaped drums nicknamed 'conundrums' (cone-ended drums).

**Armies may well move on their stomachs, but for a modern army, fuel is almost as important – particularly so after an amphibious landing where resupply may be compromised by enemy naval assets.**

Unlike the German Army that, even this late in the war, was essentially horse-drawn, the Allied armies were voracious consumers of fuel. The plan for the Normandy campaign called for a lot of it. So essential was the requirement for an uninterrupted supply that Allied planners spent much time and effort trying to work out a better solution than oil tankers, which would be at the mercy of the weather and German naval and air assets.

The answer was PLUTO – commonly translated as Pipe Line Under the Ocean – a brilliant idea that was at the edge of what was technically possible at the time. From as early as 1942 engineers worked on the practicalities of producing a flexible pipe which could be deployed by ship. In the end the original lead core idea (named HAIS after its developers Arthur Hartley, the Anglo-Iranian Oil Company and Siemens) proved impractical (it needed too much lead). A mild steel version (HAMEL, named after the engineers Hammick and Ellis) deployed from a huge 'conundrum' (cone-ended drum) did the trick. Prototypes were tested and the pipeline was eventually, after many trials and tribulations, laid. One contractor worked 18 hours a day for two years on the project.

In the end, it was unnecessary. The Germans collapsed in France after the Allies broke out following Operation *Cobra* and the Luftwaffe and Kriegsmarine were never a threat to the tankers. The battle in the west was won by the Allies with only 8 per cent of their fuel coming through PLUTO. There had been shortages of fuel because of the speed of the armies' advance, but they were overcome. Nevertheless, the technical advances made during the project would be valuable elsewhere.

Financially, the pipe was definitely worth salvaging post war and therefore little remains of the enterprise. In England, the fuel tanks at Fawley, the pumphouses and most of the run of pipe across to Cherbourg have gone. However, a small 65-yard section of pipe at Shanklin Chine on the Isle of Wight has been preserved for posterity.

Today, the area of Badminston Common, Fawley (ABOVE), once used for PLUTO (as shown on the map, RIGHT) is wasteland.

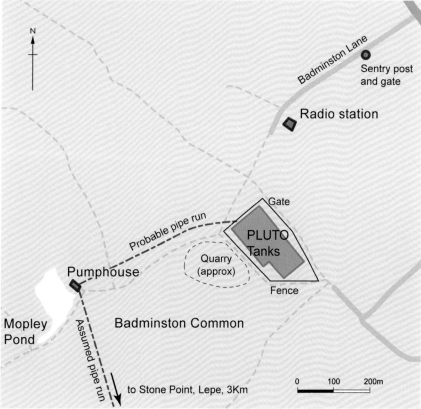

# 41  US Army Ordnance Depot O-617, Bideford, Devon

**Amphibious landings, by their very nature, set great challenges to vehicles – tracked and wheeled – that need to wade through salt water between landing craft and beach. The waterproofing had to be 100 per cent effective and enable vehicles to cope with three feet of water with waves on top.**

As well as coping with the water, vehicles had to be able to drive distances with the waterproofing in place and, as would certainly be necessary, cope with the rigours of an opposed landing. The other problem was that the vehicles were all different sizes: from Universal carriers to tanks, and from jeeps to halftracks.

The British Ministry of Supply (whose home was in the offices of Shell-Mex and BP Ltd on the Strand, London) approached Shell on 18 January 1943 to provide such a material. Just over a month later, Shell produced Compound 219. This asbestos-based product looked like putty and could be moulded around the engine and electrical points that needed to be kept dry. As well as this, engines and exhausts had to be fitted with breathers and other vehicles required more work. For example, carriers had to have three-foot-high metal plates added to the sides, welded together by the waterproofing putty.

The waterproofing could take some time to prepare. As an example, the War Diaries of the 1st/6th Queens Royal West Regiment show that they started waterproofing their vehicles on 10 May and didn't finish until 23 May. During this time they cleaned the vehicles' engines, waterproofed and had their handiwork certificated by checkers from the Royal Electrical and Mechanical Engineers (REME).

The waterproofing had to be tested, materials produced, instructors trained and instruction manuals prepared. The US location for this was the Ordnance Experimental Station (O-617) at Bideford in Devon. From December 1943 US Ordnance troops were taught to instruct the drivers, who would waterproof their own vehicles. Between 8 December 1943 and 8 July 1944, 3,570 personnel were trained as inspectors and instructors. The British Army used REME wading trials centres, No 1 being at Weymouth.

The results were good: it was reported that fewer than two vehicles in every thousand were drowned off the beaches.

**BELOW AND BELOW RIGHT**
Testing of the waterproofing took place in watersplashes created from concrete, either in a camp (BELOW RIGHT) or near where the waterproofing was carried out, such as this testing site in Dorset (BELOW).

## The waterproofing process

**Stage A:** The bulk of the waterproofing takes place 4–5 days before embarkation. Once complete, the vehicle can travel for a maximum of 200 miles.

**Stage B1:** Checking Stage A and closing all but the most important breathers, fixing a tow rope (in case of failure) and reducing tyre pressure. Now vehicles can travel a maximum of 20 miles.

**Stage B2:** Final preparation. Checking stages A and B1; closing the distributor and engine breathers and fixing a sheet over the radiator front. Vehicles can now travel a maximum of 2 miles.

**Stage C:** Dewaterproofing – taking off B2 waterproofing, checking engine oil, removing clutch and brake seals. Vehicles can now travel a maximum of 20 miles.

**Stage D:** Dewaterproofing the vehicle to return it to normal. The vehicle can now be maintained normally.

**RIGHT AND BELOW RIGHT**
Waterproofing tests at Bideford. The waterproofing of vehicles was an essential part of the landings and much thought went into it. The Combined Operations Staff Notebook of 1945 identifies the markings to be used (usually applied by the formation's REME or RASC officer or the non-commissioned officer supervising the waterproofing) to show which stage had been reached:

Nature of pigment = oil paint
Size of mark = 3" × 1" (horizontally)
Location of mark = Offside front mudguard

| Stage A | Blue |
|---------|--------|
| Stage B1 | Yellow |
| Stage B2 | Red |
| Stage C | White |

# 42  Stokes Bay, Hampshire

**Strategically placed on the western edge of the Gosport and Portsmouth naval bases, Stokes Bay has a long military history – as is evidenced by the Victorian defences. The area had a number of roles to play in the Second World War.**

The 19th-century forts of the Western Advanced Line from Gomer to Elson, the Browndown batteries, the Stokes Bay Lines, Fort Gilkicker and Fort Monckton in Stokes Bay: none of them fired their guns in anger. However, in 1939, the defensive requirements of another age led to the construction of anti-aircraft sites at Browndown and Gilkicker (*see* p 201).

As the threat of German invasion receded in 1942 and an Allied attack increased, Stokes Bay was chosen as a possible embarkation point for a cross-Channel invasion. Immediately, the area was sealed off, buildings were requisitioned and roads were widened to allow the passage of armoured vehicles.

Plans for the construction of four sloping concrete hards that would be used for the embarkation of troops and vehicles were finalised in November 1943. Constructed from locally sourced materials (sand and shingle) they were nicknamed 'chocolate blocks' by locals. Each of the hards had a central mooring dolphin over which the soldiers embarked. Additionally, there were power lines and water and fuel tanks at each hard. To help monitor and control the embarkation – men of the Canadian 3rd Division heading for Juno Beach boarded here – the D-Day Control Centre was constructed in the old bathing station.

Alongside the hards, there were other installations around the bay: the Royal Marines Small Arms School was based at Browndown (RM Snipers' courses were held there), the DD Tank Saltwater Training Wing (*see* p 61) was based at Browndown Second Battery and the School of Electric Lighting was based at Fort Monckton.

In September 1943 the Ministry of Supply decided that Stokes Bay would also be one of the locations at which Mulberry Harbour B2 caissons (aka Phoenixes) would be built, 14 of them, at 203ft 6in long, 44ft wide and 35ft high. They were constructed by two contractors, and a combined total of 1,400 men, who worked seven days a week in 12-hour shifts. Once completed, they were towed to one of the two holding sites (nearby Selsey, in West Sussex, and more distant Dungeness, in Kent) before being towed to Normandy.

**Colin M Baxter's *Prelude to D-Day, Stokes Bay, Gosport c 1944* was painted to mark the 50th anniversary of D-Day in 1994. The detailed painting shows the D-Day preparations in full swing, with vehicles backing onto the LCTs, the dolphins to which the vessels are moored and the 'chocolate block' concrete hards. Note the barrage balloons above the invasion fleet moored in the Solent and the trees of the Isle of Wight in the background.**

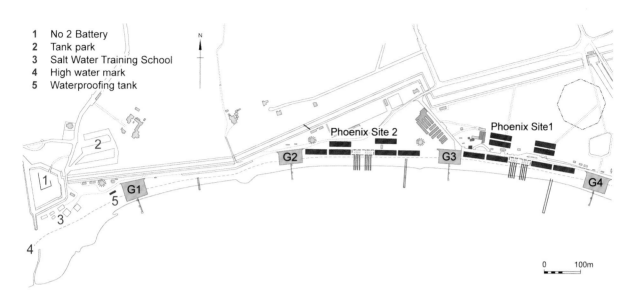

1  No 2 Battery
2  Tank park
3  Salt Water Training School
4  High water mark
5  Waterproofing tank

Phoenix Site 2

Phoenix Site 1

G1   G2   G3   G4

0      100m

**ABOVE AND RIGHT**
Historian David Moore's detailed plan of Stokes Bay (ABOVE) shows embarkation hards and Mulberry Phoenix caisson construction locations. A construction site is shown in the photograph (RIGHT).

**BELOW**
The dolphins and hards were able to accommodate LCTs allowing for the tides.

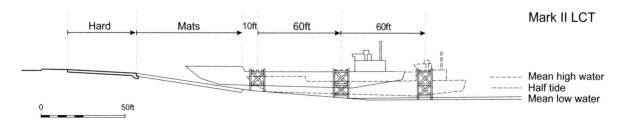

Hard | Mats | 10ft | 60ft | 60ft

Mark II LCT

Mean high water
Half tide
Mean low water

0      50ft

# 43  Phoenix construction, Stansore Point, Lepe, Hampshire

**Just east of the Beaulieu River and west of Southampton Water, today a country park, Lepe played an important role in the preparations for D-Day.**

Here were embarkation hards used by the 4th/7th Royal Dragoon Guards en route to Gold Beach. The PLUTO pipeline (*see* pp 90–1) crossed from Lepe to the Isle of Wight. However, Lepe was also a site for the construction of Phoenix Mulberry Harbour caissons, and the location today is well preserved.

The Allied planners realised that they needed to build up troops and materiel on their Continental lodgement if they were not to be pushed back into the sea. Both sides would rapidly build up their forces and it behoved the Allies to win this race if they could – but whatever happened, at least reach parity. How were they to achieve this without a costly siege of a major port?

Mulberry Harbour was a brilliant answer to the problem. Instead of trying to capture a port immediately after the invasion – something the Dieppe Raid had suggested might be very costly – why not bring the harbour with them?

This was not a new idea, but putting the concept into practice was definitely new and took many man-hours of effort. There was no single genesis: Churchill himself had proposed something similar during the First World War and was a strong proponent. Welsh engineer Hugh Iorys Hughes proposed a floating harbour in 1942. Some of his ideas were tested for use in the Mulberry project. Royal Engineer Allan Beckett designed floating roadways for the harbours and solved problems with anchoring. Professor John Desmond Bernal, scientific adviser to Lord Mountbatten, had much to do with the design – particularly with the issue of the suppression of waves by introducing barriers. Admiral John Hughes-Hallet put forward the idea of blockships.

Prototypes were built at Morfa, near Conwy, and then tested at Garlieston in Scotland, where the tides were similar to those on the Normandy coast. Once the design had been chosen and the decision to produce two taken – there was some opposition to the idea, notably American, but the rationale won over most – production started all over Britain, straining the civil engineering capacity. The components were:

**Bombardon:** The first line of defence, 50 were built for the two harbours. These were cruciform floating metal breakwaters and proved very effective. 'Both breakwaters were moored in 11–13 fathoms, giving sufficient depth inshore for Liberty ships to anchor. In this depth they reduced the height of the waves by the measured amount of 50%, which represents a 75% reduction in wave energy.'[38] The overall dimensions of each unit were 200ft long, 25ft 1in beam, 25ft 11in hull depth and 19ft draft. The cross-section was roughly the form of a Maltese cross.

**Phoenix:** There were different types of concrete caissons – made in six main versions. They were built with air-cocks to lower them to the seabed in a controlled manner. Around two million tons of steel and concrete were used in their construction. They were built in a number of locations, including Stokes Bay, Lepe, Southampton Docks,

**BELOW AND BOTTOM**

The remains of the construction line at Stansore Point, in Hampshire; the huge concrete caissons were built, rolled along to the slips and then launched.

**Phoenix versions**

| Type | No built | H (ft) | L (ft) | W (ft) |
|------|----------|--------|--------|--------|
| A1 | 60 | 60 | 204 | 56.25 |
| A2 | 11 | 50 | 204 | 56.25 |
| B1 | 25 | 40 | 203.5 | 44 |
| B2 | 24 | 35 | 203.5 | 44 |
| C1 | 17 | 30 | 203.5 | 32 |
| D1 | 10 | 25 | 174.25 | 27.75 |

Source: Ramsey 1995, 1, 198

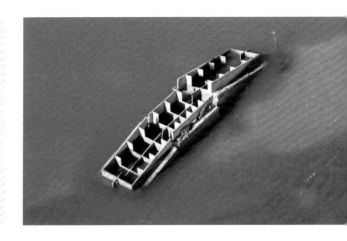

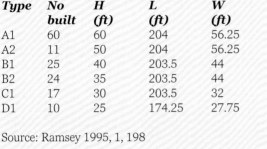

**ABOVE RIGHT**
Some Mulberry caissons have survived, such as this one at Langstone Harbour, in Hampshire.

the Thames and the Clyde. What survives at Lepe shows how the caissons were built in line along a track and then rolled to slipways, from where they were launched.

**Gooseberry:** Another form of breakwater, these were 70 old ships that set off from Oban and were sunk off each of the five beaches. They had been readied before sailing and had charges placed aboard to allow them to be scuttled more easily.

**Pierhead:** Inside the breakwaters, pierheads stood on spuds (legs), and a platform could move up and down with the tide. The roadways headed to shore from here. Some 23 were planned, of which 8 were spares. They were built at Morfa.

**Beetle:** The roadways (whales) stretched from the pierheads to shore and rested on concrete and steel floats or pontoons (beetles). Some 670 concrete beetles were built at Marchwood, on the River Beaulieu; others were built at Southsea. Steel beetles were built in Richborough, Kent.

**Whale:** Codename for the roadways; 10 miles built, much of it at Marchwood.

**Buffer:** Codename for the approach span from roadway to beach. They were built at Morfa.

Because of the size of the project, there were difficulties harnessing the disparate elements – COSSAC, Admiralty, War Office and Ministry of Supply. Planning, design and coordination of military and civil engineers was the remit of Brigadier Bruce White, the Director of Ports and Inland Water Transport, a Royal Engineer Officer in both world wars and in private life a civil engineer. The job of organising the construction was given to Major General Harold Werner, Coordinator of Ministry and Service Facilities. He didn't win any friends, but he got the job done.

Elements of the Mulberry Harbours were concentrated off Selsey Bill, in West Sussex, and Dungeness, in Kent, awaiting transport to Normandy. To achieve this they had to be propelled by tugs and these were in short supply. The convoys began sailing on D-Day and the bombardons were the first to be laid on D+1. Rear Admiral William Tennant – Rear Admiral Mulberry/PLUTO – was responsible for the cross-Channel towing. The crossing was not uneventful: weather and enemy action took a toll: five whales, two Phoenixes and two tugs were lost.

# 44 Netley Royal Victoria Military Hospital, Hampshire

**Netley was built after the Crimean War, on Queen Victoria's orders, and intentionally sited close to Southampton Water so as to be convenient for receiving injured naval and military personnel.**

With an empire to run and continuous wars to fight, the British needed a bespoke facility to treat and rehabilitate wounded soldiers. At Netley, specialist army doctors and nurses were trained to deal with the consequences of battlefield injuries. When built, it was the largest military hospital in the world. In June 1940 French soldiers from Dunkirk were treated here.

In January 1944 Captain C J Brown (Medical Corps, US Navy) was sent as part of SNAG (Special Navy Advance Group) 56 to take over Netley Hospital to use as a temporary medical HQ. On 13 January, 13 officers and 75 men arrived; more came on 19 and 26 January. Between 17 and 22 January the nurses arrived. The unit was complete by 28 February. As the US Navy moved in, the British Army moved out. It was designated Navy Base Hospital Number 12 on 1 April, with a notional 1,000 beds. The actuality was that the hospital was in a poor state of repair, with negligible facilities and few useable instruments and virtually no serviceable stores to hand over. But what they did have was 325 (mostly British) patients, and more arriving every day. They had to scramble to acquire medical stores, without even typewriters to use to request them.

However, by D-Day the hospital was cleaned and well equipped, with around 700 staff and the capacity to treat more than 900 patients at a time. The muster

Aerial view of the Royal Victoria Military Hospital in its prime. It looked grand but had many defects, as were pointed out at the time by journalist Matthew Wallingford, who highlighted: 'It was a ghastly display of deception to say the least … It is not so much the greatest military hospital in the world as much as it is a rather impractical waste of government finance.'[39]

The West Wing of the hospital. Florence Nightingale criticised the design of the hospital so forcibly to Prime Minister Lord Palmerston during construction that he wrote: 'It seems to me that at Netley all consideration of what would best tend to the comfort and recovery of the patients has been sacrificed to the vanity of the architect, whose sole object has been to make a building which should cut a dash when looked at from the Southampton river.'[40] Unfortunately the construction was so far advanced that it could not be halted.

West Wing, Netley Hospital.

by D-Day comprised 42 doctors, 98 nurses, 12 Hospital Corps officers, 4 dental, 2 supply and 2 Chaplain Corps, plus 585 enlisted men. All British patients were removed. Eight operating teams were readied, each comprising a surgeon, assistant, anaesthetist, corpsmen and nurses. For a couple of days little happened, then streams of LSTs (landing ships) and hospital ships landed at Southampton hards. On 11 June the wounded from Utah and Omaha Beaches started arriving, more than 400 in total. Patients were taken by ambulance to the hospital. Non-medical litter bearers brought the wounded in for triage, which was assessed in the passageways by medical personnel accompanied by Records and Personnel officers, who took personal details.

Between September and October the Navy handed over the facility to the Army General Hospital. SNAG 56 had been commissioned for 8 months and 11 days and treated more than 9,000 patients.

Today all that is left of the hospital is the chapel, whose interior – now a museum – has been beautifully restored using National Lottery money.

# 45  The Royal Hospital Haslar, Hampshire

**The roll call of sick and wounded sailors and marines treated at Haslar Hospital after battle reads like the story of empire: Trafalgar, Corunna, Waterloo, the Crimea, both world wars and later 20th-century conflicts.**

In the reign of King George II, Haslar Hospital in Gosport was built to provide medical care for British Navy servicemen and was open for patients from October 1753. In the early 1940s the hospital specialised in treating air raid victims. So many wounded arrived from the bombings of Gosport and Portsmouth – in the first 11 months of the war the latter had 792 air raid warnings – that the cellars were opened up by VADs (Voluntary Aid Detachments) to create two operating theatres. After the Normandy landings this increased to six theatre tables.

Between 1944 and July 1945 the United States Military ran the facility and both Allied casualties from the Normandy landings and German PoWs were treated. In the three months after D-Day, 17,566 casualties were taken in by the Portsmouth Medical Office alone; of these, 1,347 wounded were sent to Haslar.

When a hospital ship berthed at the dock, an alarm bell sounded in Haslar warning of the imminent arrival of ambulances containing casualties. Transferred directly to Haslar, servicemen were seen by the CCC (Casualty Clearing Centre) run under the auspices of the Hospital Principal Medical Officer. There they

**ABOVE**
The Royal Hospital Haslar was designed by Theodore Jacobsen and built 1745–53. Its beautiful water tower dominates the brick building.

**RIGHT**
HRH The Princess Royal, Princess Mary, during her visit to the Royal Naval Hospital Haslar on 4 January 1943. L–R front row: Acting Superintending Sister E M Blundstone, the Princess Royal, Rear Admiral William Bradbury, Medical Officer in Charge.

A 2018 aerial view looking south-west over the hospital building (centre left) towards Stokes Bay. Fort Gilkicker is in the top left of the photograph.

had systems in place to assess 300 men an hour. Patients were given emergency operations and necessary treatment, then stabilised before being moved inland within three days of arrival to other hospitals across England. Eighty QARNNS (Queen Alexandra's Royal Naval Nursing Service) and 140 nursing members of the VAD and other staff, such as pharmacists, were rushed to Haslar to cope with the extra demand for treatment after D-Day.

The first blood bank had been set up at Haslar in 1940 and after the Normandy landings the local population contributed, with their blood collected at a field hospital in nearby Stokes Bay.

The hospital, with its huge three-sided wings and distinctive water tower, was an easy target for the Luftwaffe to spot. As a safety precaution nurses moved patients to the cellars to shelter when nightly air raids on the docks were likely to occur. Bed-bound patients who had injured limbs held up by pulleys were each given a knife with which to cut themselves free if necessary, so they could escape to the cellars.

The hospital was not bombed regularly during this time and it is speculated that the German bombers deliberately refrained because they used the hospital's distinctive profile to direct them to the far more important target of Portsmouth harbour.

The Royal Hospital Haslar officially closed as the last military hospital in Great Britain in 2007. It is now both an NHS civilian and military hospital.

# 46  US 28th General Hospital, Kingston Lacy, Dorset

A 1944 aerial photograph of Kingston Lacy. The 28th General Hospital moved out in late July, staging via Bishops Court, near Exeter, and Eastleigh, in Hampshire, to Utah Beach. They arrived in France on 16 August and set up near Carentan.

**When the Normandy landings were being planned it was realised that the provision for treating the expected numbers of casualties was inadequate: more hospitals were needed.**

Three hospitals were built in east Dorset: Blandford Camp, St Leonards (near Ferndown) and Kingston Lacy. For the latter, the authorities requisitioned 72.5 acres of parkland at Kingston Lacy near Wimborne, at a cost of £131 a year. In mid-March 1943 the War Office took control and in the late summer of 1943 work started. Most of the buildings were brick with concrete foundations, they had electricity, full plumbing (including flushing toilets) and central heating. Doctors and nurses had stove-warmed bunk-bed wooden cabins housing 30 people each. The facilities consisted of more than 100 buildings, including Nissen huts, barracks, kitchens, mess halls, operating theatres, clinics, wards, chapel, mortuary, libraries, cinema and dance hall, all linked by walkways and covered corridors. It was built and (almost) ready for occupation by 3 April 1944.

The first unit to arrive (via the RMS *Queen Mary*) was the US 28th General Hospital, officially activated at Camp Rucker, Ozark, Alabama. Their fourth posting in England was Kingston Lacy; as this was a new camp they had to requisition supplies and finish off many of the buildings to make them fit for purpose. The hospital had 28 wards capable of holding 834 beds. In an emergency, an additional 330 beds could be put in ward tents. The unit completely mustered on 6 April, with operations starting on 15 April.

Kingston Lacy was run as a General Hospital from 15 April until 2 June. On 30 May it was put on alert in anticipation of Operation *Overlord*, and assigned an extra 40 medical officers and 69 enlisted men. At this time it was redesignated a Transit Hospital – by definition responsible for receiving and treating casualties straight off

Nissen huts – and their US equivalent, the Quonset – were much in demand during 1943 and 1944, as temporary structures housing men and munitions sprang up all over Britain. They were also used for hospitals as here.

the battlefield. It served in this function between 3 and 23 June 1944. From 24 June to 15 July it returned to being a General Hospital.

The first battle casualties arrived on 3 June, but from 7 June combatants from *Overlord* began to arrive. Between 3 and 27 June the hospital recorded 1,900 admissions, 1,891 dispositions (return to duty, transfer to another medical facility or death), 464 operations (113 minor surgical) and 6 combat death losses. Between 27 June and 9 July 1944 the hospital admitted 721 patients, performed 304 operations, recorded 254 dispositions and 2 deaths: the outpatient unit treated 369 patients. On 10 July there were 767 patients at the hospital.

A hospital ward set up in a Nissen hut, photographed in 1943 and similar to those at Kingston Lacy. Note the central stove, the pipe-smoking soldier in bed on the right and the convalescence area.

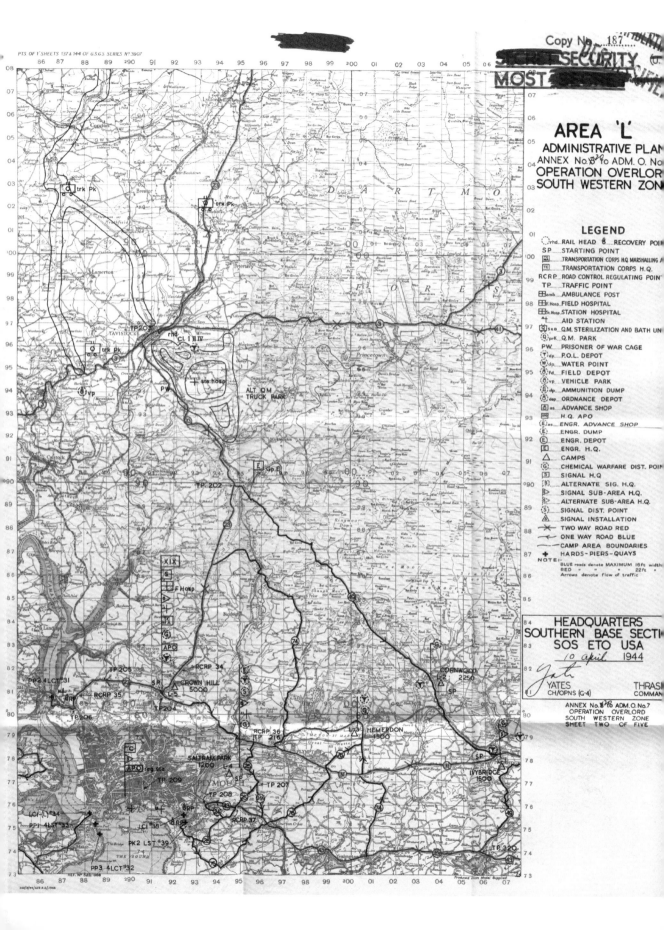

# 4 | All aboard

LEFT

Detailed marshalling plan maps were produced during 1944 showing the routes to and from embarkation points, as well as the location of waterproofing checkpoints, water and petrol stations, etc. This map covers area L – East Plymouth – and shows the routes to hards at St Budeaux, Cattedown and Hooe Point, as well as West Plymouth's Mount Edgcumbe embarkation points.

The target date for D-Day had been set: weather willing, it would be 5 June, with 6 and 7 June also options. If these dates were missed, the next opportunity would be weeks away. The Germans had seen the weather forecasts and had come to their own conclusions: commander of German Army Group B, Generalfeldmarschall Erwin Rommel, was at home in Germany. It was his wife's birthday. Seventh Army commander General Friedrich Dollmann had planned to spend a couple of days with his senior officers war gaming an Allied landing.

In England, shortly before D-Day, during May, the assault forces entered purdah. The marshalling camps were sealed off from the outside world. Surrounded by barbed wire, patrolled by guards with no passes out. Usually the camps were administered and policed by units that would follow on to Normandy. There the units learnt their objectives, and saw maps which had been kept under guard. These camps – sometimes known as 'sausage camps' because of their shape on maps – were usually in wooded areas to protect them from discovery from the air, usually tented, although there were some with more permanent structures.

A range of preparation was undertaken at the camps: waterproofing, vehicle and weapons checks and the handing out of equipment. In the case of US troops, this included lifebelts and uniforms impregnated with anti-gas paste.

When the time came, the units left the marshalling camps and boarded the awaiting vessels from hards that had been built along the south coast. The timings were, of course, different for each unit. Some boarded and sat for days at sea. The weather wasn't good and the 5 June sailing was postponed. Many vessels were

RIGHT

Chow time at a US 'sausage camp' in the west of England, June 1944. The name 'sausage camps' arose because many were located in the narrow valleys of Devon; some soldiers were camped out in tents for some time before embarkation.

The D-Day assault forces left from the south coast of England; follow-on forces left mainly from south Wales and Essex. This plaque in Barry, in the Vale of Glamorgan, is one of many remembering the presence of US troops in Wales.

already at sea – the blockships and bombardment groups, and some of the follow-up forces, had to backtrack to take up the time.

But, unlike the Germans, the Allies had a forecast that identified a window of opportunity on 6 June. Eisenhower gambled that this was correct – but wrote a statement accepting the blame if things went badly.

They may not have been the first troops to leave their camps, but the first of the assault troops to leave Britain on D-Day were the airborne assault troops: the British 6th Airborne, which included Canadian paratroopers, and the US 82nd and 101st Airborne Divisions.

## Airborne

From early on it was realised that gliders would be needed to deliver a significant percentage of the airborne forces into France – even before the location to be attacked had been chosen. Late in 1942 US forces used RAF Cottesmore, in Rutland, to store Horsa gliders that would be used in the Normandy landings. Presciently, General Henry H Arnold had ordered the dispatch of 1,400 Wacos to England in 1943 so there were sufficient for use even after 'considerable attrition in training'.[41] Using gliders would, it was hoped, allow a better concentration of forces and also allow the quick arrival of the airborne artillery.

Delivery of the gliders and the paratroopers would be by means of the aircraft of the USAAF's IX Troop Carrier Command. IX TCC was set up and activated in October 1943 as part of the newly created Ninth Air Force. Its HQ from November was Grantham, Lincolnshire, where it was commanded by Brigadier General Paul L Williams, who had commanded the troop carriers in the Mediterranean theatre. It was composed of three wings: the 50th (HQ at RAF Exeter, in Devon), the 52nd (Cottesmore) and 53rd (Greenham Common, in Berkshire). The 53rd would be responsible for glider operations and would need to train intensively. They did: as an example, in April 1944 the wing logged 6,965 hours of glider training.

There is no doubt that the haste employed to bring Troop Carrier Command up to strength for the Normandy invasion meant that not all personnel were as experienced or trained as they should be. This may, in part, have contributed to the problems experienced on 6 June. John C Warren noted: 'Drastic steps were taken to step up the rate of advanced glider training and some pilots were diverted from other theaters with the result that 380 pilots reached the United Kingdom in late March and early April and 215 more arrived in May.'[42] The first thing IX TCC needed was more crews and aircraft. That was accomplished between February

Most sausage camps were heavily camouflaged against enemy photo-reconnaissance or bombers.

## Airlifts to Normandy

### Nos 38 and 46 Groups, RAF airlift

| Date/time | Codename | Mission |
| --- | --- | --- |
| D-Day early am | Sunflower I | SAS insertion |
| D-Day early am | Sunflower II | SAS insertion |
| D-Day early am | Tonga | 6th Airborne paradrop and gliders |
| D-Day evening | Mallard | 6th Airlanding gliders |
| D-Day night | Rob Roy I | resupply |
| D+1 night | Rob Roy II | resupply |
| D+2 night | Rob Roy III | resupply |
| D+3 night | Rob Roy IV | resupply |
| D+3 night | Sunflower III | SAS reinforcement |
| D+4 night | Sunflower IV | SAS insertion |

### US IX Troop Carrier Command airlift

| Date/time | Codename | Mission |
| --- | --- | --- |
| D-Day early am | Albany | 101st Airborne paradrop |
| D-Day early am | Boston | 82nd Airborne paradrop |
| D-Day dawn | Chicago | 101st gliders |
| D-Day dawn | Detroit | 82nd gliders |
| D-Day dusk | Keokuk | 101st gliders |
| D-Day dusk | Elmira | 82nd gliders |
| D+1 dawn | Galveston | 82nd gliders |
| D+1 dawn | Hackensack | 82nd gliders |
| D+1 am | Freeport | 82nd resupply |
| D+1 am | Memphis | 101st resupply |

and May 1944, when the complement increased from 760 crew and 845 aircraft to 1,116 crew and 1,207 operational aircraft. However, the 924 crew committed on D-Day would include 20 per cent filler personnel, who had been overseas for less than two months.

Other factors played their part in what turned out to be a poorly grouped drop. First, there was a late change to the route and dropping location. Second, there was the nature of the terrain onto which they dropped: the rivers had been deliberately allowed to flood low-lying ground; in the west, there was bocage – small fields, with big hedges. Third, the fields were draped with 'Rommel's asparagus' – poles, wire and booby traps. Fourth, the training was based on the bulk of the division dropping onto prearranged signals. The trouble was, the Pathfinders were scattered, the equipment was broken and the following aircraft had problems spotting the markers.

But the biggest problem was the weather, specifically a cloudbank that sat over the Cotentin Peninsula and forced aircraft to go round or over. This allowed the German flak (anti-aircraft fire) to play a role.

The paratroopers didn't expect these problems. The exercises in England had been excellent. Exercise *Eagle* was successful enough for General Williams to anticipate 90–100 per cent delivery to the correct spot. Even Air Chief Marshal Trafford Leigh-Mallory, who had been a voice of doom about the effectiveness of the airborne mission and its likely casualties, was impressed.

On the eastern side of the invasion, around the Orne River, things were similar. The flooded terrain meant that too many brave young men drowned, unable to free themselves from the encumbrance of a paratrooper's kit. Pathfinder issues, flak, etc – all these things conspired against a tight drop. The worst effect of this was that the Merville Battery assault group went in with less than a third of its manpower and none of its demolitions. They were able to keep the guns quiet for D-Day, but the Germans were able to retake the position and Sword Beach had to be closed later because of the artillery.

At least one part of the mission worked perfectly: Operation *Deadstick* and the taking of the bridges at Bénouville.

# 47 USAAF Air Station 463, RAF Exeter, Devon

**For most of the war, RAF Exeter was used as a fighter base equipped with Hurricanes to defend the Channel coast. In April 1944 they were withdrawn and the field was handed over to the US Ninth Air Force. From here on D-Day paratroopers of the 101st Airborne Division left for Normandy.**

It had not been intended that RAF Exeter should be part of IX Troop Carrier Command (TCC); until 1944, the command – with its HQ in Grantham – was expected to fly out of Lincolnshire. However, lack of proximity to Normandy, the decision to use the British Horsa glider, which stretched the C-47's towing power to its capacity – and the increase of the original COSSAC mission to two divisions, forced a reassessment and, subsequently, a move to more southerly bases. First, the bases of Ramsbury (in Wiltshire) and Welford Park, Greenham Common and Aldermaston (in Berkshire) were taken up. Subsequently, after the size of the glider operation expanded, a further four bases were obtained by the USAAF from the RAF: Exeter and Upottery (in Devon) and Merryfield and Westonzoyland (in Somerset).

The wing that was to fly out of Exeter was the 50th, until then based at Bottesford, on the Leicestershire/Lincolnshire border, working with units that were passed to 53rd Wing. Instead, three new groups arrived from the United States. Short of training, as they had been raised less than nine months before, they settled around Bottesford before moving to southwest England, with Exeter as the Wing HQ. The 439th Troop Carrier Group (TCG) went to Upottery, the 440th to Exeter and the 441st to Merryfield. The 442nd TCG – which had trained with the 52nd Wing – flew out of RAF Fulbeck, Lincolnshire, on D-Day and only subsequently moved to Westonzoyland (which became USAAF station 447).

The 440th TCG had 70 C-47As and 70 Waco CG-4 gliders, arranged in four squadrons: the 95th, 96th, 97th and 98th Squadrons. From 22:30 on 5 June, 45 Dakotas took off as part of Mission *Albany*, carrying paratroopers from the 101st Airborne Division. Altogether, there were 723 men as well as two platoons from C/326th Airborne Engineers aboard. These aircraft then met others over the Portland assembly area and began the journey across the English Channel. Once over the Cotentin Peninsula, they flew into thick flak, losing three C-47s as they dropped the paratroopers onto DZ-D (Drop Zone D). The day after, they flew supplies, including fuel and ammunition, to the area, losing two more aircraft in the process and bringing home 11 with severe damage. For this – part of Mission *Memphis* – the aircraft had to stage via Welford to pick up their cargo. A third aircraft was lost later the same day when it was accidentally hit by a bomb from a higher-flying P-47 Thunderbolt. The 440th TCG received a Distinguished Unit Commendation for its actions over Normandy.

**Exeter opened as a municipal airfield before the war and returned to civilian use in 1947. It is still a bustling airport today, offering international and domestic flights. This memorial at the front of the airport remembers all the airmen who flew from the airfield in wartime.**

**101st Airborne troopers marching towards aircraft of the 95th and 98th Squadrons on 5 June, in preparation for their flight to Normandy.**

**RIGHT**

Lieuteant Colonel Robert L Wolverton, commanding officer of 3/506th Parachute Infantry Regiment, and his HQ Company check their equipment before boarding C-47 *Stoy Hora*, of 440th Troop Carrier Squadron, at Exeter, 5 June 1944.

**BELOW**

Part of the western end of the airfield is being redeveloped (centre top in this photograph) but the three asphalt runways are still obvious. During the war these were extended, the longest (08–26) reaching 6,000ft. There were numerous hardstandings, although there weren't enough to accommodate the 70 or so C-47/C-53s of the 440th TCG when it arrived in April 1944 and a number had to park on grass.

# 48  USAAF Air Station 462, RAF Upottery, Devon

**Constructed in 1944 specifically for D-Day, and officially opened on 17 February 1944, it was not until 26 April that RAF Upottery became the base for the 439th Troop Carrier Group, whose four squadrons – 91st (L4), 92nd (J8), 93rd (3B) and 94th (D8) – had arrived in England on 10 March.**

**BELOW**

A few miles east of Exeter, Upottery was another USAAF airfield from which 101st Airborne embarked for Normandy. A third was nearby Merryfield, in Somerset, which was retained for USAAF use until the end of October 1944. Upottery was used from 26 April 1944 until most of the aircraft moved to Ramsbury on 24 June. In November 1944 US Navy antisubmarine units moved in and Upottery was used in this role until the end of the war. The photograph shows a memorial at Upottery.

**BELOW RIGHT**

Men of F Company, 2/506th Parachute Infantry Regiment, waiting for their 439th TCG C-47 to take off on 5 June. L–R: William G Olanie, Frank D Griffin, Robert J Noody and Lester T Hegland. At 01:20 they would drop over Hiesville in Drop Zone C.

On 6 June aircraft from Upottery dropped 101st Airborne Division paratroopers over Normandy as part of Mission *Albany*, 45 C-47s taking the HQ and 1/506th Parachute Infantry Regiment (PIR) and 36 taking 2/506th – whose Easy Company was made famous by the TV series *Band of Brothers*.

The 506th PIR's commanding officer, Colonel Robert L Sink, flew in the lead aircraft which was piloted by the 439th's commanding officer, Lieutenant Colonel Charles H Young. They headed towards DZ-C (Drop Zone C), where the Pathfinders had managed to get a Eureka navigation beacon working. The experienced Young was able to drop his paratroopers successfully on target, as did the few aircraft that had remained with him. The others had succumbed to the problems of the cloud over the Cotentin Peninsula, with only 14 dropping close to the DZ. There were three casualties, all shot down, one of them flown by Second Lieutenant Marvin F Muir, who was posthumously awarded a Distinguished Service Cross for his heroism. The official citation stated:

> After his ship was mortally hit by enemy ground fire it burst into flames while at an altitude of only 750 feet and 2½ minutes from the drop zone. Although forced to leave formation, he courageously stuck to his post and battled the controls in order that he might effectively accomplish his mission and properly accomplish the evacuation of his paratroopers in the assigned dropping zone. After the evacuation of the paratroopers, he continued in an attempt to crash land the flaming aircraft in order by chance to save his crew members trapped inside.[43]

Many other aircraft were damaged, although only three seriously.

The 439th dropped 1,357 paratroopers over Normandy on 6 June; on 7 June they delivered nearly 1,000 more by glider. Part of Mission *Hackensack*, the last glider mission of the landings, saw the 439th tow 30 Horsas and 20 Wacos to LZ-W

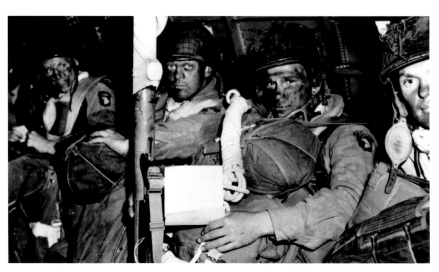

This modern-day aerial view of Upottery shows clearly the dispersals (the hardstandings on the left of the picture, intended to help disperse the aircraft so that bombing would affect as few as possible).

(Landing Zone W), taking 2/325th Glider Infantry Regiment (GIR) and most of 2/401st GIR. Only three aircraft were hit and slightly damaged by ground fire, as the delivery of the gliders went well, although enemy fire on the ground killed a number of troops before they could exit.

The group received a US Distinguished Unit Citation and a French *Croix de Guerre* with Palm for their actions.

The airfield sentry box at Moorhayes Farm contains a memorial to the 506th Parachute Infantry Regiment (101st Airborne), 325th Glider Infantry Regiment (82nd Airborne) and 439th TCG, who transported them to Normandy.

# 49  USAAF Air Station 489, RAF Cottesmore, Rutland

Memorial to those who flew from RAF Cottesmore during the Second World War.

**Built for the RAF in 1935–38 as a grass airfield and used by Bomber Command, the airfield was enlarged in 1943 with long concrete runways. Taken over by the USAAF on 8 September 1943, AAF-489 became Ninth Air Force's IX Troop Carrier Command HQ and home to the 52nd Troop Carrier Wing HQ.**

The 52nd Troop Carrier Wing consisted of five Troop Carrier Groups (TCGs): the 61st (based at AAF-463 Barkston Heath, Lincolnshire), 313th (at AAF-448 Folkingham, Lincolnshire), 314th (at AAF-538 Saltby, Leicestershire) and 315th (AAF-493 Spanhoe, Northamptonshire), as well as the experienced 316th TCG.

The 316th was based at Cottesmore in 1944–45. It started life in February 1942 as the 316th Transport Group and was redesignated the 316th Troop Carrier Group in July 1942. Trained with C-47 and C-53 aircraft, it saw action in North Africa, and dropped paratroopers into Sicily during Operation *Husky* and in Italy at Salerno.

The 316th arrived in England from the Mediterranean in February 1944, along with almost all the rest of the wing, flying via Marrakech and Gibraltar. Training in England for the landings in France started in earnest in spring 1944, with both paratrooper drops and glider-towing practice. This training had mixed results. A major daylight exercise at the end of May showed that 4,207 hours of practice towing gliders meant the wing – slated to drop paratroopers of 82nd Airborne – could handle glider operations as well. However, the 313th and 314th TCGs did not perform well in night drops, hampered by construction at their airfields, and the 315th hadn't begun training until May and practice drops on 5 and 7 May were not wholly satisfactory.

Also briefly located at Cottesmore was the Combat Pathfinder School, opened on 28 February 1944 to train Pathfinders in the use of Gee and SCR-717 air-to-surface radars. However, congestion at Cottesmore led to the move of the school to North Witham, in Lincolnshire, from where the US Pathfinders flew on D-Day.

On 6 June, the aircraft of the 52nd Troop Carrier Wing dropped the 505th PIR and 456th Parachute Field Artillery Battalion of 82nd Airborne as part of Mission *Boston*, taking off at around 23:00 on 5 June and arriving over the Cotentin Peninsula around 02:00 on 6 June. They had been able to fly over the cloudbank, encountered little flak (paratroopers in one aircraft were wounded but none were shot down), which meant that the drops by the 52nd over Drop Zone O were the best achieved of the *Albany* and *Boston* missions. John C Warren wrote: 'Of 118 sticks delivered … 31 landed on or barely outside the zone, approximately 29 more came within a mile, and at least an additional 20 were within two miles of it.'[44]

The 316th TCG dropped 1,276 men of 1/ and 3/505th PIR near Sainte-Mère-Église and then flew a resupply mission – *Freeport* – on 7 June, receiving a third Distinguished Unit Citation for these operations.

The 316th TCG at Cottesmore had four squadrons, the 36th (4C), 37th (W7), 44th (6E) and 45th (T3). The W7 on these aircraft at Cottesmore, therefore, indicates the 37th TCS. In the foreground is the tail of a Ford-built CG-4A-FO Waco glider *43-42014*; behind it, C-47A-80-DL Serial *43-15292*.

# 50 USAAF Air Station 538, RAF Saltby, Leicestershire

**Six miles south of Grantham lies the ancient Domesday Book-listed village of Saltby. The nearby heath, studded with Bronze Age round barrows, was the site of a 1941 grass airfield for 14 Operational Training Unit of No 7 Group, Bomber Command. In 1943–44 it was rebuilt for use by IX Troop Carrier Command.**

Three concrete runways – two of 4,200ft and one of 6,090ft – were laid by No 5352 Airfield Construction Wing, the main work completing by early February 1944 when the 314th Troop Carrier Group (TCG) of 52nd Wing began to arrive. It took a month for the air squadrons and ground echelons to appear from Italy and paratrooper training drops started at the beginning of April.

The 314th comprised four squadrons, the 32nd (S2), 50th (2R), 61st (Q9) and 62nd (E5). It was an experienced unit that had seen sufficient action in the Mediterranean to earn a Distinguished Unit Citation, and it needed to draw on its experience as its training time before the D-Day landings was limited by construction at the airfield. The 314th first flew exercises in April and by the time of Exercise *Eagle* had still not reached the right level in night drops. A further exercise on 14/15 May helped improve things.

On 6 June two serials of 36 and 24 aircraft from the 314th dropped elements of the 508th Parachute Infantry Regiment and B/307th Parachute Engineer Battalion as part of Mission *Boston* onto DZ-N (Drop Zone N) near Picauville, west of Sainte-Mère-Église.

As elsewhere, the cloudbank over the Cotentin Peninsula hampered the drop, and flak accounted for the loss of one aircraft, with 18 others sustaining light damage. The serials received scattered help from the Pathfinders, who had been prevented from reaching the DZ by enemy action, and as a result only 17 out of 132 sticks (groups of parachutists) landed on or near the DZ and 16 within a mile's radius. That meant a lot of the 2,183 men who dropped over DZ-N were scattered – including two sticks that dropped early nearly 10 miles away at Valognes. Half of the 508th was within two miles of its zone – including the regimental commander, Colonel Roy Lindquist, and 82nd Division commanding officer, Brigadier General James M Gavin; the rest were too far away to be able to complete their primary mission.

The 314th was later involved in resupplying the 82nd on 7 June: Mission *Freeport*. Unfortunately, as the Germans still held DZ-N at the time, the 314th encountered heavy fire that accounted for the loss of 3 aircraft, with significant damage to 11 more. Few of the supplies dropped were retrieved at the time by the paratroopers, although ultimately they did get around 140 of the 156 tons. John C Warren said: 'The paratroops on D+2 were very short of food and ammunition and subsisted largely on a captured trainload of cheese.'[45]

The 314th was awarded a Distinguished Unit Citation for its heroism during these operations.

April 1944 aerial view of RAF Saltby, showing its three runways and dispersals. Part of the longest (07–25) runway (6,090ft) is still used today by a gliding club. Most of the infrastructure has been cleared away and there's no sign of the control tower or hangars that housed Horsa gliders. However, there are still some Stanton and brick-lined blast shelters. The Stanton shelters were arch-shaped precast concrete units which were bolted together to form a shelter for 50 men. The entrances were often brick-lined with concrete steps.

# 51 USAAF Air Station 486, RAF Greenham Common, Berkshire

The turn of the 82nd Airborne's glider drop – Mission *Elmira*, which took place on the evening of 6 June – which saw 50 C-47s carry 82nd's Recon Platoon, Signals Company and Division HQ, along with the 303rd Engineer Battalion.

**Opened in 1942, RAF Greenham Common was handed over to the US Ninth Air Force in 1943. In February 1944 it became the HQ of the 53rd Troop Carrier Wing and home base of the 438th Troop Carrier Group (TCG). It played a big part in the invasion, with 50 troop-carrying gliders leaving the airfield for Normandy.**

The 53rd Wing had been selected to handle glider operations and was composed of five four-squadron groups based in Berkshire and Wiltshire: the 434th based at Aldermaston (AAF-467), the 435th at Welford (AAF-474), the 436th at Membury (AAF-466), the 437th at Ramsbury (AAF-469) and the 438th at Greenham Common. The latter's four squadrons were the 87th (3X), 88th (M2), 89th (4U) and 90th (Q7).

Of these groups, the 434th and 435th were trained in both parachute and glider missions, the 436th and 437th had only parachute training and the 438th wasn't operational until April. A heavy training schedule – the wing logged 6,965 hours of glider towing in April – particularly on the British Horsa glider, ensured that IX Troop Carrier Command rated them up to the job.

On the evening of 5 June – with Operation *Overlord* about to begin – the 101st Airborne Division troops assigned to the 438th TCG were all ready and waiting within Greenham Common airfield's perimeter. Around the outside there were armed guards to maintain security and to prevent anyone deserting. General Eisenhower then arrived and met up with General Lewis H Brereton, commander of the Ninth Air Force, to watch the first paratroopers leave as part of Mission *Albany*. The first aircraft to take off was a C-47A named *Birmingham Belle* – it became airborne at 22:48 hours with Lieutenant Colonel John M Donalson, commanding officer of the 438th, at the controls. It was followed by another 80, which took off in the dark at an average of 18 seconds an aircraft, a speed that shows a high level of training. They carried 1,430 men of 2/ and 3/502nd Parachute Infantry Regiment.

RIGHT

RIGHT
Eisenhower talks to men of the
101st Airborne at Greenham
Common on 5 June. He had joined
Lieutenant General Lewis H
Brereton to watch the first troops
leave and gave his famous 'Eyes of
the world are on you' speech.

BELOW
After the war, Greenham Common
became synonymous with protest.
The Women's Peace Camp was
a presence outside the airbase
for nearly 20 years, campaigning
against the cruise nuclear missiles
that were kept in silos on site from
1981 to 1991. The base closed in
1993 and was later returned to
common land. The control tower
(pictured here) reopened as a visitor
centre and cafe in 2018.

There was little opposition and, unlike some of the following serials, no aircraft were lost, there was no serious damage and no casualties. However, 'maladjustment or misinterpretation of his Gee [radar] set'[46] saw Donalson and 26 pilots in close formation drop three miles south of Drop Zone A. The 438th's second serial was spread over an even wider area.

The 438th TCG also towed gliders to Normandy on D-Day, as part of Mission *Elmira*, reinforcing 82nd Division. In total 50 gliders – 14 Wacos and 36 Horsas – were towed by the 438th. Along with 8 Wacos and 18 Horsas towed by the 437th, these carried Battery C/80th AAA Battalion, 'contingents of medics signallers, and divisional HQ personnel, a reconnaissance platoon and an air support party – 437 men in all. The cargo comprised 64 vehicles, mostly jeeps, 13 57mm anti-tank guns and other supplies and equipment.'[47]

For their actions during the operation, the 438th received a Distinguished Unit Citation.

116

# 52 USAAF Air Station 467, RAF Aldermaston, Berkshire

**Home base to 53rd Wing's 434th Troop Carrier Group (TCG), RAF Aldermaston was built in 1941–42 for RAF Bomber Command. It was handed over to the USAAF in August 1942 and used by Eighth Air Force until being transferred to the Ninth in October 1943.**

On 3 March 1944 434th TCG's four squadrons moved in: 71st (CJ), 72nd (CU), 73rd (CN) and 74th (ID). They were slated to carry 101st Airborne, based in the nearby Kennet Valley, to Normandy by glider, something for which they had been intensively trained.

They flew as part of Mission *Chicago*, 52 aircraft each towing a Waco to LZ-E (Landing Zone E). Of these, 44 carried A and B/81st AAA Battalion, the others elements of 326th Airborne Engineer Battalion, 101st Signals Company and the Antitank Platoon of 327th Glider Infantry Regiment: 16 57mm antitank guns, 25 vehicles (including a bulldozer), ammunition and other supplies, and 155 men, including the assistant divisional commander, Brigadier General Don F Pratt.

The serial was harassed by enemy fire over France, losing one aircraft and glider combo near Pont l'Abbé, but saw the LZ markers and found the Eureka beam to ensure a good release. Unfortunately, the poor visibility – the moon was setting and there were clouds – led to difficult conditions for the gliders, many of which landed badly. Five troops were killed including the unfortunate Pratt, who had been slated to arrive on the Continent as part of 101st's sea echelon. In spite of this, the arrival of the antitank guns and men had a beneficial impact on the battle.

Subsequently, in the evening of 6 June, the 434th flew Mission *Keokuk*, resupply of the 101st by 32 aircraft towing Horsa gliders to LZ-E. Again, delivery was no problem, but landing gliders was – thanks to the enemy fire: there were 54 casualties (14 dead, 30 wounded and 10 missing).

The 434th was in action again on D+1 (7 June) as part of Mission *Galveston*, reinforcing 82nd Airborne in two serials, one flown by the 437th from Ramsbury. The 434th flew 50 aircraft and Waco combos, carrying HQ/325th Glider Infantry Regiment, 82nd's Recon Platoon and other troops: 251 men, 24 vehicles, 11 guns and 5 tons of ammunition.

Poor weather hampered the launch, which also suffered from two early releases, only one of which was early enough to allow the aircraft to return for a substitute craft. The German ground fire hit 18 aircraft, but none seriously and the gliders were released correctly and with good accuracy: 20 gliders arrived in the zone, 19 within a mile and a further 8 within two miles – and while 16 Wacos were destroyed and 26 damaged, there were some injuries but no deaths and most of the vehicles were recovered.

# 53 RAF Blakehill Farm, Cricklade, Wiltshire

**RAF Blakehill Farm was one of three airfields near Swindon – the others being RAF Broadwell and RAF Down Ampney – that housed squadrons of No 46 Group, RAF Transport Command. Dakotas of No 233 Squadron flew from here on 6 June.**

RAF Blakehill Farm became operational on 9 February 1944 following the requisition of 580 acres of land by the War Office in 1943. Named after the farm that once stood there, it was an extensive site with more than 500 buildings of one sort or another. These included aircraft hangars, the control tower, accommodation blocks and medical centres.

After its transfer to Transport Command, where it exchanged Hudsons for Dakotas, No 233 Squadron was involved in intensive training, helped by elements of the 1st Canadian Parachute Battalion, working not only with paratroopers but also with Horsa gliders. Between 21 and 26 April, the squadron took part in Exercise *Mush*, a rehearsal for the invasion of Normandy that set the 1st Airborne Division and the Polish 1st Independent Parachute Brigade against the 6th Airborne Division.

A few weeks later, on the night of 5 June, 30 Dakotas of No 233 Squadron took off from RAF Blakehill Farm, six towing gliders and another 24 carrying paratroopers from the 3rd Parachute Brigade. The drop went well, although the lack of suitable navigation beacons meant it was widely scattered. Two Dakotas were lost. There were further flights as the squadron towed Horsas with Operation *Mallard*, the second lift bringing 6th Airlanding Brigade and the balance of 6th Airborne's men, along with their heavy equipment.

Two more No 233 aircraft were lost later on 6 June when the squadron sent 21 Dakotas to Normandy with supply flights. There were also four 'Rob Roy' resupply missions.

# 54 RAF Down Ampney, Gloucestershire

**RAF Down Ampney was home base of Nos 48 and 271 Squadrons, RAF, both of No 46 Group. They deployed Dakotas on D-Day to tow Horsa gliders and drop the main part of the 3rd Parachute Brigade.**

RAF Down Ampney, which became operational from February 1944, was part of a network of three airfields that were used by No 46 Group – the other two being RAF Broadwell and RAF Blakehill Farm – which flew exclusively Dakotas. It was home to around 3,000 personnel.

The work of the aircraft pilots and paratroopers is well known, but what is less well known is the work of the Glider Pilot Regiment, whose men came under army command but were trained by the RAF. The Glider Pilot Regiment lost 34 men in Normandy. E Squadron was based at the airfield. The Air Despatch Regiment, Royal Army Service Corps (RASC), was responsible for the supply of the division from the air. There is a memorial to the men of Nos 48 and 271 Squadrons, the 1st and 6th Airborne Divisions, the Glider Pilot Regiment and the Air Despatch Regiment, RASC, at the southern end of what was the main runway of RAF Down Ampney.

On D-Day, RAF Down Ampney aircraft flew a range of missions over France: more than 50 sorties with the first lift (No 48 Squadron dropping paratroopers and No 271 dropping paratroopers and towing Horsas); 37 sorties on the second (No 48 22 Horsas; No 271 15 Horsas); and No 271 flew 16 sorties on resupply flights, one being shot down by Allied fire and another sufficiently damaged to crash-land.

## 55 RAF Tarrant Rushton, Blandford Forum, Dorset

**The bulk of the Transport Command squadrons used on D-Day were commanded by No 38 Group, based at RAF Netheravon, in Wiltshire. RAF Tarrant Rushton hosted two of them: Nos 298 and 644, both equipped with Halifaxes.**

While No 46 Group deployed Dakotas, No 38 Group had a range of aircraft: Stirlings (Nos 190, 196, 299 and 620 Squadrons), Albermarles (295, 296, 297 and 570) and the Halifaxes at RAF Tarrant Rushton. Tarrant Rushton had become operational in October 1943 and was also the initial home of the RAF's Airborne Forces Tactical Development Unit, which was established the same year. This had the remit of refining the techniques of airborne warfare. As well as this, the base was used by No 196 Squadron, which operated the Stirling Mk IV mostly for covert purposes, such as supplying the French Resistance at night.

Tarrant Rushton also had the distinction of being the airfield from which, at 22:30 on 5 June, six Halifaxes – three from each squadron – left towing Horsas on Operation *Deadstick*, the coup-de-main attack on the river and canal bridges at Bénouville, today's Pegasus and Horsa Bridges. They carried 181 men of the 2nd Battalion, the Oxfordshire and Buckinghamshire Light Infantry, under the command of Major John Howard. Their success was a product of brilliance and bravery, and the successful capture of the bridges ensured that they could not be used by German counter-attacking forces but were retained for a future Allied thrust.

RAF Tarrant Rushton played an essential role in the wider Operations *Tonga* and *Mallard*, 298 Squadron flying an additional 45 sorties (15 Horsas and 2 Hamilcars with *Tonga*; 16 Hamilcars with *Mallard*; and 12 resupply flights) and 644 Squadron 36 sorties (15 Horsas and 2 Hamilcars with *Tonga*; 16 Hamilcars on *Mallard*; and 3 resupply flights).

The heavy-lift Hamilcar gliders were made by General Aircraft Limited. Each carried a lightweight Tetrarch tank of A Squadron, 6th Airborne Reconnaissance Regiment. These were landed near the mouth of the Orne River to help protect the eastern flank of the landings. They were not hugely successful, being outgunned by the German armour, but proved to be useful fire support.

**The memorial at Tarrant Rushton stands in front of a wartime T2 hangar. The memorial has three plaques, one of which remembers Nos 298 and 644 Squadrons, RAF, who towed gliders on D-Day – including Tetrarch tanks of the 6th Airborne Armoured Reconnaissance Regiment in Hamilcar gliders.**

Wartime view of Tarrant Rushton: Halifax bombers are ready to tow a line-up of Hamilcar gliders behind a pair of Horsas. The aircraft are ready for the reinforcement of the British airborne assault – Operation *Mallard* – on the evening of 6 June. This had the dual effect of scaring the elements of 21st Panzer Division, whose counter-attack had reached the coast, and bolstering the defences of the lightly armed paratroopers.

RIGHT
While little of the airfield survives intact today, traces are visible from the air.

# 56 RAF Fairford, Gloucestershire

**Another No 38 Group airfield, RAF Fairford was built in 1944 to support the invasion of Normandy. Base to Nos 190 and 620 Squadrons, on D-Day it dispatched Stirlings for both Operation *Tonga* (paratroopers) and *Mallard* (gliders).**

Construction of RAF Fairford began in 1943, with staff moving during January 1944. The first operational squadron was No 620, which arrived on 19 March 1944. Six days later it was joined by No 190. Both operated the Short Stirling Mk IV – these could be used either as glider tugs or for transport purposes, such as carrying paratroopers. They brought with them a number of Horsa gliders.

Once established on site, the squadrons undertook hazardous covert operations on behalf of the SOE (Special Operations Executive) and the SAS. These were undertaken at night, usually flying either singly or in pairs. The units also started training for Operation *Overlord*. Tragically, two aircraft were lost when they collided during these practices, killing everyone on board.

As part of Operation *Tonga*, 46 Stirlings, 23 from each of Nos 190 and 620 Squadrons, ferried nearly 900 paratroopers of the 5th Parachute Brigade across the Channel on the night of 5 June to their Drop Zone N across the River Orne. In total, 38 Group sent 109 aircraft on the first lift. Three aircraft from No 620 Squadron were lost during the operation.

On the afternoon of 6 June, as part of Operation *Mallard*, 36 Stirlings (18 from each squadron) each towed a Horsa glider carrying reinforcements across to Ranville.

**RAF Fairford was used by British units for D-Day but went on to have a long association with US air forces, with an extended runway (nearly 10,000ft long) that allowed B-52s to use it during the Gulf wars and also the space shuttle to nominate it as an abort landing strip. Today it is a standby field and sees little activity.**

# 57 D-Day Marshalling Area Camp D6, Piddlehinton, Dorset

**Purpose-built in 1937 after the land had been requisitioned by the War Office, Piddlehinton Camp wasn't a temporary location, unlike so many of the camouflaged camps that studded the south coast.**

Piddlehinton, near Dorchester, north of Weymouth, was a typical British army camp originally built as a brigade or divisional camp, which then was used as a reinforcement and reception camp by the 3rd Division. On 31 May 1944 it was being used by the 62nd Armored Field Artillery Battalion. A day later the assault echelon – 24 officers and 237 men – left for Portland, where they boarded six different LCTs (landing craft), leaving behind four officers and 164 men in Bournemouth. There the assault echelon remained until 02:30 on 5 June, when they left for Omaha. Later in June, the camp was used by the 67th Armored Field Artillery Battalion, who reached Omaha Beach much later.

The camp was used by both American and British soldiers during the war: by the 1st US Infantry Division, the Parachute Regiment, Royal Engineers, Kings Dragoon Guards, Royal Artillery, Welch Fusiliers and 46 Royal Marines Commando, who gathered at Piddlehinton before forming at the Keep, Dorchester.

The camp had a capacity of 3,600 men and 510 vehicles but as it had not been camouflaged throughout the war there were no changes around D-Day, so as not to arouse the suspicions of the Germans.

Later in 1944, on Christmas Eve, troops from Piddlehinton were aboard SS *Leopoldville*, a Belgian liner acting as a troopship, sailing from Southampton to Cherbourg, when it was torpedoed by *U486*. More than 800 men from the US 262nd and 66th Infantry Divisions – who had been in camps scattered around Dorset – died.

Today, the camp is an industrial estate, and on 23 December 2004, 60 years after the men from the 66th Infantry Division left the camp, 800 trees were planted in their memory.

Piddlehinton Camp covered a large area outside the village, as the wartime aerial photograph shows (BELOW). It was used well into the 1980s, but today most of the camp has been redeveloped, although there are still a couple of huts and a firing range extant, as can be seen in the 2018 view (BELOW RIGHT).

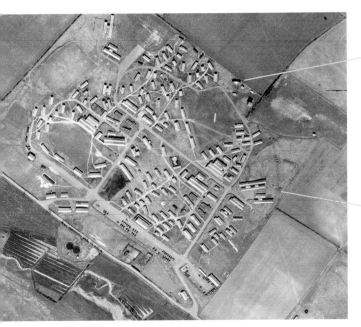

# 58  D-Day Marshalling Area Camp D3, Yellowham Woods, Dorset

**Apart from concrete hardstandings, little remains of the marshalling camp in Yellowham Woods.**

**'1944 Buffalo' carved onto a tree trunk in Yellowham Woods, perhaps referring to the US city of Buffalo, a reminder that men of the 1st Infantry Division were marshalled for D-Day in camp D3.**

**OPPOSITE**
**The aerial photograph shows the line of the A35 heading to Dorchester (top right; the top of the photograph is south). Yellowham Woods Camp D3 is at 'A', with little visible beneath the trees.**

**Unlike Piddlehinton, an army camp that had been built before the war, Yellowham, just off the A35 east of Dorchester, was a temporary *Overlord* Camp that was in deep woodland and well camouflaged.**

The camp had a capacity of 1,500 personnel and 220 vehicles and was very close to the fuel depot at Kingston Maurward (*see* pp 84–5). Camp D3 was one of three camps operated by the 773rd Tank Destroyer Battalion, which would itself reach Normandy on 8 August. Yellowham was only a few miles north of Weymouth (*see* pp 142–3) and the isle of Portland (*see* pp 144–5), from where the troops of 1st Infantry embarked for Omaha Beach. Nearby camp D1, at Puddletown, housed men of A Company, 16th Infantry, part of the US 1st Infantry Division (known as the 'Big Red One').

Today, there are only sparse reminders of the camp: a few brick and concrete hut bases, some trenches and a few screw picket posts. The camp would have been encircled by barbed wire and guarded to ensure no one could leave and let slip what was happening. It made the area feel like a PoW camp – and, later, many of these camps became exactly that to cater for German prisoners of war.

# 59 D-Day Marshalling Area Camp L1, Ivybridge, Devon

**The Royal Engineers built Uphill Camp at Ivybridge in 1943 and in May of that year the 29th Infantry Division – a National Guard unit – moved from Tidworth, in Wiltshire, and took up residence in Devon.**

More than 1,300 men of the 29th Division were accommodated in the camp at Ivybridge, with 1/116th Regiment the only infantry unit there. This regiment was firmly rooted in Virginia, in the US, with the four original companies located in Bedford, Virginia (A Company – the 'Bedford Boys'), Lynchburg (B Company), Harrisonburg (C Company) and Roanoke (D Company). During their time at Ivybridge, the 29th were visited by Eisenhower and Montgomery and spent 12 days at the Assault Training Center at Woolacombe, on the north Devon coast (*see* pp 64–5).

On 15 May the regiment moved to Blandford Camp in Dorset, where it entered high security and was briefed on the landings. On 3 June the 116th was in Portsmouth ready to board its transports to Normandy: 1st Battalion was assigned to the SS *Empire Javelin*, an Infantry Landing Ship that took them to Dog Green, Omaha Beach.

The Bedford Boys had the longest training programme (from October 1942 to May 1944) of any of the American infantrymen who landed on Omaha Beach. It made little difference, on 6 June, within a few minutes of landing, 19 boys were dead. A total of 22 men died – from a town with a population of just 3,000.

A war memorial in Harford Road car park, Ivybridge, is inscribed: 'Dedicated to all the American Servicemen based in Ivybridge 1943–1944, particularly the 1st Battalion 116th Infantry Regiment who made many friends with local residents. Sadly many of these men were to die on, or after, D-Day the 6th June 1944.'

**BELOW AND RIGHT**
Today the site of the camp is an open space, MacAndrews Field. Two beautiful memorial benches were created by Peter Lanyon and a host of volunteers and installed in 2014. Lanyon explained: 'The benches consist of two slabs of chestnut, with hand-cleaved oak uprights – each upright symbolises one of the young men involved in the D-day landing on Omaha Beach. The height of each upright is proportional to the man's age when he died, and has been incised with his name and age.'[48]

# 60  D-Day Marshalling Area Camps A11 and A12, Creech Woods, Denmead, Hampshire

**With space for 3,850 men and 300 vehicles, Creech Woods was a sizeable encampment. It was just over 10 miles from the Stokes Bay embarkation hards.**

Creech Woods had a number of visitors before D-Day, among them Montgomery's Tactical Headquarters, the HQ of the 3rd British Infantry Division and 2nd Battalion, the Royal Lincolnshire Regiment. The latter was moved from Creech Woods on 2 June: it would board its LCIs (landing craft) alongside Southsea pier.

The Lincolnshire Regiment was replaced in the marshalling camps by the Canadian Stormont, Dundas and Glengarry Highlanders of the 9th Infantry Brigade of the 3rd Canadian Infantry Division, destined to land on Juno Beach on D-Day.

The 1st Battalion, King's Own Scottish Borderers, was also at Denmead, embarking for France on 4 June. The Scots landed on Sword at Queen Beach.

The Highlanders had practised the marshalling and loading of troops and vehicles on 27–29 April 1944, during Exercise *Fabius*. On 30 May it was the real thing: the assault troops went to the marshalling areas at Creech Woods and later moved to Stokes Bay, where they boarded seven landing craft, moving into Southampton Waters on 3 June, before being held for a day because of the weather.

After D-Day, Creech Woods was used as a PoW camp for German troops captured in Normandy.

**Sergeant W Woolridge of No 2 AFPU (Army Film and Photographic Unit) captured scenes at the camp near Denmead on 29 April 1944. He went on to take photographs in Italy in 1945. Here his photograph of Sergeant Ernest Docherty, composing a letter in his unit's tented camp.**

Aerial views of Creech Woods, then (RIGHT) and now (BELOW). The location of the camp is shown on the overlay.

# 61 Follow-up Force L loading port, Felixstowe, Suffolk

**Felixstowe had hards NST 1–3 that could accommodate six LSTs (landing ships) and four LCTs (landing craft). From here, follow-up forces left for Normandy on 7 June. They had to brave 'Hellfire Corner' at Dover, where German long-range guns had the range to pick off shipping.**

Landguard Point, at the mouth of the River Orwell south of Felixstowe, was a well-defended area with anti-invasion defences, anti-aircraft positions and HMS *Beehive*, a Coastal Forces base that housed a seaplane base during the First World War. This part of the country had indeed been a hive of military activity since being threatened by invasion. On D-Day, it was where the 22nd Armoured Brigade of the 7th Armoured Division boarded landing craft to head towards Gold Beach.

Returning from Italy, the 7th Armoured refitted with Cromwell tanks in the Thetford area, each troop having three Cromwells and one Sherman Mk Vc Firefly. The 22nd Armoured Brigade – 1st and 5th Royal Tank Regiments (RTR), 4th County of London Yeomanry (CLY) and 1st Battalion, the Rifle Brigade – had waterproofed their vehicles at marshalling camp R5 Orwell Park School, near Ipswich, arriving there on 8 May and completing this by 26 May. They headed by road for Felixstowe Docks on 3 June and sailed on 5 June. The 4th CLY landed in France on the evening of 6 June, the rest of the division arriving over the next few days.

**RIGHT**
This Cromwell Mk IV in Thetford Forest, Norfolk, is a replica of 'Little Audrey' – of B Squadron, 1RTR, whose call sign was '5 Able'. Thetford was where the division converted to Cromwells and trained for the assault on Europe. The division sailed from Felixstowe on 5 June and the first tanks landed on Gold Beach on the evening of 6 June. A plaque at the replica tank reads: 'The memorial is dedicated to all who served in the 7th Armoured Division (The Desert Rats), the 4th Armoured Brigade (The Black Rats) and the 7th Armoured Brigade (The Green Jerboa), throughout history.'

**RIGHT**
Slipway at Landguard Point, Felixstowe, built for use in the build-up for Operation *Overlord. See also* 'C' in aerial photograph.

# 62  Follow-up Force L loading port, Tilbury, Essex

**Elizabeth I made her famous defiant speech at Tilbury in 1588; 356 years
later it was a landing craft maintenance base, a marshalling area and
embarkation point for the landings.**

Its five hards – NZ 1–5 – could accommodate four LSTs (landing ships) and eight
LCTs (landing craft). From 6 June through to early August 1944, more than 40 runs
were made between London Docks, Tilbury and Juno Beach. Tilbury also played an
important role in the assembly and transport of the PLUTO cross-Channel petrol
supply pipe (*see* pp 90–1) and the prefabricated Mulberry Harbours.

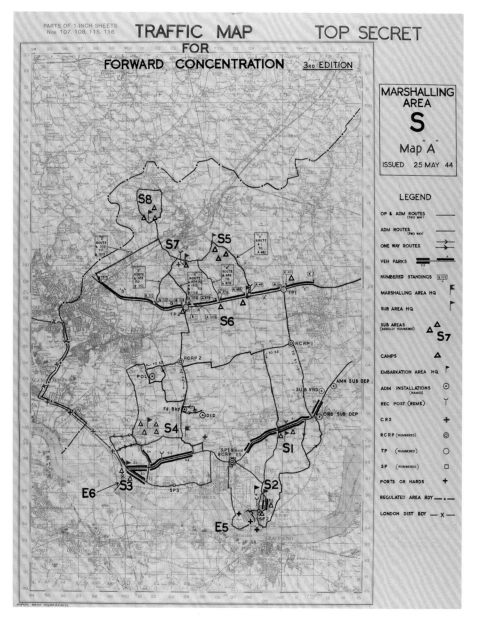

Sited on the north
shore of the River
Thames, 25 miles
downstream from
London Bridge, Tilbury
is an important part
of the Port of London,
with access to deep
water. Like much of
southern England in
1944, it was a military-
restricted marshalling
area, holding 40,000
men and 6,500 vehicles
prior to embarkation
and charged with
transporting 4,000
men and 600 vehicles
per day for as long
as necessary after
D-Day itself. Eastern
Command, which
included Essex,
provided for more than
100,000 men and their
equipment embarking
through Tilbury
and London Docks,
including elements of
Force L's 1st Brigade
Group, 7th Armoured
Division, 51st
Highland Division,
support units of I and
XXX Corps, 21st (BR)
Army Group HQ and
the Canadian 3rd
Infantry Division.

Coal House
Fort housed HMS *St
Clement* Combined
Operations base.

# 63 'Wetbobs', Folkestone Harbour, Kent

**In the midst of all the preparations for D-Day, the dummy landing craft known as 'Wetbobs' or 'Big Bobs' in Folkestone and other south-eastern ports were part of a deception plan – Operation *Fortitude South* – designed to make the Nazis think that the Normandy landings were a feint.**

Admiral Bertram Ramsay's 1944 *Report by ANCXF on Operation Neptune* states: 'Because the power of manoeuvre at sea was so limited and because it was vital to hold the enemy reserves in sectors other than that to be assaulted as long as possible, the need for cover and deception was paramount, both strategically during the preparatory period and tactically during the approach.'[49] The report makes clear in a number of places how important the deception was. In conjunction with the creation of the notional FUSAG (First US Army Group) and the use of General Patton as its putative commander, the use of troops who were being readied to go to Normandy as part of the scheme, the work of No 5 Wireless Group, Royal Signals, and the use of physical dummies helped to make the deception work. No 5 Wireless Group helped deceive the German *B-Dienst* (*Beobachtungsdienst* – radio observation and monitoring service) by playing back recordings of scripted radio traffic which had been made on a wire recorder over No 19 wireless sets.

From January 1944 the 4th Battalion, Northamptonshire Regiment, and 10th Battalion, Worcestershire Regiment, were chosen to play a part in the deception. Trained secretly near Ipswich, they learnt how to erect dummy landing craft and launch them – a more complicated job than it sounds. The 4th Northamptonshires were deployed on the east coast of England and the Worcesters were sent to work at Dover, Folkestone and on the River Orwell, where hards were created.

The units moved into position in late April and a month later deliveries – more than 700 lorries – had been completed. On 20 May the first 'Big Bob' was floating on the Orwell. By D-Day there were a number of dummy craft on the coast as the table below shows. There were problems: designed to float for four weeks in sheltered waters, the dummies at Dover and Folkestone were badly affected by the weather, but the troops were able to keep them working. On 13 June, they realised the deception was working: German long-range artillery fired 46 shells at Folkestone, and German propaganda radio claimed that the shelling had stopped the craft from sailing.

**Dummy landing craft in East England**

| Location | Qty of Craft | Suggested Storing Place | Launching Hard | Area of Berthing |
|---|---|---|---|---|
| Yarmouth | 50 | Pitches Quay & Railway Yard | Pitches Quay & Railway Yard | Breydon Water |
| Lowestoft | 20 | Chambers Yard | Chambers Yard | Lake Lothing |
| River Deben – Waldringfield | 66 | Waldringfield | Waldringfield | River Deben |
| River Orwell – Cat House & Woolverstone | 70 | Woolverstone Park | Cat House | River Orwell Woolverstone Pin Mill |

# 64 Southsea Pier embarkation point, Hampshire

**As with most of the south coast, Southsea had been declared a restricted zone in summer 1943, as part of the 10-mile-deep strip that was closed to visitors.**

Nearby, at the end of May in the woods north of Portsmouth, the marshalling camps were sealed. Once the final briefings had been given and orders delivered, the embarkation began. Southsea was one of the Portsmouth embarkation points that was slated for use by Force S, along with those at Newhaven, in East Sussex, and Shoreham, in West Sussex. Southsea Pier had been reworked with scaffolding piers alongside to help increase the number of troops that could be loaded aboard LCIs (landing craft). Hampshire was the location for Marshalling Area A, which included Rowlands Castle (A1), Emsworth Common (A2), Horndean (A4), Waterlooville (A5–A7), Hambledon (A10), Denmead (Creech Woods; *see* pp 128–9) and Southwick (A11 and A12), Wickham Park (A13–A15), Funtley (A16), Park Gate (A17), Sarisbury (A18), Gosport (A1) and Botley (A22).

Force S would land on Sword Beach, specifically Queen White and Queen Red Beaches. The assault brigade, the 8th Infantry, would be followed up by the 9th and 185th Infantry Brigades. Attached for the assault were the DD tanks of the 27th Armoured Brigade, and two Special Service brigades: the 1st, commanded by Brigadier Lord Lovat, to the east and the 4th to the west. The Beach Group, No 5, with groups from the 80th AA (Anti-Aircraft) and the Royal Engineers, landed in the assault.

Force S was commanded by Captain Eric Bush, Royal Navy, from HMS *Goathland*, leaving with Convoy S5 from Spithead. Other elements of the convoy were 10 landing craft transporting the AVREs (Armoured Vehicles Royal Engineers), 4 LC (Flak), 5 LCT(R), 18 LC(SP) and 9 LCAs (*see* p 49 for explanation of landing craft types).

By the end of D-Day, 28,845 men had landed over Sword Beach. They were helped by a bombardment squadron of 2 battleships (*Ramillies* and *Warspite*), a monitor (*Roberts*), 5 cruisers and 13 destroyers, the latter including *Stord* and *Svenner* of the Royal Norwegian Navy. *Svenner* was sunk by German torpedo boats off Sword Beach on D-Day.

Unveiled on Eastney Esplanade, in Southsea, on 6 June 1948 by Field Marshal Montgomery, this concrete antitank block is inscribed on two sides:

1940 France and the Low Countries having been overrun, we laboured alone to obstruct our coasts with such blocks as this against invasion by the enemies of freedom

1944 Yet from this very beach in the company of powerful allies many thousands of our men embarked on the great adventure of liberating Europe and achieved their objective

# 65  Gosport embarkation hards, Hampshire

**Portsmouth has been at the centre of British naval power for more than 800 years and, unsurprisingly, was a key location for the planning and execution of both Operation _Neptune_ and Operation _Overlord_. Its less well-known neighbour, Gosport, was also crucially involved.**

Gosport has a rich and important naval history and played a significant role in the run-up to D-Day and after. As well as housing the Royal Hospital Haslar (_see_ pp 100–1), HMS _Hornet_ (the HQ for RN MTB (motor torpedo boat) flotillas), HMS _Dolphin_ (then home to the RN Submarine Service), the Royal Clarence Victualling Yard and Priddy's Hard RN Armament Depot (_see_ pp 88–9), there were a number of embarkation points around Gosport. They were used by British and Canadian troops bound for Sword and Juno Beaches; once embarked, the vessels moored up in the Solent awaiting the order to depart.

 The most intensively used were the four hards – G1 to G4 – at Stokes Bay (_see_ pp 94–5). Here, alongside the Mulberry Harbour construction sites, troops embarked onto four LCTs (landing craft) on each hard. Today, a memorial to the Canadian 3rd Infantry who boarded here looks out over the Solent at Stokes Bay Sailing Club.

 Anyone who has crossed on the ferry from Gosport to Portsmouth has passed close to the Beach Street hard, today remembered with a memorial. Alongside the ferry, GF hard (at 'A' on the photograph on page 137) could take two LCTs. Some of the best-known photographs of the loading for D-Day were taken here – of the British 3rd Infantry Division and 27th Armoured Brigade embarking.

 Further into Portsmouth Harbour, at Hardway, from 3 June troops began to board: the hard (GH hard) could accommodate two LSTs. Subsequently, both German PoWs and Allied wounded returned to Gosport's hards.

**ABOVE**

Memorial in Ferry Gardens, Gosport.

**RIGHT**

AFPU (Army Film and Photographic Unit) photographer Sergeant Jimmy Mapham took a series of photographs of _LCT-610_ and _LCT-789_ on 4 or 5 June at Gosport hard. _610_ carried elements of Regimental HQ and C Squadron of 13/18th Hussars, 27th Armoured Brigade. Other elements of this regiment landed DD tanks on Sword Beach. Note the porpoise ammunition sledge and the 3rd Division markings (circle and triangles) on the LCT.

**OPPOSITE**

Post-war aerial view of Gosport, with the mooring dolphin and hard still in evidence at 'A'.

# 66 Warsash Commando Memorial, Hampshire

**D-Day embarkations from the River Hamble may not have been as numerous as at the larger ports, but few were as significant. From Warsash, Lord Lovat led his 1st Special Service Brigade to Sword Beach, where it took Ouistreham and then linked up with the 6th Airborne at Pegasus Bridge.**

Lord Lovat tells the story with his customary elan in his autobiography, *March Past*. He was at Brigade HQ when he received the call to action: 'Top Priority. From Movement Control, Southern Command. Commandos will be collected and moved under separate arrangements ... as detailed: proceeding to C18 Transit Camp, Southampton. Acknowledge and alert all units concerned.'[50] Marshalling Area C – Southampton – had at least 24 camps, four of which (C18–C21) were on Southampton Common. In total these catered for 8,500 men and 1,000 vehicles.

Lord Lovat continues:

> Brigade headquarters was waiting packed and ready. Despatch riders roared out of town with sealed orders for commanding officers. The wheels of invasion began to turn. Our waterproofed Jeeps had already gone ahead, loaded into ships for France ... The rear party took over files and switchboard; John Cowdray (who had lost a limb at Dunkirk) gave me breakfast before departure. The fighting men had far to travel, and there was time to say goodbye to Rosie [Lovat's wife] and the children. Then the convoy rolled.[51]

At the marshalling area there was time to go to a cinema tent, in addition to the final preparations that needed to take place. Lord Lovat remembers:

> Officers busied themselves with final arrangements and the check-ups that save lives; dinghies were inflated, bayonets sharpened, automatic springs tested, magazines oiled, waterproof wrapping wound round all weapons, escape maps were issued with ammunition, rations and first-aid kits. Hand grenades were not primed until the day of departure. The intelligence section made a sand table to supplement air photographs showing half-hidden details of enemy fortifications, wire and suspected minefields. Place-names and destinations were withheld until embarkation, but Frenchmen [of No 10 Inter-Allied Commando] identified the destination at a glance. Sappers and signals attended to the mysteries of their trade. The briefings were a formality: everybody knew his job.[52]

The brigade's war diary takes up the story more tersely: 'The Brigade left Camp C18 and embarked for operation OVERLORD at WARSASH in LCI(S) of the 200th and 201st LCI(S) Flotilla. (Senior Naval Officer Lieut Commander L R Curtis RNVR).'[53]

There's a memorial and a plaque at Warsash, the latter identifying that 3,000 commandos – 1st and 4th Special Service Brigades – embarked on 36 landing craft based on HMS *Tormentor* for Normandy.

Commandos of the 1st Special Service Brigade board five LCI(S)s – which could carry 96 fully equipped men – at Warsash, on 3 June 1944. They landed at 09:10 hours on 6 June on Queen Red Beach, west of Ouistreham, one of their objectives.

Warsash today. There's a memorial on the quay from which the commandos left and one on the pub opposite. Note the yacht club building (on the far right): this was the Combined Operations HQ.

# 67 Plaque for the Essex Regiment, Lymington, Hampshire

**The pretty little town of Lymington, on the river of the same name, had a rail link to a ferry across to Yarmouth on the Isle of Wight. Forces heading to Gold Beach, including the Pompadours – the 2nd Battalion, Essex Regiment – boarded here.**

Raised in 1755, with battle honours that include Badajoz, Waterloo, Somme and Gallipoli, the Pompadours were part of the 56th Independent Infantry Brigade, along with the 2nd Battalion, South Wales Borderers and the 2nd Battalion, Gloucestershire Regiment. They landed on Gold Beach as part of the assault group.

On 25 May they had moved to the marshalling camps in the New Forest: Brigade HQ at Pennerley Lodge, the Borderers at Pennerley Farm (camp B4, near Beaulieu), the Pompadours at Stubbs Wood (B3) and the 2nd Glosters at Brockenhurst (B7).

There, Andrew Holborn relates:

> Sergeant Dick Philips, the Intelligence Section NCO of 2nd South Wales Borderers, equally remembers that: "The briefings were wonderful really. There were these photographs of the area where we were going to land and relief maps showing every cottage and every tree. When we actually landed and got off the beach we would have no problem in finding our way."[54]

On 3 June, the boarding started: first the rifle companies, then the Borderers, followed by 2nd Essex and then the Glosters. The LCIs sailed to Southampton, their vehicles had already started driving there or to Gosport. They were marked with white numbers on a brown square: 2nd Essex was 69, 2nd Glosters 68 and 2nd South Wales Borderers had 67.

On 5 June, as part of Convoy G3, they headed to Normandy.

Memorial to the Pompadours at the quayside, Lymington. On 3 June the battalion boarded LCI(L)s and spent the night moored in Southampton Docks. They endured the extra day after the 5 June postponement cooped up in the ships, although they were allowed some time on the quayside for 'Char and Wads'. On 5 June, in the late evening, they cast off.

Aerial view of Lymington (2018), looking upriver. Note the hard used by the Pompadours at 'A' and the rail terminal at 'B'. Part of the 56th Infantry Division, the Pompadours landed on the right flank of Gold Beach on D-Day.

# 68  US 14th Port, Southampton, Hampshire

**Henry V's departure for France and the Battle of Agincourt took place from Southampton, and the city was the lynchpin of the British elements of Operation *Neptune*. Southampton saw two-thirds of the British and Canadian assault force – all of Force G and much of Force J – embark through the port.**

It was beyond question that the invasion of France from the south coast of Britain would include Southampton. In 1936 the port handled 46 per cent of the UK's ocean-going passenger traffic, handling more than 600,000 passengers and more than 6,500 freight and passenger trains. It had 5.5 miles of quays but had suffered badly from bombing and had lost some of its equipment to other ports.

The US 14th Port moved in towards the end of 1943. (The 12th operated in London, Hull and Immingham before moving to Normandy after D-Day. The 13th looked after Plymouth and the western ports.) Under the 14th, Southampton became the principal US port on the south coast. After getting over the problems of strikes – associated with Military Police action against pilferage – the HQ moved down from London in early 1944. In May 1944 Southampton stopped receiving cargo and concentrated on preparation for D-Day; it would become a significant player in the movement of US troops, equipment and supplies to the Continent. Operation *Bolero* had seen nearly 1.8 million troops and 15.5 million tons of cargo come to Britain since January 1942; most of that now needed to be shipped to Europe. The port went on to see a lot of use beyond the end of the war, including repatriating US troops and British war brides to the US.

**As the south coast's most celebrated passenger port, Southampton was a significant player on D-Day. More than a quarter of a million vehicles were shipped out of Southampton and more than 3.5 million men between D-Day and the end of the war.**

Southampton's South Western Hotel became HQ of the Combined Operation Military Movement Control as the number of landing craft built up from spring 1942. In late 1943, camps were set up, designated Marshalling Area C, including: Harefield (C1), Thornhill Park (C2), Netley Common (C3), which had US troops at one stage, as did Bushfield, Winchester (C5), Chandler's Ford (C6–C9), Bassett Green (C10), Bassett Wood (C11), Hursley Park (C12 and C13), Cramp Moor, Broadlands and Nightingale Wood, Romsey (C14–C16), Upton (C17), Southampton Common (C18–21), Toothill (C22) and Chilworth Common (C24).

Southampton had six LST (landing ship) loading points and two LCT (landing craft) hards (S 1–4). They loaded from D-6 (31 May), vehicles first, and the soldiers – many Canadians destined for Juno Beach. Once loaded – and some of the loading was delayed by problems with the tides – the ships moved into the Solent. They sailed for Normandy on D-1.

Finally, opposite Southampton Docks is Marchwood, a Royal Naval Armaments Depot since 1812, and Marchwood Military Port, joined to the main line railway by the Marchwood Military Railway from the end of November 1943. Among other things, Marchwood was a construction site for 'beetles' (pontoons) used in the roadway sections of Mulberry Harbours.

# 69  Weymouth, Dorset

**There were 14 camps in Marshalling Area D, where men of the Rangers – the US Army's version of commandos, who had undergone similar training in Scotland – and the 'Big Red One', the US 1st Infantry Division, readied themselves for embarkation at Weymouth and Portland.**

There's a classic selection of colour photographs – rare enough during the Second World War – and newsreel of the Rangers walking along the seafront at Weymouth on 3 June and embarking on the LCAs (landing craft) that would take them out to the LSIs (landing ships) of Assault Group O4 in Weymouth Bay. The Rangers were going to assault the Pointe du Hoc (although, thanks to a misprint, most of them thought it was Pointe du Hoe). They were given coffee and doughnuts en route. A memorial on the Esplanade at Weymouth remembers the Rangers, the Slapton Sands incident (*see* pp 72–3) and also states:

> The major part of the American assault force which landed on the shores of France 6 June 1944 was launched from Weymouth and Portland harbors. From 6 June 1944 to 7 May 1945, 517,816 troops and 144,093 vehicles embarked from the harbors. Many of the troops left from Weymouth pier. The remainder of the troops and all the vehicles passed through Weymouth en route to Portland points of embarkation. Presented by the 14th Major Port, US Army.

The men of the 1st Infantry Division had trained in Dorset and Devon (at the Assault Training Center, Woolacombe; *see* pp 64–5). They had been billeted throughout Dorset – there's a wartime photo article about life in Burton Bradstock, outside Abbotsbury. As an example, take the 18th Infantry Regiment, whose Regimental Combat Team (RCT) was to assault Omaha's Easy Red. The 1st Battalion was at Chickerell (having moved from Piddlehinton on 12 January), the 2nd Battalion and Cannon Company were at Broadmayne and West Knighton, the 3rd Battalion was in Dorchester, the AntiTank Company was in Piddlehinton (*see* p 123). HQ was in Ilsington House, Puddletown.

The marshalling camps – there were 14 of them in the area – included fixed camps such as Piddlehinton and those in the woods, such as Yellowham (D3; *see* p 124). On 26 May the assault units moved into them preparatory to embarking. When they did embark, on 3 June, they did so under the cover of smoke generated on trailers.

Also leaving from Weymouth was the 116th RCT of the 29th Infantry Division, moving from Devon to Blandford Camp on 15 May and embarking on 3 June.

**BELOW**
US forces embark from Weymouth in readiness for D-day. Note the old Weymouth Pavilion in the background, since rebuilt in rather brutalist style.

**BELOW RIGHT**
US Rangers traverse the Esplanade to their waiting LCAs (landing craft). There were two Ranger units involved on D-Day: the 2nd and 5th Battalions. Commanded by Lieutenant Colonel James E Rudder, three companies of the 2nd Battalion assaulted Pointe du Hoc. The rest, through a series of errors, diverted to Omaha, where they were instrumental in leading the way off the beach and up the bluffs.

**ABOVE**
Modern aerial view of the Esplanade
curving round to the ferry port
and Weymouth Pavilion. The
light is never extinguished on the
memorial on Weymouth Esplanade
('A' and inset). The memorial was
unveiled on 3 December 1947
and remembers all the American
servicemen who passed through
Weymouth and Portland to
Normandy.

**RIGHT**
LCAs ferry the Rangers out to larger
vessels to cross the Channel.

# 70  American Memorial, Portland, Dorset

**Portland and Weymouth provided US forces with both troop embarkation and port facilities, but these south-western ports struggled to cope with the size of the forces being sent to Normandy.**

The south of England was divided up between the Americans and British, with US forces allotted all the marshalling and embarkation facilities from Poole westwards. The Allies shared facilities from east of Poole as far as Southampton. After that, it was all British. The American division between base sections saw most of the staging area in the Southern Base Section, which had, therefore, the largest share of the mounting, and all of the seaborne assault forces.

  The Southern Base Section had an enormous task on its hands, and not much time to make it work. It's when one sees just how much was done in 1944 that one realises just how difficult it would have been to deliver sufficient fighting forces into

**ABOVE**
Portland's role in D-Day is remembered by the 'America Stone' in Victoria Gardens, dedicated on 22 August 1945 by the American Ambassador, John G Winant. The plaque reads: 'The major part of the American assault force which landed on the shores of France on D-Day, 6 June 1944, was launched from Portland Harbor. From 6 June 1944 to 7 May 1945, 418,585 troops and 144,093 vehicles embarked from this harbor. This plaque marks the route which the vehicles and troops took on their way to the points of embarkation. Presented by the 14th Major Port US Army.'

Portland hard in wartime (ABOVE RIGHT) and now (RIGHT).

ABOVE
Aerial photograph showing the
Portland hard (at 'A'). Note the pair
of Mulberry caissons at 'B'.

Europe any earlier than this (and that's before counting landing craft). To quote Roland Ruppenthal's *Logistical Support of the Armies*:

> Eight US divisions were quartered in the Southern Base Section area by January 1944. Within the next five months the number rose to fourteen, and the total US military population of the Southern Base Section doubled, rising from approximately 360,000 to 720,000. This sudden growth in strength made it necessary not only to build new camps but to convert old buildings which had been rejected earlier as unsuitable for military purposes.[55]

The rehearsals of *Tiger* and *Fabius* helped and after the latter finished in early May, the countdown was started: D-Day was less than a month away. The assault troops moved into the marshalling camps, sorted out the waterproofing, did their housekeeping and final training and waited for the off. Once they left, follow-on forces would move in, ensuring that the marshalling camps were full.

Portland harbour was completed in 1872 and at the time was the largest man-made harbour in the world. On 1 May 1944 the harbour was commissioned as USNAAB (US Navy Advanced Amphibious Base) Portland-Weymouth. It had five LST and four LCT hards (R2 and 3). For the cross-Channel movement, Force O was organised into five convoys. Most of its craft were assembled at Portland and Weymouth, and the remainder at Poole. Assembly was completed by 30 May, and loading began the following day.

# 71  US Coast Guard Memorial, Poole, Dorset

**ABOVE**

The US arrived in Poole in early 1944, creating an advanced amphibious base. Originally, Force G was going to leave from here, but the expansion of the plan saw Force O and U using the port.

**OPPOSITE, CENTRE LEFT AND RIGHT**

There are a number of memorials along the quayside at Poole, including that for the Coast Guard cutters, which is sited at 'A' on the photograph above.

**OPPOSITE, BELOW**

Poole was also an embarkation point. The hard used was originally RAF *Hamworthy* – a seaplane base – but became HMS *Turtle* when set up in 1942 as an amphibious warfare centre, training the men who would crew the LCG and LCT(R) landing craft. On 5 June more than 400 landing craft left the hard at HMS *Turtle* for Normandy, including those of O2A, the Close Gunfire Support Group for Omaha.

**The story goes that President Franklin D Roosevelt (some would say, at Churchill's behest) suggested that Operation *Neptune* would have need of a rescue service during the landings. The US Coast Guard was chosen to provide this dangerous duty.**

Poole was a large embarkation point for Operation *Overlord*, being slightly closer to France than some of the Devon sites. From here units of both Force O and Force U left for the beaches, from the town and also from HMS *Turtle*. The port was operated exclusively by US logistics crews, although many of the crews were British.

It was also, as remembered by a memorial erected in 1994 near the RNLI station on the quayside, home to 60 US Coast Guard 83ft cutters, which formed Rescue Flotilla 1. Designated *USCG1–60*, these wooden-hulled vessels – the so-called 'Matchbox Fleet' – were shared between the American beaches (30 vessels) and British beaches (also 30). Their mission was to rescue sailors, soldiers and airmen in difficulties. To do that while under fire in wooden boats that provided little protection showed considerable bravery.

They saved many lives: more than 400 men on D-Day, and by the time the unit was decommissioned in December 1944, the figure had increased to 1,438 (1,437 men and a woman). Amazingly, none of the cutters was lost in action.

Examples to exemplify their duties abound:

- Before 07:00 on the morning of 6 June, *USCG-1* rescued 28 survivors from a landing craft off Omaha.
- *USCG-34* pulled 32 British soldiers and seamen from the Channel on D-Day.
- *USCG-53* rescued five men from a swamped landing craft while under fire from the German guns, which were silenced by HMS *Rodney*.

From this Quay, 60 cutters of the United States Coast Guard Rescue Flotilla 1 departed for the Normandy Invasion 6 June 1944. These 83-foot boats, built entirely of wood, and the 840 crew members were credited with saving the lives of 1,437 men and one woman. In remembrance of the service rendered by Rescue Flotilla 1, and with appreciation of the kindnesses of the people of Poole to the crews, this plaque is given by men and women of the United States Coast Guard.

"Semper Paratus"
June 1994

# 72  Torquay embarkation hard, Devon

**On 5 June 1944 the 4th US Infantry Division, part of VII Corps, embarked from the Torquay hard. Their next stop was Utah Beach, where they rapidly pierced the opposition crust and advanced inland.**

OPPOSITE

4th Infantry Division troops march past Torquay's clock tower towards their embarkation point (ABOVE); the clock tower in more peaceful times (BELOW).

BELOW AND BOTTOM

The embarkation hards at Torquay are well preserved in the town marina.

The excellent information panels near the Grade II*-listed hard at Torquay explain the infrastructure that had to be built between Falmouth and Felixstowe: 68 hards that provided 172 berths for LCTs (landing craft) and 47 berths for LSTs (landing ships). In Torquay the four-berth LCT hard (designated PY) was built by 931 Port Construction and Repair Company, Royal Engineers, 14 January–28 May 1943. The panels note the unusual composition of the hard: a steeply inclined slope supported by a reinforced concrete framework. They also mention the crew that manned the hard – 40 when in operational use:

- commanding hardmaster
- embarkation staff officers
- a maintenance and repair crew
- supply quartermasters, cooks, stewards and medical orderlies.

The 4th Division had arrived in England, at Liverpool, in January 1944 and taken the train journey down to Devon, with Division HQ. There was a significant presence in the rural south-west, with many of the country houses requisitioned, travel restricted and mail censored.

The spread of the 4th Division around Devon saw elements of the three infantry regiments based around Seaton (2/8th), Exmouth (2/12th) and Budleigh (3/12th). The 8th Infantry Regiment was one of the first Allied units to hit the beaches at Normandy, helping to relieve 82nd Airborne at Sainte-Mère-Église and going on to take part in the capture of Cherbourg less than three weeks later, on 25 June.

# 73 Brixham embarkation hard, Devon

**Force U had the farthest to travel of all the troops assaulting on D-Day. It left from a large number of ports, from Falmouth to Poole, the convoys joining together off the Isle of Wight when the armada sailed. One of the ports was Brixham, a historic fishing port on the south coast of Tor Bay, opposite Torquay.**

In Brixham the four-berth LCT (landing craft) hard – designated PU and similar to that in Torquay – was built by the same company who had worked at Torquay (931 Port Construction and Repair Company, Royal Engineers) by 30 May 1943. The hard was used, as a bronze plaque close by attests, by the 4th Infantry Division, who assaulted Utah. The hard was then used to shuttle men and supplies to Normandy and wasn't derequisitioned until February 1945.

Not all the vessels moored up in Brixham picked up from the hard there. Take *LCT-2304*, one of eight LCT Mk 5s tasked with taking the 238th Engineer Combat Battalion (ECB) to Utah. These eight landing craft were part of the 107th Flotilla/O LCT Squadron. *LCT-2304* had been transported across the Atlantic in pieces, reconnected in England and checked over at Dartmouth. On 31 May it sailed to Torquay, where it embarked 70 combat engineers, their equipment and vehicles. Having done this, *2304* was taken back to Brixham, moored up and awaited the decision to go. On 3 June that was given and *2304* moved out to Start Point, where it waited to join a Force U convoy from the western ports. Reaching a point just south of the Isle of Wight on 4 June, the operation was postponed and the convoy turned round. The seas were high and without lights there were some difficulties as they circled, awaiting developments. On 5 June the order to continue came and *2304* eventually ran in to Utah, dodging obstacles as it went, but it was impossible to miss all of them. The LCT sustained damage and, having dropped its cargo, returned to Southampton.

Map showing the embarkation points around Tor Bay.

Brixham hard can be seen at the top right of this photograph. The 4th Infantry Division embarked for Utah Beach from here.

**RIGHT AND BELOW RIGHT**
Then and now views of Brixham
hard. The wartime view shows LSTs
attached to the mooring dolphins
running out from the hards.

# 74  HQ US XI Amphibious Force, Dartmouth, Devon

**Dartmouth has a long association with America: the Pilgrim Fathers stopped here en route to America and Britannia Royal Naval College, Dartmouth, which dominates the skyline, was the location of HQ US XI Amphibious Force.**

To provide the amphibious forces required for the cross-Channel assault, Commander-in-Chief, United States Fleet (COMINCH) revived Amphibious Forces Europe on 15 July 1943, redesignating it XI Amphibious Force, and assigning it to the command of the 12th Fleet. Rear Admiral John L Hall was given the task of building it up for Operation *Neptune*. He left the Mediterranean, arriving in Plymouth on 27 November 1943.

At that time, the 11th Amphibious Force consisted of:

- landing craft and Bases Organization for their support and maintenance
- 235 landing vessels
- miscellaneous special units (Shore Fire Control parties, elements of beach battalions and others).

In December the amphibious forces started to arrive: by 1 June 1944 there were 2,458 ships and craft in force, plus 35 temporarily associated destroyers, cruisers and battleships of the Atlantic fleet. As they arrived they were organised into an invasion force by Hall. A COMINCH directive identified that it should use the standard US Navy allocation of six vessels to a division, two divisions to a group and three groups to a flotilla.

In addition to the strictly amphibious forces (LSTs, LCIs, LCTs, etc), nearly all other ships and special parties required for an amphibious assault were turned over to XI Amphibious Force to be organised, trained and supported. Included among these were the transports, most of the destroyers, the minesweepers, PTs (patrol torpedo boats), SCs (submarine chasers) and various far shore groups.[56]

Dartmouth was an embarkation point for troops heading for Utah Beach. This photograph shows an earlier training exercise.

To commemorate XI Amphibious Force's involvement with Britannia Royal Naval College there's a marker that was dedicated on 6 June 2017:

The United States of America honors the courage, sacrifice and achievements of the US XI Amphibious Force, headquartered in this building as Allied Forces prepared for and launched the liberation of Europe from these shores. Under XI Amphibious Force supervision, thousands of soldiers, sailors and airmen prepared for the landings in France, which came ashore on 6 June 1944. Hundreds of thousands of troops and millions of tons of supplies moved steadily across the English Channel as the United States and its Allies carried the battle to the enemy, overthrowing the grip of Nazi tyranny. The Allies forged ahead with ever increasing strength and confidence, securing the blessings of freedom and liberty for generations yet unborn. This marker further commemorates the enduring bonds between the United Kingdom and the United States, forged through shared sacrifice in peace and war, serving the cause of justice for all.

Troops await embarkation, Dartmouth, June 1944 (ABOVE). Nearby Kingswear Hoodown Terminal (ABOVE RIGHT), was an embarkation point on the east side of the River Dart.

## Dartmouth

Dartmouth and the surrounding area was home to some 4,000 US Navy personnel. Coronation Park was used as base, store and somewhere to repair damaged vehicles.

Task Force U was marshalling in the Torquay–Dartmouth sector. The US troops and their equipment set sail from Dartmouth on 4 June, taking shelter in Weymouth Bay on 5 June until the storm abated, and reaching Normandy the next day.

After D-Day the importance of USNAAB (US Navy Advanced Amphibious Base) Dartmouth as a base began to wane and the facilities were handed back to the British before the end of 1944.

### Preparations for Operation *Neptune*

#### LCT hards built

| Location | Number | Berths |
| --- | --- | --- |
| Brixham | 1 | 4 |
| Torquay | 1 | 4 |
| Dartmouth | 3 | 8 |
| Plymouth | 6 | 20 |
| Falmouth | 4 | 12 |
| Helford River | 1 | 2 |

#### LCT slips built

Plymouth: Queen Anne's Battery, Waddeton, Millbay, Silley Cox Yard

Dartmouth

Salcombe

Falmouth

Concrete grids for major landing craft were constructed at Appledore, Falmouth, Fowey, Plymouth and Dartmouth in order to expedite repair work and hull examination. (As the tide receded the craft would ground, allowing inspection of their undersides before they refloated on the tide.) This avoided the need to pull the craft onto a slipway at a maintenance base. The grids were operated principally by private firms, employing their own labour and equipment. The D-Day landing craft maintenance site on the River Dart, 270m south-east of Maypool Cottage, has survived with the grid retaining all 12 piers.

Maintenance bases for minor landing craft were established at Plymouth (Calstock and Saltash), Falmouth, Dartmouth and Teignmouth. Suitable LCM slips or trolleys were also constructed. LCM slipways were constructed at Plymouth, Falmouth and Teignmouth.

At Dartmouth, minor landing craft were placed on trolleys at the hards and taken to the maintenance base, Coronation Park, nearby.

By invasion day, maintenance facilities capable of dealing with 20 per cent of the amphibious force (some 300 vessels) at one time had been prepared.

# 75  Plymouth embarkation hards, Devon

**Plymouth is one of Britain's great ports, from which no less a figure than Sir Francis Drake – mayor of the city in 1581 and 1593 – set sail against the Spanish Armada. In the Second World War it was one of the ports worst hit by the Luftwaffe, particularly in 1941, but it was able to play a significant role in 1944 when the US 29th Infantry Division embarked from the port for Omaha.**

As mentioned on page 144, the American and British marshalling and embarkation areas overlapped. Roland Ruppenthal writes in *Logistical Support of the Armies*:

> The entire coast in the Southern Base Section zone, extending from Portsmouth westward, was divided into nine marshaling [sic] and embarkation areas, four of them falling within the XVIII District and five in the XIX. Of the four in the former, one area in and around Portsmouth and Gosport was operated entirely by the British, two around Southampton were to be used by both the British and Americans and were jointly operated, and a split area around Weymouth, the Isle of Portland, and Poole was operated solely by the Americans. All five areas in XIX District were US-operated. The nine areas (lettered from A to D in XVIII District and from K to O in XIX District) had a total of ninety-five marshaling camps with a capacity of 187,000 troops and 28,000 vehicles. The number and size of the camps in each area were determined by the outloading capacity of the adjoining embarkation areas, of which there was a total of nineteen.[57]

From their 'sausage camps' in the area, around 26 May the troops headed towards the boats, passing depots where they picked up equipment. Force U's loading ports were more widely scattered than Force O, which was mainly concentrated around Weymouth, Portland and Poole – as is shown by the fact that O was in 5 convoys and U in 12. Force U's ports extended all the way from Falmouth in Cornwall to Poole in Dorset.

The craft were ready to load on 30 May, and this complicated procedure was completed by 3 June. Once the weather delay was over, the dispatch of troops got under way.

The majority of the troops who embarked from the Plymouth area were from the 29th Infantry Division – including those from Ivybridge (*see* pp 126–7). Moving from their training areas into the marshalling area, most entered 'sausage camps' in late May. These camps, so named because they were often in narrow valleys, were heavily protected by camouflage and patrolled to ensure details did not leak out. There were 'sausage camps' in Antony Park, Saltram Park and Mount Edgcumbe.

**OPPOSITE**

In January 1944, a temporary camp was opened on Vicarage Road, St Budeaux, Plymouth: some 60,000 US soldiers passed through. The nearby Saltash Passage hard ('B') was built at around the same time as the Vicarage Road Camp ('A'). 'C' shows site of today's memorial.

**RIGHT**

Mount Edgcumbe embarkation hard.

**RIGHT**

With Isambard Kingdom Brunel's Royal Albert Bridge over the Tamar in the background, landing craft fill up at Antony.

**BELOW**

Brunel's bridge is even closer in this 2018 photograph of the embarkation hard ('A' in the aerial photo). Note the memorial to the right ('C'). It reads: 'This tablet marks the departure from this place of units of the V and VII Corps of the United States Army on the 6th June 1944 for the D-Day landings in France and was unveiled by His Excellency John Hay Whitney the ambassador of the United States of America 14th May 1958.'

# 76 Falmouth embarkation hards, Cornwall

**One of the world's great deep-water harbours, Falmouth had a number of hards used to embark troops for D-Day – the most westerly of the assault troops.**

It was from Falmouth that the greatest raid – the commando attack on Saint-Nazaire – set off in 1942. In 1943 the Americans arrived, making it both a naval base and a US Army centre.

During the 1943–44 period the area was used extensively for training, and in preparation for the invasion the Admiralty built 'sausage camps' and hards. These included:

- hard PH at Polgwidden Cove, Trebah, on the Helford River– two-berth LST
- hard PF1 at Polgerran Wood, Tolverne, on the Fal River – two-berth LST
- hard PF2 at Turnaware Point, St Just in Roseland, on the Fal River – four-berth LST
- hards PF3 and 4 at Falmouth town – two-berth LCI; four-berth LCT and two-berth LCT.

These hards were manned by US Navy personnel and approach roads had to be built to access them.

'Sausage camps' A, B, G and H would embark from PF1 and 2; C and F at Falmouth town; D and E were at PH. The personnel in the 'sausage camps' was a mixture of the 29th Infantry Division (D, E, F); 5th Engineer Special Brigade (C); and other V Corps units (A, B, G, H). On D-Day, elements of the US 29th Infantry Division embarked from here. The plan had called for 36 LSTs to carry some 10,800 men and 2,160 vehicles from these hards around Falmouth.

**Right and below right**

Some 7,500 men of the 29th US
Infantry Division, including the
175th Infantry Regiment, embarked
at Polgwidden Cove for the assault
landing on Omaha. Here a unit
marches through Trebah (RIGHT)
towards the beach, where the LSTs
await (BELOW RIGHT). Today, the
mooring dolphin is no longer there,
but the chocolate block hard and
some accoutrements remain.

**Below**

Map showing the Falmouth town
and Polgwidden embarkation points.

# 77  Follow-up Force B loading port, Cardiff, Wales

**Men of the 90th Infantry Division aboard *LCI(L)-326*. The *After Action Report* identifies that most of the division was loaded onto nine MT (motor transport) ships at Cardiff and Newport between 1 and 3 June. The remainder went aboard the Excelsior at Newport and the *Explorer* and the *Bienville* at Cardiff.**

**Once the largest coal port in the world and employing more than 15,000 people, almost 75 per cent of all supplies for the US forces in Europe were shipped out through Cardiff docks following the D-Day landings in June 1944.**

The leading elements of Follow-up Force B's US 90th Infantry Division (VII Corps) saw action on D-Day itself, attached to the 4th Infantry Division. This was Group A, the foot elements of the 1/ and 3/359th Infantry Regiment and 40 vehicles, who had been at Syon Abbey marshalling area camp K7, in Devon (embarking at Dartmouth on D-5 and D-4). Group A landed on Utah Beach on D-Day, becoming part of the 4th Infantry Division's reserve.

Some residual elements of the 90th Infantry Division were in Bournemouth, in Dorset, but the bulk was loaded on nine motor transports at Cardiff and Newport bound for Utah Beach. The *After Action Report* of the 90th Infantry Division identifies the division marshalling at the following locations:

- Llangattock Camp – 358th Infantry Regiment
- Court-Y-Gollen Camp – Regimental Combat Team (RCT) 9 (Group A – elements embarking at Dartmouth) and the 90th Recon Troop
- Chepstow Camp – RCT 7, 344th Field Artillery Battalion, B/315th Medical Battalion and B/315th Engineer Battalion
- Heath Camp, Cardiff – Division Headquarters, Division Artillery Headquarters, 345th Field Artillery Battalion, Special Troops, 315th Engineer and 315th Medical Battalions (each less three companies) also at Heath Camp.[58]

They embarked from D-5 (June 1) to D-2, sailing across the Channel on D+1. During this process, the *Susan B Anthony*, carrying the division's advance detachment and RCT 9, hit a mine and sank – but not before all 2,689 men on board were saved. They were transferred onto USS *Pinto* and two destroyers. The 90th Division debarked on D+2.

Cardiff was also a TURCO HQ (Turn-Round Control; *see* p 201), ensuring a continuous resupply of men, ammunition and equipment to Normandy.

## 78  Follow-up Force B, Marshalling Area X, Swansea, Wales

**A vital construction base allocated to US engineering companies to build pontoons and barges for the invasion beaches, Swansea was also the chief embarkation port for the Marshalling Area X's follow-up Force B and an important resupply port furnishing the Allies with reinforcements, ammunition and some 158,000 tons of petrol in jerrycans.**

Marshalling Area X's tented camps included Singleton Park (X3) in Swansea, where 1,566 personnel of the 5th Engineer Special Brigade, 12th Port of Embarkation, and the 52nd Quartermaster Base Depot were camped; X4 Mynydd Lliw I and II in Grovesend and X5, in Scurlage, Gower, each had a capacity of 2,000 men. These troops were part of follow-up Force B, which landed on the American beaches in Normandy in the days after D-Day. The main unit involved was the US 2nd Infantry Division – the Indianhead Division – who began landing on Omaha Beach on 7 June and led the attack inland.

The loading of vehicle ships, coasters, LCTs and barges got under way in the second week of May, most cargo – for up to 15 days after the invasion – being pre-stowed to meet the needs of the First (US) Army. Several ports specialised in certain commodities. Llanelly, Sharpness, and Port Talbot were used exclusively for POL (petrol, oil and lubricants); Penarth and Fowey were primarily ammunition ports; heavy engineer and other out-of-gauge equipment was handled at Cardiff. Western Base Section set up a simple, centralised system of control whereby movement orders were the responsibility of the Transportation Corps, which controlled the location and movement of all units through a headquarters established at Newport and a subsection headquarters at Swansea, in the Bristol Channel area.

Embarkation of both assault forces and the follow-up force was completed on 3 June.

**Classic view of the 2nd Infantry Division – the Indianheads – making their way up the bluffs at the St Laurent draw on Omaha Beach and heading inland. They disembarked on 7 June.**

# 5 | Air operations

**LEFT**
Loading 3-inch RP-3 rockets with 60lb warheads onto Typhoon fighter-bombers. Although analysis of their results against armour suggest they were less effective than thought at the time, against other vehicles and infantry they were devastating, as was shown at Mortain and Falaise.

After all the debates about command and control of the Allies' aviation assets and their best use, there is little disputing that every aspect of the air plan was undertaken energetically, although not always effectively. Operation *Neptune* was completely dependent on airpower – and air supremacy gave the invading forces the edge they needed. It's hard to imagine that the successful prosecution of the attack, or the maintenance of the lodgement in the first few weeks after the landings, could have taken place had the Germans been able to bring suitable air forces together over Normandy.

Instead, even before the Allies were able to create landing strips in France – although they did that swiftly enough, the first being ready to use on 8 June – air cover of the invasion force and the battlefield was total and very few sightings of the Luftwaffe were made. The Air Commander-in-Chief, Allied Expeditionary Air Force (AEAF), Air Chief Marshal Trafford Leigh-Mallory, may not have wrested control of RAF Bomber Command and the US Eighth Air Force from the 'Bomber Barons', Air Chief Marshal Arthur Harris and General Carl Spaatz, but he still had under his direct command US Ninth Air Force and the British Second Tactical Air Force (2TAF), as well as Air Defence Great Britain (ADGB) fighter groups.

**RIGHT**
In spite of General Carl Spaatz's objections, when push came to shove the US Eighth Air Force switched from strategic bombing to assisting the invasion. This is the plan.

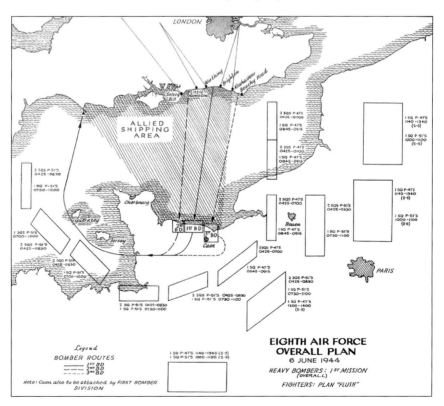

163

The heavy bomber squadrons, too, were diverted from their strategic campaign against Germany to support the invasion from mid-April until September 1944. On D-Day itself the Allies had more than 12,000 aircraft to hand, including 3,467 heavy bombers, 1,545 medium and light bombers and no fewer than 5,409 fighters. Against this, the Luftwaffe's Luftflotte 3 in northern France could assemble only 125 fighters and 198 bombers.

The Luftwaffe had been deliberately put out of business in late 1943 and the early part of 1944 as part of Operation *Pointblank*, the directive made at the Casablanca Conference of January 1943 and pushed at the Quebec Conference in August 1943 that the Allied heavy bombers should focus on the German aviation industry. This reached a crescendo between 20 and 25 February 1944, in the so-called 'Big Week' raids to lure the Luftwaffe into a huge attritional battle.

The figures show that this major effort did considerable damage to both sides: in the period Eighth Air Force lost 97 B-17 Flying Fortresses and 40 B-24 Liberators, with 20 more scrapped. Fifteenth Air Force in Italy also took part and lost 90 bombers; RAF Bomber Command lost a further 131. On the German side, more than 350 fighters were destroyed (rather fewer than the 500 claimed by US aircrew) and, more importantly, around 100 pilots died. However, the German Luftwaffe had not been completely eradicated. Indeed, amazingly, German aircraft production was the highest of the war in 1944 when 35,076 aircraft were produced as compared to 20,599 in 1943. Nevertheless, the Luftwaffe could not sustain the deaths of so many trained pilots, and the continued strategic bombing campaign – in March the USAAF targeted Berlin – did much to reduce Luftwaffe effectiveness in Normandy.

After 1 April 1944, Eisenhower took control of all the Allied air forces and was able to turn to the Transportation Plan. Based on advice from scientist Professor Solly Zuckerman, this directed the strategic bombers against the French transport infrastructure to slow German reinforcements, particularly targets such as repair facilities, marshalling yards, bridges, traffic nodes and crossroads. As an example of its effectiveness, take the progress of Kampfgruppe Heintz – some 4,000 men of the German 275th Infantry Division – ordered up from the south coast of Brittany towards the fighting on 6 June. This 120-mile journey – usually two days' travel – was impeded by air attacks on the railways and although the Kampfgruppe was ready to entrain inside 10 hours, the first elements only arrived at the Allied lines on 11 June, five whole days later. Another example is 17th Panzergrenadier Division, whose progress north was stopped in its tracks by the destruction of the Saumur tunnel, southwest of Paris, on the night of 8/9 June. No 617 Squadron (the Dambusters) sent 25 RAF Lancasters armed with Barnes Wallis's latest creation, the new 12,000lb Tallboy bomb. Both entrances were blocked and one bomb penetrated and exploded inside the tunnel. The division played no part in the fighting around the beachhead.

**ABOVE AND RIGHT**
**The build-up of American air forces in Britain before D-Day, and in Europe subsequently, required considerable work extending runways, creating airfields or simply converting grass runways into concrete to allow their use by heavier aircraft types. In December 1941 it was agreed that eight airfields, then under construction for the RAF, would transfer to USAAF usage. By May 1942 there were plans for the construction or transfer of 127 fields to the Eighth Air Force. With a shortage of labour and materials in Britain's already strained economy, this meant material help from the US. The photographs here show the 829th Engineer Construction Company at Eye, Suffolk, in September 1942.**

RAF Membury, in Berkshire, provides a good example of the work done to USAAF airfields in the UK. It was planned as an RAF training base and built in 1942. The USAAF took it on as AAF-466 in 1943 and extended the 17–35 runway (the secondary – the primary couldn't be extended because of the terrain). It had, the American Air Museum in Britain identifies, 'three concrete runways, 26 loop and 25 pan hardstandings, two T2 hangars on the airfield site and two T2 hangars in the depot area'. This August 1944 aerial view shows the airfield with C-47s and gliders in profusion.

To ensure that the Germans couldn't work out the location of the landings, up to D-Day the bombers ranged all over northern France and paid particular attention to the Pas de Calais area, destroying 75 per cent of railway rolling stock within 150 miles of the Normandy beaches, completely dislocating the railway system throughout north-west Europe, and destroying virtually every road and rail bridge accessing the battle zone.

On D-Day itself, the heavies did not cover themselves in glory. The problems on Omaha Beach were not helped by the inaccuracy of the Eighth Air Force B-17s who – understandably, perhaps – were afraid of hitting their own troops and so dropped their bombs too far from the beach and had little effect on the battle. A few days later, Bomber Command's raid on Le Havre by Lancasters and Mosquitos saw more than 30 German vessels, including three small destroyers and ten E-boats, sunk. The cost to Le Havre, however, was considerable. By the end of the war it was one of the most damaged cities in France, with 82 per cent of its buildings destroyed and around 5,000 civilian casualties. A total of 1,838 French municipalities – including 20 out of France's 27 largest cities – were officially declared *sinistrées* (war-damaged) and many of them were as a result of Allied bombing.

The assault beaches were heavily protected by the continuous cover of six squadrons of RAF Spitfires flying at low level and three squadrons of Ninth Air Force P-47 Thunderbolts at high level, while four squadrons of P-38 Lightnings kept the shipping lanes and assembly areas clear of the Luftwaffe. By night, Mosquito nightfighter squadrons were on hand.

The units covered in this chapter provide a selection of types of aircraft, nationalities and missions to exemplify the extraordinary contribution of the Allied air forces to the success of the landings.

# 79  USAAF Air Station 357, RAF Duxford, Cambridgeshire

**The 78th Fighter Group – part of US Eighth Air Force's VIII Fighter Command's 66th Fighter Wing – flew its P-47 Thunderbolts in escort and ground-attack missions from Duxford throughout D-Day.**

Located some 10 miles from Cambridge, RAF Duxford is still a working airfield. In 1977 it also became Britain's largest aviation museum, housing the Imperial War Museum's aircraft collection. In 1997 the American Air Museum was also opened here and dedicated to the 30,000 American airmen who died flying from UK bases during the Second World War.

The airfield has a long pedigree stretching back to the end of the First World War, when it opened as No 35 Training Depot Station and was used by the Royal Flying Corps and US Aero Squadrons to train pilots.

In 1938 Duxford became the first home airfield of the legendary Supermarine Spitfire. The following year it supported the evacuation of Allied forces from Dunkirk, and then played a pivotal role in the 1940 Battle of Britain.

The base was officially handed over to the USAAF on 15 June 1943, becoming the home of the 78th Fighter Group (FG) until October 1945. The 78th FG consisted of the 82nd, 83rd and 84th Fighter Squadrons that flew Republic P-47 Thunderbolts, armed with eight .50-calibre machine guns; in its fighter-bomber ground-attack role it could carry 5-inch rockets or a bomb load of 2,500lb. Aircraft belonging to the group were identified by their distinctive black-and-white chequerboard-pattern nosecones. Its primary roles were to escort US Eighth Air Force bombers on daylight

Line-up of P-47D Thunderbolts at Duxford. The 'MX' markings identify the 82nd Fighter Squadron of 78th Fighter Group – the other squadrons were the 83rd (HL) and 84th (WZ). Note the 108-gallon underwing paper tank.

raids into occupied Europe and Germany, to destroy enemy fighters and to attack
ground targets.

On D-Day the 78th undertook just such a mixture of missions. First, every
available Thunderbolt provided air cover to the Allied invasion fleet as it crossed the
Channel. The group then switched to escorting bombers to targets in the invasion
area, then changed roles again to launch ground attacks on railways and other
infrastructure ahead of the advancing Allied forces.

# 80  USAAF Air Station 156, RAF Debden, Essex

**AAF-156 was the home of the famous Eagle squadrons and the 4th Fighter Group – the highest scoring in the USAAF, with more than 1,000 enemy aircraft kills on the ground and in the skies over Europe.**

Located three miles southeast of Saffron Walden, in 1940 RAF Debden was a sector station for No 11 Group, RAF, and was attacked several times during the Battle of Britain. In 1942 it became the base of Nos 71, 121 and 133 RAF Eagle Squadrons, made up mainly of American pilots who had joined the RAF to fight the Germans before the US entered the war. They gained a reputation for their aggression and were absorbed into the USAAF's 4th Fighter Group when it was activated, the Eagles becoming the 334th (No 71 Squadron), 335th (No 121) and 336th (No 133) Fighter Squadrons of the US Eighth Air Force on 29 September 1942. For a while – until March 1942 – Spitfires flew with US markings but they were then re-equipped with P-47 Thunderbolts and later, in April 1944 before the D-Day landings, P-51 Mustangs.

The 4th Fighter Group spent much of its time escorting bombers – it was the first US fighter group to both penetrate German airspace and escort bombers to Russia – and it played an important role in the 'Big Week' attacks on the Luftwaffe on 20–25 February 1944. Its aggression in seeking out enemy fighters and air bases between 5 March and 24 April 1944 earned it a Distinguished Unit Citation.

One of the consequences of such aggression was high casualties – 125 killed and 105 missing during the war. On D-Day the group took off at 03:20 on the first of the five fierce, interdictory air-cover and ground-attack missions that they flew in support of the Normandy landings. On the day's last mission, a fighter patrol of the 335th FS was attacked by a German force four times its size in the vicinity of Rouen/Dreaux and all four pilots were killed, bringing the casualty rate to a total of 10 that day. The 4th Fighter Group went on to fly throughout the Normandy campaign and by the end of the war claimed the distinction of destroying more enemy aircraft in the air and on the ground than any other fighter group of the US Eighth Air Force.

**LEFT**
**Memorial in Grosvenor Square, London, to the Eagle Squadrons who fought with the RAF before America entered the war.**

**RIGHT**
**Two 108-gallon drop tanks could extend considerably the range of the P-51 Mustang, enabling it to escort bombers deep into the Reich, or for prolonged loiter time over Normandy.**

# 81  USAAF Air Station 162, RAF Chipping Ongar, Essex

## 387th BG's bombing missions

| Date | Targets |
| --- | --- |
| January | |
| 9 | 8 V-1 sites; others: coastal defences – La Glacerie (Cherbourg) |
| February | |
| 24 | 15 V-1 sites; 8 airfields; others: marshalling yards – Amiens |
| March | |
| 18 | 10 V-1 sites; 3 airfields; others: marshalling yards – Amiens (twice), Criel-sur-Mer, and Haine-Saint-Pierre; E-boat pens – Ijmuiden |
| April | |
| 22 | 9 V-1 sites; 3 airfields; others: coastal defences – Le Havre, Dunkerque, Dieppe and Benerville-sur-Mer; marshalling yards – Namur (twice), Charleroi-St Martin, Malines (Mechelen), Cambrai and Somain |
| May | |
| 24 | 1 airfield; others: marshalling yards – Monceau-sur-Sambre, Louvain, Criel-sur-Mer, Douai and Somain; coastal defences – Hardelot, La Pernelle, Benerville-sur-Mer (twice), Fort Mardyck, Ouisterham, Fécamp, La Pernelle-Barfleur and Étaples Sainte-Cécile; railroad bridges/sheds – Liege-Val Benoit, La Manoir, Orival, Maisons-Lafitte and Conflans; bridges – Oissel, Liege-Renory, Bennecourt and Antwerp |
| June | |
| 29 | 4 V-1 sites; 1 airfield; others: batteries/defended areas – Épreville, Calais-Marck, Bretteville, Valognes, Villers Bocage (twice) and Laye-Le Belles Martin; coastal defences – Étaples-Camiers and La Madelaine; railroad bridges/junctions/sidings/marshalling yards – Rennes (twice), Villedieu and Pontaubault (twice); troop concentrations – Saint-Lô; road junction – Vire, Falaise and Ambrières-les-Vallées; fuel dump – Domfront, Forêt de Conches (twice), Forêt de Senonches, Forêt d'Écouves; Cherbourg tank trap |

**AAF-162 was home to bombers of the Ninth Air Force's 387th Bombardment Group which attacked German coastal defences for Utah Beach on D-Day.**

Sited two miles outside the town of Chipping Ongar and some 20 miles north-east of London, RAF Chipping Ongar had three asphalt runways and was one of the first of a small number of UK airfields built by the Americans for use during the war, then handed over to the RAF at its end. The US 831st Engineer Battalion began construction in late August 1942 and was still finishing off the base when it opened in August 1943.

Its first occupants were the B-26 Marauder medium bombers of the Eighth Air Force's 387th Bombardment Group, consisting of the 556th (FW), 557th (KS), 558th (KX) and 559th (TQ) Squadrons, which flew its first bombing mission on 15 August. The 387th was transferred to the newly formed Ninth Air Force in October 1943. Prior to D-Day, the 387th's combat role had been search and destroy missions against V-1 flying bomb sites in northern France. It then switched to attacking coastal batteries, airfields and bridges – both inside the invasion area and outside, so as to keep the Germans' focus away from Normandy.

On D-Day itself the squadrons of the 387th first supported the landings with assaults on coastal targets at Utah Beach, then moved inland, attacking railways, bridges, transport links, fuel dumps and enemy strongpoints, giving support to the ground troops.

The 387th left Chipping Ongar on 21 July 1944, moving closer to the battlefield, and the airfield was used only intermittently for the rest of the war. It closed officially in 1959, reverting mainly to agricultural use. Today it has only a small private landing strip.

**387th BG B-26 Marauders at Chipping Ongar.**

# 82 USAAF Air Station 121, RAF Bassingbourn, Cambridgeshire

**The airfield at Bassingbourn may have been small, but it packed a big punch. Here, a B-17 Flying Fortress taxies past a line-up of light aircraft. Bassingbourn was the location for filming of *Memphis Belle: A Story of a Flying Fortress*, released in 1944.**

**The home base of the Eighth Air Force's 91st Bombardment Group – the 'Ragged Irregulars' – one of three groups in the 1st Bombardment Wing, AAF-121 was one of the earliest USAAF airfields in Britain. For D-Day it switched from precision bombing of enemy infrastructure to assault of coastal strongpoints and troop concentrations.**

Located just over three miles from Royston and 10 miles from Cambridge, Bassingbourn was built in 1937–39 for RAF Bomber Command. Its three grass runways were concreted and asphalted in the winter of 1941–42 and in August 1942 they were extended to 6,000ft, 1,300ft and 1,000ft, before the airfield was handed over to the US Eighth Air Force.

The 91st BG – with four squadrons, 322nd (LG), 323rd (OR), 324th (DF) and 401st (LL) – was one of a pioneer group, flying Boeing B-17 Flying Fortresses and tasked with the development of doctrine, tactics and operational experience for the mass bomber formations, but left struggling initially without adequate fighter support. By 1944 this strategic bombing system had reached fruition. Now with fighter support, but still against tough anti-aircraft defences, overwhelming force was brought to bear on all German infrastructure. From 1943 the group engaged chiefly in attacks on aircraft factories, aerodromes and oil facilities deep in the German heartlands. As could be expected, the length of the 91st's service is reflected in its losses: 197 aircraft missing. However, it also claimed the most enemy aircraft destroyed: 420.

In June 1944, as part of the plan for *Overlord*, the 91st BG was assigned tactical targets. On 2–5 June its targets were gun emplacements and troop concentrations around Cherbourg. On D-Day itself, 36 aircraft of the 91st BG bombed gun positions at La Rivière. The USAF Historical Division summed it up:

> Fortresses of the 91st Bombardment Group bombed the submarine construction and repair centers at Kiel, Vegasack, Wilhelmshaven, Brest, Emden, Lorient, St Nazaire, and La Pallice. They attacked railroad communications centers at Hamm, Bremen, Abbeville, and Rouen. At Antwerp the 91st hit the Erla Auto-Works and the former factories of Ford and General Motors; near Paris it bombed the great Renault tank and truck plant, and at Lille it attacked the steel and locomotive plants. At Bremen the Group smashed a Focke-Wulf factory, at Meaulte an aircraft repair base, and at Romilly-sur-Seine an airpark and airdrome. Many of these targets were raided more than once – St Nazaire was hit by the 91st Group nine times. With the invasion of the continent successful, the 91st not only continued striking strategic targets but used its outstanding precision bombing skill on tactical targets in support of ground troops.[59]

The 91st left Bassingbourn in June 1945. Since 1974 the Tower Museum, in the original pre-war air traffic control tower, has told the story of the station from both RAF and USAAF perspectives.

# 83  USAAF Air Station 485 Andrews Field, RAF Great Saling, Essex

**The first of 14 airfields to be built by the US Army in the UK during the Second World War, AAF-485 was renamed Andrews Field in honour of General Frank M Andrews, USAAF, who was killed in an air accident in Iceland in May 1943.**

**AAF-485 was the first of 14 'Type A' airfields built in Britain. Intended for heavy bombers or transports, it's said the 'A' in 'Type A' came from the crossed runways (*see* example at Hurn on p 175). The nine original airfields for the USAAF (Alconbury, Bassingbourn, Chelveston, Grafton Underwood, Kimbolton, Molesworth, Podington, Polebrook and Thurleigh) had to have their runways extended in late 1942/ early 1943 to achieve this standard. There's a plaque at Great Saling remembering the 819th Engineer (Aviation) Battalion and the 'first airdrome constructed by American troop.' It goes on to mention British friends and 'our comrades who later made the ultimate sacrifice in Western Europe.'**

Constructed by the 819th Engineer (Aviation) Battalion, RAF Great Saling had three runways – a main one of 2,000 yards and two secondaries of 1,400 yards. Opened in January 1943 and assigned to the VIII Bomber Command of the US Eighth Air Force, its first unit, the 96th Bombardment Group (Heavy), flying Boeing B-17 Flying Fortresses, arrived in May of that year. The 96th did not stay more than a month before it was replaced by the 322nd Bombardment Group (Medium), with 449th, 450th, 451st and 452nd Squadrons flying tactical combat missions in their Martin B-26B/C Marauders. The 322nd had been the first B-26 unit to enter combat and suffered heavy losses when used at low level: on its second sortie, a strike mission flown from RAF Bury St Edmund over the Netherlands on 17 May 1943, it lost all ten of the aircraft that reached the target, six to flak, two to collision and two to enemy fighters on the way back. The Eighth Air Force pulled the B-26s out of the line to retrain as medium altitude bombers, the 322nd returning to combat from Andrews Field in June 1943.

Also posted to Andrews Field was 1st Pathfinder Squadron (Provisional), attached to the 322nd and also flying B-26s, but equipped with the Oboe blind-bombing system developed for night strikes.

All Marauder squadrons were transferred from Eighth to Ninth Air Force in October 1943, tasked primarily with attacking enemy airfields but also with secondary targets of power stations, shipyards, construction works and marshalling yards. On D-Day the 322nd attacked coastal defences and gun batteries in the vicinity of the landing beaches, followed by ground troop support attacks on fuel and ammunition dumps, bridges and road junctions. It received a Distinguished Unit Citation for the period 14 May 1943 to 24 July 1944.

The 322nd transferred to France in September 1944 and Andrews Field was then handed over to the RAF's Fighter Command, and thereafter used to provide fighter cover for Bomber Command's daylight operations.

# 84 USAAF Air Station 454, RAF Warmwell, Dorset

**Dorset's only fighter base protected Portland Harbour and Weymouth during the Battle of Britain. Taken over by the USAAF, it was home to the Ninth Air Force's 474th Fighter Group during the D-Day landings.**

Five miles from Dorchester and just over the same from the coast near Weymouth and Portland, RAF Warmwell has now vanished under extensive gravel extraction and house building. It was constructed in 1936 as an RAF armament training facility and as a base for aircraft using the Chesil Beach Bombing Range. In 1940 control passed to 10 Group Fighter Command and Warmwell became a satellite of RAF Middle Wallop, in Hampshire. Fighters from Warmwell contributed to the winning of the Battle of Britain but they also provided vital protection to the nearby Portland Naval Base and other important south coast areas. The airfield was, consequently, bombed in various raids 1940–42, with ensuing casualties. A large number of Spitfire and Hurricane squadrons rotated through Warmwell, but also other squadrons of Whirlwinds, Walruses and Typhoons.

The Americans took possession of the airfield in 1943 and in March 1944 the 474th Fighter Group arrived, flying Lockheed P-38 Lightnings. The 474th was part of Ninth Air Force's 70th Fighter Wing in IX Tactical Air Command and consisted of 428th, 429th and 430th Fighter Squadrons.

On D-Day, Warmwell's proximity to the route of the armada and Normandy itself made it an important asset. Aircraft from the airfield first provided air cover for the invasion fleet, then switched to attacking enemy transportation targets and military convoys, bridges, armour formations and airfields. The 474th FG remained at Warmwell until August 1944, when it handed the airfield back to the RAF and moved to more forward airfields in France.

P-38 Lightnings of the 430th Fighter Squadron (K6) at Warmwell – the other two squadrons based here were the 428th (F5) and 429th (7Y). A total of 80 aircraft of the 474th FG were based on the grass strip of Warmwell. Nearly 30 of its aircraft were lost – mainly to ground fire – during its time in Dorset. Note the control tower in the background.

RIGHT

**RIGHT**

The memorial for RAF Warmwell (originally called Woodsford and known as Moreton to the USAAF because of the nearby railway station). Today the memorial is surrounded by a housing estate.

**BELOW**

Aerial view of the area, taken in 1947. Note the two Bellman hangars at 'A'.

**BELOW RIGHT**

The site of the hangars today – a suspected arson attack has led to the demolition of one of them.

# 85 RAF Manston, Kent

**This famous front-line fighter station saw constant action throughout the war, and D-Day was no exception, with Typhoons, Mosquitos and Beaufighters in action.**

Located on the Isle of Thanet in Kent, the Admiralty Aerodrome at Manston was first used by the Royal Naval Air Service, although by 1917 it was being used by the Royal Flying Corps (precursor to the RAF) as an anti-Zeppelin fighter base. The newly constituted RAF used it as a technical training facility; then in the 1920s and 1930s it was used for pilot refresher and navigation training. During the early years of the Second World War the base provided fighter cover for the Allied forces in France and then supported the evacuation from Dunkirk. In the ensuing Battle of Britain, Manston played a major role, although its proximity to France inevitably made it a target and it was attacked many times.

In June 1943 the grass airfield underwent extensive modification, with a longer hard runway, perimeter loop and crash bays constructed. Manston ended up with a 9,000ft-long, 750ft-wide runway that was used as an emergency strip for damaged bombers returning from missions.

Typhoons and rocket-armed Hurricanes conducted increasing numbers of cross-Channel sorties, and as the Allied invasion grew closer, Manston saw the arrival of the Mosquito intruders of No 605 Squadron and anti-shipping Beaufighters of No 143 Squadron to join the Hawker Typhoon 1Bs of No 137 Squadron. The Fleet Air Arm, as part of the Coastal Command, also deployed aircraft from the airfield.

On D-Day, the airfield saw considerable action:

- No 137 Squadron Typhoons provided support to ground forces, particularly on the eastern flank.
- 18 Mosquitos of No 605 Squadron attacked anti-aircraft and searchlight positions in preparation for the 6th Airborne landings.
- No 143 Squadron Beaufighters were on patrol, keeping the invading armada free from interference by German E-boats and submarines.
- Six Beaufighters from each of the 'Anzac Strike Wing' squadrons – No 455, Royal Australian Air Force, and No 489, Royal New Zealand Air Force – landed at Manston and stood by.
- The Spitfire VIs of 1401 (Met) Flight provided weather reconnaissance across the invasion area.

**Memorial dedicated to 'The Few' at RAF Manston.**

**Typhoon Mk 1B of No 609 Squadron, RAF, seen at Manston. It has 18 locomotives beneath the cockpit identifying its tally – 609 Squadron was well known for its prowess, initially with Spitfires and, after spring 1942, with the Typhoon, reaching 200 kills in early 1943 while at RAF Duxford.**

# 86  RAF Hurn, Dorset

**Situated across the Channel from the invasion beaches, Hurn played an important role during D-Day as a base for two 83 Group wings – Nos 124 and 143 – of the Second Tactical Air Force.**

**BELOW**

The U2 and 9F markings on these B-26 Marauders indicate they belong to the 598th and 597th Bombardment Squadrons respectively, of the 397th Bombardment Group.

**BOTTOM**

Post-war aerial view of Hurn showing its three runways: 26–08 (2,000yd); 17–35 (1,600yd); 13–31 (1,130yd).

Located on the edge of the village of Hurn, near Christchurch and Bournemouth, RAF Hurn is today's Bournemouth Airport. It was constructed in 1941 and initially used for aircrew training, then the research and development of airborne radar and other techniques such as glider towing.

At first it was a satellite station of RAF Ibsley, in Hampshire, but following the extension of its runways – it ended up with three runways, 30 pan and 46 loop hardstandings and 17 hangars – it became a major airbase for fighters and bombers, including Spitfires, Typhoons and Wellingtons of the RAF and Royal Canadian Air Force (RCAF). In August 1944 RAF Hurn was handed over to the USAAF and became Station AAF-492, home to the Northrop P-61 Black Widows of the 422nd Night Fighter Squadron and the 397th Bombardment Group's Martin B-26 Marauders.

The airfield was very active over the D-Day period, with six squadrons of RAF and RCAF Typhoons involved in ground-attack roles ahead of the beachheads,

followed later by the USAAF flying B-26 Marauder bombers. The fighters were soon able to use the temporary Normandy airstrips built behind the advancing Allied forces, returning to Hurn only for servicing, and by August 1944 all the aircraft had moved completely to Normandy.

The *Operations Record Book* of No 438 Squadron, RCAF, records the first flight of 6 June:

> ... 11 aircraft off, led by the Wing Commander, Flying. Squadron was assigned the task of dive bombing two concrete block houses overlooking the beach on which the 50th British Division was to land tanks. This operation had to be performed just as the tank landing craft lowered their ramps. Cloud conditions were 5/10 from 2,000ft up with the result that the dive bombing had to be done from a much lower level ... direct hits were scored on both targets with 1,000lb bombs and it is believed they were totally destroyed. All pilots came back safely with their aircraft though one had a piece of flak bounce off the prop and bash in the leading edge of the wing.[60]

There were two other strafing operations and all told, 'Total flying for the day: operational – 45:40 hrs'.

# 87  RAF Tangmere, West Sussex

**RAF Tangmere was a major front-line fighter station famous for its heroic role in the Battle of Britain and its renowned aces Douglas Bader and Johnnie Johnson. On D-Day, Tangmere housed Nos 126 and 127 Wings, Royal Canadian Air Force.**

Three miles east of Chichester in West Sussex lies the village of Tangmere, home to the RAF fighter base that took its name, and in fact most of the village as well, for beyond the duration of the Second World War – it was eventually handed back in 1966.

It was first built in 1917, briefly handed over to the American Air Force in 1918 but then promptly mothballed as the First World War ended. It reopened in 1925 as a Fleet Air Arm station and in 1939 was substantially enlarged (and almost all the villagers expelled) to become a major coastal airbase of Sector A in No 11 Group RAF Fighter Command, covering the area from Brighton to Bournemouth. It was soon found to be too small to accommodate all the fighter squadrons and two new satellite airfields were constructed at Westhampnett (now Goodwood; *see* pp 178–9) and Merston, both also in West Sussex.

Tangmere was also vulnerable – on 16 August 1940 substantial damage was caused and 13 killed when the station was attacked by Stuka dive-bombers. As a result, the Operations Room was moved to Chichester, then in February 1944, to Bishop Otter College, from where it controlled 56 squadrons on D-Day.

Just prior to D-Day, two Canadian Spitfire IX wings were brought to Tangmere, from where they carried out 'Ranger' operations over northern France, attacking any military targets. On D-Day itself the Canadians provided air cover and standing patrols over the beachheads. By mid-June they had moved to new airfields in Normandy. Other Tangmere-based squadrons provided air protection to the invasion fleet, then also attacked ground targets, including V-1 and V-2 installations. By the summer of 1944, four temporary airfields, advanced landing grounds, had been built close to Chichester at Funtington, Apuldram, Selsey and Bognor to support the Allied invasion.

Throughout the war, the station was also used as a secret base for the Special Operations Executive, flown in and out of occupied France by the black-painted Westland Lysanders of No 161 (Special Duties) Squadron – commanded by Squadron Leader Hugh Verity, whose account of the operations was suitably entitled *We Landed by Moonlight*.

**Aerial view of RAF Tangmere, photographed on 10 April 1944. Today there are still a few reminders of the airfield, in particular the excellent museum that has a number of exhibits, including a Westland Lysander Mk III, and two accurate replicas – one of the Spitfire prototype K5054 and one of Hurricane Mk I L1679.**

# 88 RAF Coolham, West Sussex

**Created solely for D-Day, RAF Coolham's grass strip was used by the Second Tactical Air Force's 133 Wing in their Spitfires and Merlin-engined Mustang Mk IIIs to reach the Normandy beachheads.**

Coolham ALG (Advanced Landing Ground) was in use for only about 18 months, and had almost no permanent buildings: the pilots and aircrew lived under canvas. Construction by the Airfield Construction Service began in August 1943 and was complete by the beginning of March 1944. RAF Coolham was used by the RAF's Second Tactical Air Force 133 Wing (who arrived in April 1944 and left on 22 June) and 135 Wing (30 June–5 July): on D-Day 135 Wing flew out of nearby Selsey ALG.

The squadrons were made up of pilots from British Commonwealth countries and exiles from German-occupied Europe. 135 Wing, flying Spitfires and Mustangs, contained the following squadrons: Nos 129 (from Mysore, India; although on D-Day No 129 Squadron flew with 133 Wing), 222 (Natal), 349 (Belgium) and 485 (New Zealand). 133 Wing was Polish, consisting of Nos 306 (City of Torun) and 315 (City of Deblin) Squadrons, formed in 1940–41 after the defeat of Poland. Both were initially equipped with Hawker Hurricanes, converted to Spitfires, then American Mustang III fighters in March 1944. (The Mustang was developed for the RAF, its first user, and built to British requirements.)

On D-Day, 133 Wing – Nos 129, 306 and 315 Squadrons – flew low-level reconnaissance and braved sustained flak anti-aircraft fire, while 135 Wing carried out intensive seek and destroy operations and 'Ramrods' (day bomber raids escorted by fighters).

By 5 July all aircraft had transferred elsewhere and no other squadrons operated from Coolham after that date, although equipment removal did not start until the autumn of 1945. However, that isn't the end of the story. As well as a memorial in Coolham village, there's a tribute to the men of 133 Wing – an avenue remembering their dead.

The avenue remembering the fallen of Nos 133 and 135 Wings, to the east of Coolham, has 15 crosses, including this one for Henryk Sworniowski, who shot down an FW190 on 7 June 1944 but was hit by flak on 10 June south of Caen. He was shot after crash-landing.

The Coolham ALG War Memorial outside The Selsey Arms pub, itself full of memorabilia and photographs of the airfield, aircraft and crew. The memorial 'commemorates and honours the airmen of many nations who fought valiantly in defence of Britain while serving at Coolham ALG during Operation *Overlord* in 1944 and those who made the ultimate sacrifice and died far from their homeland will be remembered for evermore.'

# 89 RAF Westhampnett, West Sussex

**Constructed as an emergency strip in 1938 before upgrading to become a satellite airfield for RAF Tangmere, Westhampnett lives on as Goodwood Airfield.**

Westhampnett was a sizeable airfield which had four grass runways – 1,500, 1,100, 1,000 and 900 yards long – which could be adversely affected by wet weather, making it unsuitable for heavier aircraft such as the Mosquito. Personnel were housed in tents and the aircraft serviced in blister hangars, portable aircraft hangars of corrugated steel-sheet cladding. In 1941, famed RAF ace Douglas Bader left on his final flight from this airfield, before being shot down and captured. The airfield was allocated to the USAAF Eighth Air Force in 1942 and was transferred to the Ninth but wasn't used by USAAF squadrons after the 31st Fighter Group moved to Africa in October 1942.

There was only one squadron present on D-day, No 184 of No 129 Wing, equipped with rocket-firing Typhoon 1Bs, having swapped their Hurricane fighter-bombers in October 1943, and being tasked with attacks on enemy communications. On D-Day itself No 184 Squadron carried out sorties over the assault beaches, attacking ground targets and suffering casualties from heavy flak. On 7 June the squadron lost three pilots attacking flak 88mm guns near Caen.

During August and September Westhampnett became home to three Spitfire IX squadrons – Nos 118, 124 and 303 – flying coastal reconnaissance, conducting fighter sweeps over northern France and providing escort to No 2 Bomber Group and fighter escort to the Typhoons of No 83 Group.

**Pilots of No 245 (Northern Rhodesia) Squadron, RAF, pass their Hawker Typhoon Mk IBs at Westhampnett after a *Noball* operation against V-1 flying bomb sites. After converting to Typhoons in March 1943, the squadron became part of the Second Tactical Air Force from its formation in June 1943.**

**RIGHT**

On 3 June all Allied aircraft had so-called 'Invasion Stripes' applied to wings and fuselage in the hope that these would reduce incidents of friendly fire. During Operation *Husky*, 23 Dakotas had been shot down by friendly fire and a further 37 were damaged. Here, two Canadian aircraftsmen repaint D-Day markings on Spitfire Mk IXb DB-R (DB being the No 411 Squadron code), at RAF Tangmere – Westhampnett was its satellite.

**BELOW**

Now known as Goodwood Airfield, Westhampnett was a satellite for RAF Tangmere (*see* p 176). It had three grass airstrips, 19 pan hardstandings, 32 small pens and a T1 and eight blister hangars.

# 90  RAF Shoreham, West Sussex

**With a beautiful Art Deco terminal, Shoreham has a long history, well told in its on-site museum.**

**Used by Air-Sea Rescue and as a Battle of Britain fighter base, on D-Day RAF Shoreham's Spitfires provided air cover for the Normandy landing beaches and escorted gliders across the Channel.**

A mile from Shoreham alongside the A27 sits Brighton City Airport, once RAF Shoreham. The airport has a long history: first used by pioneering flight enthusiasts, it opened as a civil airport in June 1911 and saw military use in both world wars, before resuming its civil role. The Royal Flying Corps arrived in 1914 and left as the Royal Air Force in 1920. A forward operating base for Fighter Command's 11 Group Fighter Interception Unit and later the Hurricanes of 422 Flight, in 1941 the base was extended and No 277 Air-Sea Rescue Squadron, equipped with Spitfires, Walrus amphibians, Defiants and Lysanders, continued to operate from there, rescuing more than 600 airmen by the war's end.

**Shoreham gained a Combined Operations Landing Craft Base – HMS *Lizard* – in 1942 (there was a sister base in Newhaven, HMS *Newt*). By D-Day, 50,000 marines and sailors had been trained there.**

Elements of S Force – British 3rd
Infantry Division – left Shoreham
on their way to Sword Beach. In
2007, Holmbush roundabout in
Shoreham acquired a wartime
Higgins boat.

In 1943 another runway was added and Shoreham came under the control of
RAF Tangmere (*see* p 176). As a frontline base it inevitably suffered several air raids.
In April 1944 two Spitfire V squadrons of the Second Tactical Air Force (2TAF) were
posted to the base – Nos 277 and the Free French 345 – and Shoreham entered its
busiest period of the war. On D-Day, under the control of 11 Group, Nos 277 and
345 Squadrons flew sorties over the landing beaches and escorted glider-towing tugs
across the Channel. Over the next few days the two squadrons used their Spitfires to
provide fighter cover for the Utah and Omaha beachheads, supporting the Americans.

Shoreham remained under 2TAF operational control until October 1944, when
it was reduced to a care and maintenance status, with very occasional use. It was
handed back to civilian use in 1946.

## 91  HMS *Daedalus*, Lee-on-Solent, Hampshire

**On 24 May 1939 the Fleet Air Arm (FAA) was established. HMS *Daedalus* was one of four FAA stations commissioned. It played a major role during D-Day and deployed more units for Operation *Overlord* than any other UK airfield.**

Sited on the coast near Lee-on-Solent in Hampshire, approximately four miles west of Portsmouth, the airfield was first established as a Royal Naval Air Service seaplane base in 1917 during the First World War. When the Royal Navy's Fleet Air Arm was established in 1939 – until then it had come under the RAF – four shore establishments were created at Worthy Down, Hampshire (HMS *Kestrel*), Ford, West Sussex (HMS *Peregrine*), Donibristle, Fife (HMS *Merlin*) and HMS *Daedalus*. *Daedalus* became the main training establishment and administrative centre of the Fleet Air Arm, who used it for the formation and development of newly commissioned operational squadrons.

Immediately, the station was given concrete runways, which ended up by 1942 being 3,000ft, 4,290ft and 3,300ft long. After being bombed by 20 Ju87 Stukas in 1940, new hangars and the control tower were completed, and by 1943 no fewer than 10 front-line squadrons had been formed at *Daedalus*, with the base having the capacity to operate five front-line and three second-line squadrons at any one time.

By February 1944 it had assembled Nos 808, 885, 886 and 897 Squadrons, FAA – 3rd Naval Fighter Wing – with Supermarine Seafire L III and Seafire Vb aircraft replacing the Sea Hurricane. Also transferred were Nos 26 and 63 Squadrons of the RAF and together these squadrons formed 34th Reconnaissance Wing of the Second Tactical Air Force, providing mainly target-spotting for RN gunners.

HMS *Daedalus* was the busiest airfield on the south coast during D-Day, as the FAA and RAF were joined by Canadian Typhoons and Mustangs and the US Navy Squadron VCS-7, with its Spitfire Vbs. The latter was a unique squadron created primarily to spot for the US Navy bombardment vessels supporting the invasion – Task Force West under Rear Admiral Alan G Kirk. The squadron was composed of US

Pilots of Navy Squadron VCS-7 with a Spitfire. The only US Navy squadron to use Spitfires (Mk Vbs), VCS-7 gave up their floatplanes (Kingfishers and Seagulls) for faster aircraft. Operational only during 1–16 June, they flew around 200 sorties, lost eight aircraft – mainly to flak, with one pilot killed – and won 9 Distinguished Flying Crosses and 11 Air Medals. Here, US Navy Lieutenant Robert F Doyle shakes the hand of his wingman, Ensign John F Mudge, after a spotting mission over the beaches.

A Royal Navy Fairey Barracuda II carrying an 18-inch torpedo. One of the strange omissions on D-Day was Allied aircraft carriers – particularly as so many Allied aircraft were at the edge of their combat radius. In fact, as Tim Benbow argues, there were good reasons why not. First, they would have had to steam west to launch and east to retrieve aircraft – straight across the north–south shipping lanes. Second, most of the naval assets used for Operation *Neptune* were British and the Royal Navy didn't have sufficient carriers. And finally, the carriers *were* involved: three escort carriers conducted ASW (antisubmarine) operations in the South-West Approaches.[61]

Navy pilots from battleships and cruisers who usually flew scouting or observation sorties in floatplanes. They trained at RAF Middle Wallop, Hampshire, and then moved to HMS *Daedalus* for D-Day. Three other RAF air-spotting squadrons, Nos 2, 268 and 414, which flew the Mustang, also flew from the airfield.

Operations began at 04:41 on 6 June, when the first aircraft to take part in Operation *Overlord* took off. They worked mainly in pairs, with one aircraft target-spotting naval gunnery targets while the other provided protection against air attack. The Mustangs were withdrawn at 12:00 on D-Day for tactical reconnaissance, leaving 95 Spitfires and Seafires for air spotting. The aircraft were pooled and used as necessary. In all, the number of units deployed from HMS *Daedalus* on D-Day was 435 – the most from any UK airfield on the day. Between 1939 and 1945 some 81 squadrons operated 21 aircraft types from there.

Aerial photograph of Lee-on-Solent, taken in 2018.

# 92  Navy Station 804, US Naval Air Facility, Dunkeswell, Devon

**Sitting on a ridge of the Blackdown Hills, Navy Station 804 was the base from which the US Navy's Fleet Air Wing 7 flew aerial antisubmarine (ASW) operations, keeping the western end of the English Channel clear of U-boats and protecting the invasion armada.**

Lieutenant Frank Perdue and the crew of *Biscay Belle*, a Liberator of the 19th AS Squadron of the 479th AS Group, Eighth Air Force. Originally based in St Eval, the group ceased operations on 31 December 1943.

Construction of an RAF Fighter Command airfield at Dunkeswell began in 1941. During May 1942 it was transferred to 19 Group Coastal Command and opened as RAF Station Dunkeswell on 26 June 1943. On 6 August 1943 the Americans arrived: USAAF Antisubmarine Command's 479th Antisubmarine Group, made up of four antisubmarine squadrons (4th, 6th, 19th and 22nd). The 479th had been activated at St Eval, Cornwall (*see* pp 186–7), and worked up under RAF Coastal Command. Its mission was antisubmarine operations in the Bay of Biscay.

The first operational missions were flown from Dunkeswell on 7 August 1943. The dangerous nature of the missions was shown the very next day when Captain R L Thomas and his crew failed to return from an antisubmarine patrol. This was the first of four aircraft the 479th lost while at Dunkeswell.

On 21 August 1943 the 6th and 22nd Squadrons arrived but the planned reorganisation of the ASW operations – their transfer to the US Navy – saw the 6th Squadron leave after a month and Navy Squadron VB-103 Patrol Bomber Squadron take its place on 24 September 1943. The 19th and 22nd Squadrons returned to the USAAF in September (on 24 and 28 September respectively); the 4th Squadron on 6 November.

VPB-103 was joined by VB-105 on 12 October and VB-110 to form, on 30 October 1943, Fleet Air Wing 7. This designation, however, changed a number of times, to Dunkeswell Air Group, Land Plane Air Group and finally Patrol Air Group One. It wasn't the only thing to change its name: the Liberators became PB4Y-1s in US Navy service. In June 1944 there was another arrival – a detachment from VB-114 with searchlight-equipped PB4Y-1s that could fly night patrols. Each of the squadrons had its own patrol aircraft service unit (PATSU). The operations continued to be dangerous as Dunkeswell Memorial Museum graphically remembers:

> The weather was often unfavorable, take-offs of heavily loaded Liberator aircraft in instrument conditions and in darkness were routine. Long patrols at low altitude usually in conditions of reduced visibility demanded constant vigilance in the search for enemy submarines and against the ever present threat from enemy fighters. Landings often in darkness with minimum ceilings and visibility required expert airmanship on the part of tired pilots and navigators.[62]

When Fleet Air Wing 7 left Dunkeswell, the squadrons had flown nearly 6,500 missions and had sunk five U-boats and taken part in the sinking of another four, but at the high cost of 183 officers and men.

On D-Day the PB4Y-1s patrolled the sea to the west of the invasion at 30-minute intervals. While no submarines were destroyed – one, at least, was sighted – none penetrated to the invasion fleet and the fighter air cover ensured no damage to the ASW aircraft.

The US Navy's antisubmarine squadrons moved to RAF Upottery (*see* pp 110–11) in November 1944 and both Dunkeswell and Upottery were returned to RAF control on 31 July 1945.

**RIGHT**
2018 view of Dunkeswell from the
south-west. Note the dispersals still
visible at the top of the photograph
(hardstandings intended to help
disperse the aircraft so that
bombing would affect as few as
possible).

**BELOW**
Liberators – PB4Y-1s in naval
service – on their pans.

# 93 RAF St Eval, Cornwall

**RAF Coastal Command was founded in 1936 and played a significant role throughout the war and particularly on D-Day. Its key western location was St Eval, on the north Cornish coast, from where photo-reconnaissance, antisubmarine and search-and-rescue missions and meteorological flights were made.**

Neglected in the interwar period, it wasn't long before the importance of RAF Coastal Command became obvious. While Fighter Command fought off the German bombers and Bomber Command plotted to strike strategically at the enemy's industrial heartland, Coastal Command was helping to fight the U-boats, keeping open the sea lanes to America and the Commonwealth and protecting the vital convoys that brought essential supplies to Britain. The second battle of the Atlantic – the German Kriegsmarine had almost brought Britain to its knees in the First World War with its U-boats – proved the value of Coastal Command as it sank more U-boats than any other Allied service.

St Eval was chosen as a Coastal Command airfield in the late 1930s: work began in 1938 and the site opened on 2 October 1939. It played a part in the Battle of Britain – and was bombed severely in 1940, 1941 and 1942 – and throughout the war a variety of aircraft were used for antisubmarine and anti-shipping patrols: Beauforts, Blenheims, Hudsons, Wellingtons, Liberators and Spitfires. Overall, Coastal Command accounted for the sinking of 212 U-boats and lost 741 aircraft during antisubmarine sorties.

US air forces were also present to gain experience: the 1st Antisubmarine Group spent some weeks at St Eval before taking up position in French Morocco to protect the Atlantic approaches to the Strait of Gibraltar. The 479th Antisubmarine Group was also there for some weeks before moving to Dunkeswell on 6 August 1943 (*see* pp 184–5).

St Eval had an extremely powerful antisubmarine presence around D-Day: four Liberator squadrons (Nos 53, 206, 224 and 547), many of the aircraft equipped with the effective Leigh Lights (searchlights mounted under the aircrafts' wings). There were at least three U-boat kills in June and no Allied losses to U-boats in the English Channel.

**ABOVE**

Memorial at St Eval to 996 airmen and WAAFs who lost their lives during operations and bombing raids during the war.

**RIGHT**

Bombing up a Liberator Mk VA of No 53 Squadron with 250lb Mk VIII depth charges.

**OPPOSITE**

Aerial view of St Eval in March 1944: more than 30 aircraft are visible around the field.

# 6 | Sea operations

The naval element of Operation *Neptune* was meticulously planned by Admiral Bertram Ramsay, who, as Vice-Admiral Dover, had saved the British Army at Dunkirk. Ramsay had retired from the navy in 1938 but returned to become Commander-in-Chief Dover in time to plan Operation *Dynamo*, the evacuation of Dunkirk. His knowledge of amphibious warfare came from his involvement in Operation *Torch* (landings on the North African coast) and Operation *Husky* (Sicily). His instructions were all-encompassing and prefaced by a special order of the day.

### Ramsay's special order of the day, 31 May 1944

It is to be our privilege to take part in the greatest amphibious operation in history – a necessary preliminary to the opening of the Western Front in Europe which, in conjunction with the great Russian advance, will crush the fighting power of Germany.

This is the opportunity which we have long awaited and which must be seized and pursued with relentless determination; the hopes and prayers of the free world and of the enslaved peoples of Europe will be with us, and we cannot fail them.

Our task in conjunction with the Merchant Navies of the United Nations, and supported by the Allied Air Forces, is to carry the Allied Expeditionary Force to the Continent, to establish it there in a secure bridgehead and to build it up and maintain it at a rate that will outmatch the enemy. Let no-one underestimate the magnitude of this task.

The Germans are desperate and will resist fiercely until we outmanoeuvre and outfight them, which we can and will do. To everyone of you will be given the opportunity to show by his determination and resource that dauntless spirit of resolution which individually strengthens and inspires, and which collectively is irresistible.

I count on every man to do his utmost to ensure the success of this great enterprise which is the climax of the European War. Good luck to you all, and God Speed.

### Admiral Sir Bertram Ramsay KCB, KBE, MVO[63]

**HMS *Warspite* enjoyed a 30-year career in the Royal Navy, commissioning in 1915 and serving until February 1945. *Warspite* was part of the Eastern Task Force, in conjunction with HMS *Ramillies* and HMS *Roberts*, 12 cruisers and 37 destroyers.**

Ramsay's mission was to convey upwards of 150,000 men, together with their vehicles and equipment, across the English Channel, through minefields and past any E-boats, U-boats or other warships the Kriegsmarine could put in their way, and deliver them onto the Normandy beaches on D-Day.

Each of the five landing beaches was allocated its own convoy and escorts, which were preceded by minesweepers. Additionally, each beach had its own bespoke fire plan – warships allocated to provide suppressing fire before and during the landings,

The unmistakeable silhouette of the Firth of Forth rail bridge. The Royal Navy warships on the North Sea coast had to ensure that the Kriegsmarine (German Navy) couldn't affect the battle in the Channel.

and support of the troops ashore. The German gun batteries – and there were a great number of them – had been identified and Allied vessels were allocated to neutralise the threat. These bombarding groups included battleships – HMS *Warspite*, HMS *Ramillies*, USS *Nevada*, USS *Texas* and USS *Arkansas* – monitors HMS *Roberts* and HMS *Erebus*, and 23 cruisers, including the Free French Navy ships *Montcalm* and *Georges Leygues*. Additionally there were numerous destroyers, gunboats and LC(G)s and LCT(R)s – Landing Ship (gun) and Landing Craft Tank (rocket), the latter firing spectacular salvos of up to 1,000 5-inch rockets. The destroyers played an important role on Omaha, risking grounding to get close enough to supply accurate supporting fire. Indeed, this naval help continued well into the land battles and on more than one occasion naval gunfire was able to break up German attacks. *Texas*, for example, had 10 14-inch guns with a range of 10 miles. *Ramillies*' eight 15-inch guns (the same as fitted to the two monitors) could fire almost double that. She expended more than 1,000 shells during the battle, including on 10 June a bombardment of Caen railway marshalling yards, some miles away.

The convoys to the beaches were each given the code letter of their respective beaches: US divisions to Omaha and Utah Beaches were designated Force O and Force U respectively. This Western Task Force was commanded by Rear Admiral Alan G Kirk, US Navy, from the heavy cruiser USS *Augusta*, and also later included follow-up Force B from south Wales. The Eastern Task Force was commanded by Rear Admiral Philip L Vian, Royal Navy, flying his flag aboard the cruiser HMS *Scylla*, and comprised Forces S, J and G intended for Sword, Juno and Gold Beaches respectively and follow-up Force L from the Thames, through the Dover Strait.

The convoys anchored some 11 miles off the coast and transferred troops and equipment to the waiting landing craft. There was intended to be an initial wave of DD tanks launched around 8,000 yards offshore, but the choppy seas made this too hazardous an operation so the tanks were launched closer in or landed directly onto the beaches. The DD tanks on Omaha were launched too soon and all but two foundered in the waters.

Ramsay's plan worked like a dream and, while there were difficulties, as could be expected, the Atlantic Wall was pierced in five places on D-Day and Admiral Ramsay reported: 'Despite the unfavourable weather, in every main essential the plan was carried out as written.'[64]

ABOVE

Rear Admiral W G Tennant, who took charge of both Mulberry and PLUTO, suggested that the Mulberry Harbours would benefit from blockships sunk to act as breakwaters. Some 60 vessels – obsolete US and British merchantmen, some old warships – were sunk in line to construct the five 'gooseberries' that were used as breakwaters at the beaches. A number of the blockships were assembled off Oban, in the west of Scotland – shown here – and sunk in place off the Normandy coast by 10 June.

BELOW

The Historic Portsmouth Dockyard, with its wonderful collection of famous vessels – *Warrior*, *Victory*, *M33* and *Mary Rose* (in the grey building just left of centre) – contrasts with the modern warships at anchor nearby. Portsmouth was of crucial importance to the naval operations of *Neptune*.

# 94  RAF Coastal Command HQ, Northwood, London

**Formed on 14 July 1936, RAF Coastal Command's primary task was convoy protection and on D-Day its function was the same: to keep the U-boats away from the immense, slow-moving armada as it travelled across the Channel.**

Controlled from its Northwood headquarters in Eastbury Park, RAF Coastal Command was very successful – in conjunction with surface vessels – in ensuring there were few Allied losses from U-boat attacks in June 1944.

In 1939 Eastbury House was originally used as HQ – later it became the Officers' Mess while underneath a network of subterranean bunkers and operations rooms were created.

At the start of the war the Admiralty believed that ASDIC (an early form of sonar used to detect submarines) had nullified the U-boat threat so Coastal Command was originally tasked with keeping an eye on German ships attempting to break out into the Atlantic rather than antisubmarine duties. That changed pretty quickly after U-boats began sinking Atlantic convoys and soon the command became the critical factor in pushing the battle of the Atlantic away from British coastal waters – the scene of most of the action in the First World War.

Together with the clever re-routing of convoys thanks to *Ultra* decrypts, Coastal Command aircraft began to win the fight against the U-boats and consequently, as explained by Air Vice Marshal W Oulton, the command 'grew in size, efficiency and scope, exercising its control and authority – through Group and Air Headquarters – over airfields and flying boat bases running from Iceland through the Hebrides and the whole of the UK and Northern Ireland to Gibraltar and on as far as Freetown on the coast of West Africa.'[65]

The Operations Room at RAF Northwood, Coastal Command HQ. The WAAF on the ladder (to the left) is plotting the position of a convoy.

The one thing the command lacked was an aircraft specifically designed for antisubmarine warfare (ASW). They had good aircraft put to this use – flying boats such as the Short Sunderland and the American Catalina; bombers such as the Beauforts, Wellingtons and Blenheims – even B-17s; for close operations, Beaufighters and Mosquitoes proved successful. But it was the US Consolidated B-24 Liberator that proved the most effective of Coastal Command's aircraft: its long range and versatility as a weapons carrier and the effectiveness of the command was shown in June 1944, when it assisted the Normandy landings.

On 20 January 1944 Air Chief Marshal William Sholto Douglas became Commander-in-Chief RAF Coastal Command and over the D-Day landings executed Operation *Cork*: keeping the English Channel free of U-boats. The operation was hugely successful and it wasn't until 15 June that the first casualty of a U-boat attack was recorded in the Channel.

## June sinkings

| June | Name | Type | Remarks |
|------|------|------|---------|
| **Allied Vessels** | | | |
| 15 | HMS *Blackwood* | Frigate | Torpedoed by *U764*; sank under tow on 16 June. |
| 15 | HMS *Bourne* | Frigate | Torpedoed by *U767*; sank; *U767* sunk by depth charge on 18 June. |
| 25 | HMS *Goodson* | Destroyer | Damaged by *U984*. Sub sunk by depth charge on 20 August. |
| 27 | HMS *Pink* | Corvette | Torpedoed by *U988*. Towed to Plymouth but total loss. |
| 28 | HMS *Maid of Orleans* | LSI | Torpedoed by unknown or mined.* Sank. |
| 29 | SS *Edward M House* | Merchant | Torpedoed by *U984*. Damaged. |
| 29 | SS *James A Farrell* | Merchant | Torpedoed by *U984*. Total loss. |
| 29 | SS *James A Treutlin* | Merchant | Torpedoed by *U984*. Total loss. |
| 29 | SS *H G Blasdel* | Merchant | Torpedoed by *U984*. Total loss. |
| 29 | SS *Empire Portia* | Merchant | Torpedoed by unknown or mined.* |
| **U-boats** | | | |
| 7 | *U955* | VIIC | Bay of Biscay; No 201 Sqn Sunderland out of RAF Pembroke Dock. |
| 7 | *U629* | VIIC | Channel; No 53 Sqn Liberator out of St Eval. |
| 7 | *U373* | VIIC | Bay of Biscay; No 224 Sqn Liberator out of St Eval.** |
| 8 | *U970* | VIIC | Bay of Biscay; No 228 Sqn Sunderland out of RAF Pembroke Dock. |
| 8 | *U740* | VIIC | Channel; No 224 Sqn Liberator out of St Eval. |
| 10 | *U821* | VIIC | Bay of Biscay; No 206 Sqn Liberator out of St Eval. |
| 24 | *U971* | VIIC | Channel; ships and No 311 (Czech) Sqn Liberator out of RAF Predannack. |
| 22 | *U988** | VIIC | Channel; VB-110 Squadron Liberator out of RAF Dunkeswell. |
| 30 | *U441*** | VIIC | Bay of Biscay; ships and No 224 Sqn Liberator out of St Eval. |

* Discovery of wreck of *U988* shows that it did not sink these vessels as hitherto assumed.
** Flt Lt Kenneth O Moore destroyed two U-boats within 20 minutes on 7 June – this was the second; the first was possibly *U441*.

# 95 Admiralty House, Mount Wise, Plymouth, Devon

**For centuries Plymouth has been synonymous with the Royal Navy. When the Armada threatened Britain, the first major action against the English fleet was off Plymouth. On D-Day, forces detailed by the Commander-in-Chief Plymouth protected the western flank of the invasion force.**

Commander-in-Chief Plymouth was Admiral Sir Ralph Leatham and his HQ was in what had been the home of the military commander of Plymouth, then named Government House. The house was taken over by C-i-C Plymouth in 1934 and became Admiralty House (previously housed next door in Hamoaze House, which was taken over by the commanding officer of the Royal Marines). At the start of the war it was hardened against attack by the digging of deep subterranean tunnels, as were the Area Command HQs at Portsmouth, Chatham and Rosyth. This Plymouth Underground Extension housed not just the naval C-i-C and improved communications but also RAF No 19 (General Reconnaissance) Group. Hamoaze House was also used by Captain C F M S Quimby, US Navy commanding officer of the US Advanced Amphibious Base at Queen Anne's Battery.

With Admiral Bertram Ramsay as Allied Naval Commander-in-Chief, Expeditionary Force (ANCXF) in Portsmouth, the forces of C-in-C Plymouth were placed to safeguard the attacking forces. The disposition was

- the Hurd Deep Patrol – destroyers patrolling mid-Channel north of the Gulf of Saint-Malo
- the Western Patrol – another division of destroyers NNW of Ushant to combat any attempt by the Narvik class destroyers
- four US destroyers patrolling west of Force U.

At night these patrols were reinforced by Coastal Forces, Wellingtons and Albacores. Further away, a significant force of three escort carriers (*Tracker*, *Pursuer* and *Emperor*) and six escort groups were stationed by C-i-C Western Approaches (based in Liverpool) west of Land's End.

In fact there were few German incursion attempts. Rear Admiral Alan G Kirk, Western Task Force commander, reported on the largest: 'The Plymouth covering forces, assisted by radar stations in the United Kingdom, repulsed an enemy destroyer sortie of three (3) Narviks and one (1) Elbing in the early morning of 9 June, destroying one (1) enemy DD and forcing another to beach.'[66]

Also part of Plymouth's responsibilities was ASW (antisubmarine) protection from U-boats – possibly as many as 40 of them – based in the Bay of Biscay ports. To counter this, there were substantial Allied air assets, but close to the French coast these were harried by German anti-aircraft guns and fighters. The coastal areas were, therefore, heavily mined to stop the U-boats using them. There were also four ASW support groups available, two patrolling and two on standby.

Plymouth was also a major embarkation area, with hards at Cattedown, Turnchapel, Saltash Passage, Mount Edgcumbe and Torpoint.

**Admiralty House, on Mount Wise in Plymouth, was built at the end of the 18th century. Early in the Second World War, underground tunnels were excavated.**

# 96  HMS *Vernon*, Portsmouth, Hampshire

**The historic city of Portsmouth was – and still is today – the home of the Royal Navy and one of the world's greatest ports. It was pounded by German bombs – 67 air raids between 1940 and 1944 – but still it housed a number of key locations associated with D-Day.**

HMS *Vernon* – named after 18th-century Admiral Edward Vernon, nicknamed 'Old Grog' – was a shore establishment that, from the end of the First World War, housed the Admiralty Torpedo, Mining and Electrical Training establishment located on the old Gunwharf. It specialised in torpedoes, mines, mine dispersal and countermeasures. So successful did it prove that the Germans introduced booby traps.

*Vernon* was hit several times during air raids from 1940, and in May 1941 the HQ and Central Administration of the Training Establishment were moved to Roedean School for Girls in East Sussex (the school had evacuated to Keswick in September 1940). The Torpedo and Mine Warfare Schools and their training sections also went there (other elements were sent to Scotland and the West Country). The school was officially commissioned as HMS *Vernon* (R) on 3 May 1941 and tasked to provide intensive training courses in mines, torpedoes, depth charges and shipboard electrics. The ratings were billeted three to a room, while married officers were allowed to stay nearby. The school quadrangle became the parade ground and the sports facilities were also put to good use. Armed sentries (junior ratings) patrolled the perimeter day and night.

This aerial photograph shows the damage done to HMS *Vernon* (A), in Portsmouth, by the bombing.

From September 1942, 16 Wrens a week arrived to take the six-week Seaman Torpedoman's course so as to free up shore-based men for sea duty. By the end of the first year 684 Wrens had completed the course. The number of naval personnel continued to increase, with the establishment having to requisition other sites around the Brighton area to accommodate them.

In August 1943 the Mining Instruction School relocated to Portsmouth as HMS *Vernon* (P). HMS *Vernon* (R) remained at Roedean until 8 June 1945.

In the run-up to D-Day, HMS *Vernon* served as base for a section of Force S, the naval force that landed the 3rd British Division on Sword Beach.

On 6 June 1944 Roedean's flagstaff flew a No 1 White Ensign (9 × 11 feet) in honour of the men invading Normandy. It still hangs in the school's chapel.

Roedean School sits on white cliffs near Brighton. After the bombing of HMS *Vernon*, in Portsmouth, it proved a suitable substitute for the Mining Instruction School.

## 97  The Royal Navy Patrol Service, HMS *Europa*, Lowestoft, Suffolk

**Mine warfare around the coasts of Britain could have crippled the country. The threat was identified before the First World War, as was the solution: the use of east coast trawlers – Grimsby providing the most – and HMS *Europa* was the HQ.**

As soon as the Second World War started and Royal Naval Reserves were mobilised, the Royal Naval Patrol Service (RNPS) went into action – as minesweepers and ASW (antisubmarine) vessels. They would go on to fight in every theatre of the war, in 'trawlers, whalers, drifters, motor fishing vessels, motor launches, and later motor minesweepers, American-produced British yard minesweepers and numerous requisitioned vessels.'[67]

The RNPS suffered heavily in the war. It was a dangerous job: 50 vessels were lost (out of 3,000), more than 15,000 personnel were dead (out of more than 60,000), and some 35,000 mines cleared – and not just from around the British Isles.

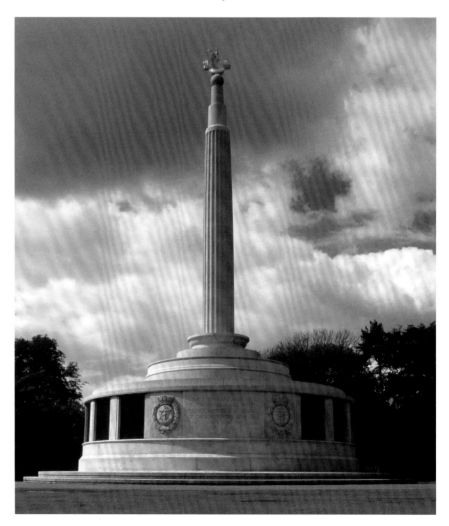

This handsome memorial in Lowestoft remembers those of the RNPS who died 1939–1945 and who have no known grave – 'no grave but the sea' as the inscription says. There are almost 2,400 of them.

HMS *Ailsa Craig* (*T377*) was an MS trawler of the Isles class. *T377* was commissioned at the end of 1943 and saw service throughout the war. The 197-strong Isles class was used by the Royal Navy, Royal Canadian Navy and Royal New Zealand Navy on minesweeping or harbour defence duties.

On D-Day, the RNPS was part of the minesweeping force that was, according to Rear Admiral Alan G Kirk, the senior US Navy commander during the landings, 'the keystone of the arch in this operation'. Kirk opined: 'The performance of the minesweepers can only be described as magnificent.'[68]

The plan was fourfold:

- to cut and mark (with Dan buoys) channels for the assault forces through the mine barrier that was known to stretch across the invasion beaches (255 minesweepers were involved)
- to clear areas for the bombarding forces
- to continue the clearance after the assault, to give more room for follow-up convoys
- to clear mines laid after the assault.

Overall it was extraordinarily successful. This is not to say that there were no mine losses on D-Day. Little could have prevented that. The table below shows vessels that hit mines in June 1944. Additionally, three LSTs (landing ships) and a number of other landing craft were destroyed by mines.

### Vessels that hit mines in June 1944

| Date | Vessel | Date | Vessel |
|---|---|---|---|
| 6 | HMS *Wrestler* | 9 | FFS *Mistral* |
| | USS *Osprey* | 11 | HMS *MGB17* |
| | USS *Corry* | 13 | HMS *MMS229* |
| 7 | USS *Tide* | 21 | HMS *Fury* |
| | MT *Susan B Anthony* | 24 | HMS *Swift* |
| 8 | HMS *Minister* | | HMS *Lord Austin* |
| | USS *Rich* | | HMS *MMS8* |
| | USS *Meredith* | 27 | HMS *MGB326* |
| | USS *Glennon* | | |
| | USS *YMS406* | | |

# 98  HMS *Dolphin*, Gosport, Hampshire

**The Royal Navy's Coastal Forces played a crucial role during the landings, providing protection against the German E-boats, whose intervention during Exercise *Tiger* showed how damaging they could be.**

The RAF had its dashing fighter pilots: the Royal Navy's equivalent was equally dashing. Protecting convoys and seaways, dropping agents ashore in clandestine operations, the motor torpedo boats (MTBs) and motor gun boats (MGBs) – today's fast-attack craft – were the 'Spitfires of the Seas'.

The RN's Coastal Forces were based around the UK, originally under the command of Flag Officer, Coastal Forces, based in Portsmouth at HMS *Vernon* (*see* p 195). During the war, however, control of these forces had moved to the home commands. The northeast had the most, based on the east coast at sites in Brightlingsea, Felixstowe, Lowestoft, Great Yarmouth and Immingham. The three Channel commands – Plymouth, Portsmouth and Dover – also had significant quantities of these Coastal Forces and as their role was so important it was vital that they were carefully controlled and meshed well with other elements of the plan. A centralised control – in the form of Captain, Coastal Forces (Channel), was created and Captain P V McLaughlin, RN, took up the position on the staff of Commander-in-Chief Portsmouth. He was responsible for planning the use of Coastal Forces during Operation *Overlord*, and on 21 May 1944 a control office was set up in HMS *Dolphin* – the home of the RN Submarine Service and Submarine School – to keep in contact with the boats and to ensure that turn-round operations, maintenance and repairs were suitably conducted.

Dover Command had nine flotillas of MTBs (two Dutch, seven British), four fleet destroyers and two frigates. Plymouth Command had 12 fleet destroyers (including four US Navy destroyers during the assault phase) and four flotillas of MTBs, one of which was French. Portsmouth had four fleet destroyers, two frigates and five flotillas of MTBs.

The Coastal Forces performed admirably on D-Day and throughout the campaign: German E-boat incursions were limited and their successes on D-Day

**HMS *Dolphin* was originally named HMS *Blockhouse* and is one of the oldest military establishments in the UK, dating back to the 15th century. Between 1905 and 1999 it was the home of Britain's submarine service.**

Around 20 submarines are visible in this 1946 aerial view of HMS *Dolphin*, but its importance for D-Day was its role in Coastal Forces. The E-boats were a real threat, as had been shown during Exercise *Tiger*. Indeed, on D-Day itself the attack that sank *Svenner* could easily have hit *Warspite* (*see* pp 188–9). The screen provided against the German threat worked very well.

amounted to one Royal Norwegian Navy destroyer, the *Svenner*, and four other small ships in June. Altogether the Kriegsmarine lost 22 of their 35 E-boats in the Channel in June, including 15 during the bombing of Le Havre by 325 Lancasters on 15 June.

The success of RN and US Coastal Forces during the landings is well summed up by Rear Admiral Alan G Kirk, Western Task Force commander:

> The Area Screen was devised against E-boats and matched the plan for the Eastern Task Force Area. It was designed to furnish protection against surface and sub-surface attack from seaward, and it was so skilfully handled that at no time was there any penetration by enemy naval forces into waters off the US beaches ... After a few attempted E-boat penetrations, shortly after D-Day, which were firmly repulsed, the Germans left the screen severely alone.[69]

### Total Coastal Forces used by each task force on D-Day

| Type | Eastern | Western | Other |
|---|---|---|---|
| MTBs, MGBs | 23 | 41 | 139 |
| Sub chasers | 0 | 18 | 0 |
| MLs (motor launches) | 31 | 19 | 90 |
| Small Coast Guard cutters | 30 | 30 | 0 |
| Harbour defence MLs | 6 | 5 | 31 |
| | | | |
| Totals | 90 | 113 | 260 |

# 99 The Solent

Protected by the Isle of Wight, the Solent played an important role as the armada troopships waited for the off. The waters offered some protection against the heavy seas on 4/5 June and – as the berthing plan opposite shows – could hardly have taken more ships. This satellite photograph is looking north-east.

**Protected to the north by the mainland and to the south by the Isle of Wight, the Solent, with its double tides, feeds two of Britain's greatest ports – Southampton and Portsmouth. It was of crucial importance during D-Day, with much of Forces J, G and S assembling there.**

The Solent runs for 20 miles from Hurst Point in the west to Spithead. It separates the Isle of Wight from mainland England at a maximum width of 5 miles. The Isle of Wight shelters the Solent and causes a double high tide every day that allows deep-draught ships longer to navigate the waters into Portsmouth and Southampton.

For the build up to D-Day the waters and sheltered shorelines of the Solent were crucial. The low beaches, numerous docks and quiet waterways were used to build embarkation hards and components of the Mulberry Harbours. The Solent was also used as an assembly area for the armada that would head towards Normandy for D-Day.

An anchorage plan of the Solent, Southampton Water and Spithead was drawn up to organise the vessels detailed for the invasion of Normandy prior to crossing the Channel. Divided into 31 main berthing areas, each craft was allocated an anchorage position. The vessels ranged in size from battleships to motor torpedo boats. To keep radio traffic silent, all communication was via 10-inch signal lamps or messenger launches. Departures started before dawn on 5 June.

In the end, only HMS *Alresford*, a Hunt-class minesweeper commissioned in 1919 (and veteran of the Dieppe Raid and Dunkirk), was left behind to do her duty sweeping the channels, leaving the Solent otherwise empty except for small servicing craft. On D-Day, two-thirds of all those who took part in the initial assault sailed from here.

# 100 Fort Gilkicker, Gosport, Hampshire

**Operation *Neptune* didn't end on D-Day, of course. Follow-up forces, resupply, casualty evacuation, air and naval support: these requirements continued for weeks. Fort Gilkicker's position overlooking Spithead, on the Solent, made it the perfect location for a TURCO (Turn-Round Control).**

After 6 June it's easy to focus attention on the battle of Normandy and to forget the huge effort that continued in the UK. Almost everything that had been needed for the assault was necessary in the forthcoming days, but with the added problems that action brought: attrition by accidental damage or action, casualties, timetable issues and, added to these factors, the weather (this June was not a sunny summer month). The day of the assault had been moved from 5 to 6 June because of bad weather and, of course, there was the storm on 19–21 June that destroyed the Omaha Mulberry.

However, as Rear Admiral Kirk summarised: 'Experience of joint British-American forces in the Mediterranean and in this theater, coupled to those acquired in the Pacific and Southwest Pacific theaters, prove by their unbroken series of successes that our system is correct.'[70] Admiral Ramsay's naval plan had taken these factors into account and he had set up a number of organisations in the major ports to help deal with the issues:

- BUCO (Build-Up Control): to deal with the problems of matching available shipping with loads needed in France. The operational orders for *Neptune* covered the first 47 follow-up convoys for 7 to 9 June (D+1 to D+3), which were then repeated.
- TURCO (Turn-Round Control): to help organise the movement of ships to the correct berths for follow-on loads.
- COREP (Combined Operations Repair): to ensure that damaged vessels were quickly repaired and returned to work.
- COTUG (Tug Control): essential to ensure that the shortage of tugs (only 132 tugs were available) didn't affect the load management.

Fort Gilkicker had been built in the 19th century as part of Palmerston's defences of Portsmouth and was unmanned save for a Trinity House observation post after 1939. Following Dunkirk, it gained a searchlight and guns, and in summer 1943 a signal station and an operations room, as part of the TURCO set-up. In April 1944 Gilkicker received radio equipment for communication with Solent Patrol vessels, which handled traffic control.

Stokes Bay had a collecting area for returning LCTs (landing craft) and this was linked with a maintenance and repair centre set up at Gilkicker. It was well used. By the end of July 1944 it had serviced 1,300 LCTs, 250 LCI(L)s and 50 LSTs (*see* p 49 for landing ship/craft definitions).

**Fort Gilkicker from the air in 2018 during redevelopment – it is due to become 'a collection of unique coastal homes'.**

# Notes

1   Bradley 1951, 206.
2   https://uk.usembassy.gov/our-relationship/policy-history/
    rcgrsvnr (the website gives the source as Winant, John G *A
    Letter From Grosvenor Square*. Hodder & Stoughton, 1947).
3   Eisenhower 1948, 225.
4   *History of COSSAC (Chief of Staff to Supreme Allied
    Commander), 1943–44*, prepared by Historical Sub-Section,
    Office of Secretary, General Staff, Supreme Headquarters,
    Allied Expeditionary Force Staff, p 15. (Historical Manuscripts
    Collection 8-3.6A CA). Accessed at https://history.army.mil/
    documents/cossac/Cossac.htm.
5   Ambrose 1991, 123.
6   D'Este 2002, 490.
7   Baxter 1999, 63.
8   Bradley 1951, 175.
9   Ibid, 11.
10  Ibid, 176.
11  Bradley 1951, 340.
12  Blumenson 1974, 254.
13  Hughes 2004.
14  'Air Operations by the Allied Expeditionary Air Force in NW
    Europe From November 15, 1943 to September 30, 1944';
    dispatch from Leigh-Mallory to Supreme Allied Commander,
    November 1944; https://www.ibiblio.org/hyperwar/UN/UK/
    LondonGazette/37838.html (p 41).
15  Ibid, 39.
16  D'Este 2002, 785 (Chap 43, note 2).
17  D'Este 2002, 401.
18  Bradley 1951, 250.
19  https://en.wikiquote.org/wiki/Arthur_Travers_Harris (the
    online reference gives the source as Robin Cross 1995 *Fallen
    Eagle*. John Wiley and Sons, 78).
20  Freeman 1970, 165.
21  Schofield 2008, 150.
22  Ibid, 46.
23  Ibid, 47.
24  Roberts 2010, chapter 9.
25  Quote taken from the original letter, on display at Bletchley
    Park; *see also* https://www.theguardian.com/uk-news/2016/
    mar/15/eisenhower-letter-uk-code-breakers-display-
    bletchley-park.
26  Bradley 1951, 344.
27  Hall 2015, 12.
28  Neillands and Normann 2001.
29  Major R Howard, 'The 52nd Light Infantry preparation
    for D-Day', based on extracts from the *Regimental War
    Chronicles of the Oxfordshire & Buckinghamshire Light
    Infantry*, vol 3 1942–1944. Accessed at http://www.
    lightbobs.com/1944-preparation-for-d-day.html.
30  Ibid.
31  Keane 2012.
32  Ruppenthal 1995, 334.
33  Williams 1997, 41–2.
34  Risch 1995, 323.
35  Eisenhower 1948, 63.
36  Stacey 1955, 209.
37  Helmich and Peters 1945 [?], 22.
38  Lochner *et al* 1948, 269.
39  https://www.dailyecho.co.uk/heritage/15452955.amp.
40  As quoted in Woodham Smith 1950, 276.
41  Warren 1956, 19.
42  Ibid, 18–19.
43  https://valor.militarytimes.com.
44  Warren, 1956, 50.
45  Ibid, 76.
46  Ibid, 38.
47  Ibid, 66.
48  https://www.peterlanyonfurniture.co.uk/new-page.
49  Barbier 2009, 69.
50  Lovat 1978, 297.
51  Ibid.
52  Ibid, 301.
53  *1st Special Service Brigade HQ War Diary*, National Archives
    WO 218/59, sourced via The Pegasus Archive.
54  Holborn 2009, 94.
55  Ruppenthal 1995, 359.
56  Much of the information in this section is taken from
    Historical Section, COMNAVEU 1946, 338–80.
57  Ruppenthal 1995, 359–60.
58  http://www.90thidpg.us/Research/90thDivision/History/
    AAR/june44.html.
59  http://www.91stbombgroup.com/91st_info/91stbg_history.html.
60  6 June 1944 entry from *Operations Record Book* of No 438
    Sqn, RCAF; https://www.junobeach.org/canada-in-wwii/
    articles/rcaf-fighter-squadrons-overseas.
61  Benbow 2017.
62  http://dmm103105110.btck.co.uk/BreifHistoryofDunkeswell.
63  Schofield 2008, 60–1.
64  Ibid, 90.
65  Oulton 1991, 15.
66  COMINCH P-006 'Amphibious Operations: Invasion of
    Northern France, Western Task Force, June 1944'; United
    States Fleet, HQ of the Commander in Chief, 1944 (p 1–23).
    Accessed at http://www.ibiblio.org/hyperwar/USN/rep/
    Normandy/Cominch/Neptune1.html.
67  Royal Naval Patrol Service Association website: http://www.
    rnpsa.co.uk/cms/?History.
68  Report of Naval Commander Western Task Force (CTF 122),
    Report of Normandy Invasion; United States Fleet, HQ of
    the Commander-in-Chief, 1944. Accessed at https://apps.
    dtic.mil/dtic/tr/fulltext/u2/a550844.pdf (Kirk, *After Action
    Report*, pp 8–9).
69  Ibid, 15.
70  Ibid, 1.

# Bibliography

Adcock, A 2003 *Warships Number 17 WWII US Landing Craft in Action*. Carrollton: Squadron/signal publications

Ambrose, S 1991 *Eisenhower: Soldier and President*. London: Simon & Schuster

Anderson, B 1985 *Army Air Force Stations*. Washington, DC: USAF Historical Research Center

Barbier, M K 2009 *D-Day Deception: Operation Fortitude and the Normandy Invasion*. Mechanicsburg: Stackpole Books

Baxter, C F (ed) 1999 *Field Marshal Bernard Law Montgomery, 1887–1976: A Selected Bibliography*. Santa Barbara: Greenwood Publishing Group

Beamish, D F 1984 *D-Day: Poole*. Poole: Poole Borough Council

Benbow, T 2017 'Absent Friends? British naval aviation and D-Day'. (www.defenceindepth.com)

Benneweis, D R 2013 'On War Planning: The 29th US Infantry Division as a Case Study in Manning and Training an Army during the Second World War'. DPhil Thesis, University of Calgary. (prism.ucalgary.ca/handle/11023/1243)

Bijl, N van der and Hanson, P 1994 *Elite 57 The Royal Marines 1939–93*. Oxford: Osprey

Blumenson, M 1974 *The Patton Papers 1940–1945*. Boston: Houghton Mifflin

Bradley, O 1951 *A Soldier's Story*. New York City: Henry Holt & Co

Bykofsky, J and Larson, H 1990 *United States Army in World War II: The Technical Services: The Transportation Corps: Operations Overseas*. Washington, DC: Center of Military History, Department of the Army

D'Este, C 2002 *Eisenhower: A Soldier's Life*. New York City: Henry Holt

Dawson, L 1989 *Wings Over Dorset*. Wincanton: Dorset Publishing

Dunstan, S 2003 *Spearhead 11 Commandos*. Shepperton: Ian Allan Ltd

Eisenhower, D 1948 *Crusade in Europe*. London: Heinemann

Elder, W D 2009 *A Coast Guardsman's Story*. (www.amphibiousforces.org/Interest/WilliamElderStory/WilliamElderLCI89.pdf )

First Army Plan *Neptune*, 28 February 1944; retrieved from Combined Arms Research Library Digital Library. (comarms.ipac.dynixasp.com/ipac20/ipac.jsp?profile=)

Ford, K 2003 *D-Day Commando*. Stroud: Sutton Publishing

Ford, K 2004 *Battle Zone Normandy 2: Sword Beach*. Stroud: Sutton Publishing

Ford, K 2004 *Battle Zone Normandy 3: Juno Beach*. Stroud: Sutton Publishing

Forty, G 1994 *Frontline Dorset*. Wincanton: Dorset Books

Freeman, R A 1970 *The Mighty Eighth*. London: Macdonald & Co

Futter, G W 1974 *The Funnies*. Hemel Hempstead: Bellona/MAP

Hall, D I 2015 'The German View of the Dieppe Raid, August 1942'. *Canadian Military History* 21/4. (scholars.wlu.ca/cmh/vol21/iss4/2)

Harrison, G A 1951 *United States Army in World War II: The European Theater of Operations Cross-Channel Attack*. Washington, DC: Center of Military History, US Army

Helmich, A M and Peters, C H 1945 [?] *History of the 756 Ry Shop Bn*. Self-produced, read on SCRIBD. (www.scribd.com/document/260800593/756-th-Railway-Shop-Battalion-Unit-History)

Historical Section, Commander US Naval Forces in Europe (COMNAVEU) 1946 *Administrative History of US Naval Forces in Europe, 1940–1946, Vol 5: The Invasion of Normandy Operation Neptune*. London: Historical Section, COMNAVEU

HMSO 1994 *Battle Summary No 39 Operation 'Neptune' Landings in Normandy, June 1944*. London: HMSO

Holborn, A 2009 'The Role of 56th (Independent) Infantry Brigade During the Normandy Campaign June–September 1944'. DPhil Thesis, University of Plymouth. (pearl.plymouth.ac.uk/bitstream/handle/10026.1/1996/ANDREW%20HOLBORN.PDF?sequence+1)

HQ V Corps Operations Plan *Neptune*, 26 March 1944; retrieved from Combined Arms Research Library Digital Library. (comarms.ipac.dynixasp.com/ipac20/ipac.jsp?profile=)

Hughes, T A 2004 'Anglo-American Tactical Air operations in World War II'. *Air and Space Power Journal*, winter 2004

Ivybridge Heritage and Archives Group, 2017 *Ivybridge and the Americans during WW2*. Ivybridge: Ivybridge Heritage and Archives Group

Jacobs, P 2009 *Airfields of the D-Day Invasion: 2nd Tactical Air Force in South-East England in WWII*. Barnsley: Pen & Sword

Jacobs, P 2013 *Southern and West Country Airfields of the D-Day Invasion Air Force: 2nd Tactical Air Force in Southern and South-West England in WWII*. Barnsley: Pen & Sword

Keane, M 2012 *George S Patton: Blood Guts and Prayer*. Washington, DC: Regnery History

Kershaw, R J 1993 *D-Day Piercing the Atlantic Wall*. Shepperton: Ian Allan Ltd

Lavery, B 2006 *Churchill's Navy*. London: Conway

Legg, R 2004 *Dorset's War Diary*. Wincanton: Dorset Publishing

Liddiard, R and Sims, D 2014 *A Guide to Second World War Archaeology in Suffolk*, 4 vols. Aylsham: Suffolk County Council

Lochner, R, Faber, O and Penney, W G 1948 'The "Bombardon" Floating Breakwater'. *The Civil Engineer in War: A Symposium of Papers on Wartime Engineering Problems*. London: Institution of Civil Engineers.

Lovat, Lord 1978 *March Past*. Worthing: Littlehampton Book Services Ltd

Mark, E 1994 *Aerial Interdiction Air Power and the Land Battle in Three American Wars*. Washington, DC: Center for Air Force History

Mountford, E R 1989 *Locomotion Papers 170: The USA 756th Railway Shop Battalion at Newport* (Ebbw Junction). Catrine: The Oakwood Press

Naval Historical Branch 2014 *Operation Neptune*. London: Royal Navy

N&M Press 1945 [?] *The Story of 79th Armoured Division*. Uckfield: N&M Press

Neillands, R and Normann, R de 2001 *D-Day 1944: Voices from Normandy*. London: Cassell

Oulton, W 1992 'Organisation, structure and tasks of Coastal Command'. *Royal Air Force Historical Society: Seek and Sink, Bracknell Paper No 2, A Symposium on the Battle of the Atlantic*. (www.rafmuseum.org.uk/documents/Research/RAF-Historical-Society-Journals/Bracknell-No-2-Battle-of-the-Atlantic.pdf)

Place, T H 2000 *Military Training in the British Army, 1940–1944*. London: Frank Cass

Ramsey, W G 1995 *D-Day Then and Now*, two vols. Old Harlow: After The Battle

Rapport, L and Northwood, A Jr 1965 *Rendezvous with Destiny: A History of the 101st Airborne Division*. Old Saybrook: 101st Airborne Division Association

Risch, E and Kieffer, C L 1995 *United States Army in World War II: The Technical Services: The Quartermaster Corps Organization, Supply, and Services: Vol II*. Washington, DC: Center of Military History, Department of the Army

Roberts, A 2010 *The Storm of War: A New History of the Second World War*. London: Penguin

Ruppenthal, R G 1995 *United States Army in World War II: The European Theater of Operations: Logistical Support of the Armies: Vol I: May 1941–September 1944*. Washington, DC: Center of Military History, US Army

Schofield, B B 2008 *Operation Neptune*. Barnsley: Pen & Sword

Sommers, M 2013 *Tank Training Site, Fritton Lake, Somerleyton, Ashby & Herringfleet, Archaeological Survey Report*. Bury St Edmunds: Suffolk County Council Archaeological Service

Stacey, C P 1955 *Official History of the Canadian Army in the Second World War, Vol I: Six Years of War, The Army in Canada, Britain and the Pacific*. Ottawa: Department of National Defence

Stacey, C P 1966 *Official History of the Canadian Army in the Second World War, Vol III: The Victory Campaign, The Operations in North-West Europe, 1944–1945*. Ottawa: Department of National Defence

Summers, J 2018 *Our Uninvited Guests: The Secret Life of Britain's Country Houses 1939–45*. New York City: Simon & Schuster

Tangmere Military Aviation Museum 2008 *Americans at Tangmere*. Tangmere: Tangmere Military Aviation Museum

Tangmere Military Aviation Museum 2008–2013 *D-Day at Tangmere and its Surrounding Airfields*. Tangmere: Tangmere Military Aviation Museum

Trenowden, I 1995 *Stealthily By Night: Clandestine Beach Reconnaissance and Operations in World War II*. Manchester: Crécy

Trew, S 2004 *Battle Zone Normandy 4: Gold Beach*. Stroud: Sutton Publishing

United States Coast Guard (USCG), Historical Section, Public Information Division, 1949 *The Coast Guard at War, Transports and Escorts*. Washington, DC: USCG HQ

United States Government Printing Office 1953 *History of the Medical Department of the US Navy in World War II*. Washington, DC: United States Government Printing Office

Verity, Hugh 1998 *We Landed by Moonlight*. Manchester: Crécy

Vince, A A 2015 *The Pompadours: D-Day to VE Day in Northwest Europe*. Uckfield: The Naval & Military Press Ltd

Wakefield, K 1994 *Operation Bolero*. Manchester: Crécy

Walford, M 2012 'Hampshire's highways under military occupation', *Proceedings of Hampshire Field Club and Archaeological Society*, 67, part 2, 407–40. (www.hantsfieldclub.org.uk/publications/hampshirestudies/digital/2010s/Vol_67ii/Walford.pdf)

Warren, J C 1956 *USAF Historical Studies No 97: Airborne Operations in World War II, European Theater*. Washington DC: USAF Historical Division

Williams, E R 1997 '50 Div in Normandy: A Critical Analysis of the British 50th (Northumbrian) Division on D-Day and in the Battle of Normandy'. DPhil Thesis, United States Naval Academy, Annapolis, Maryland. (www.researchgate.net/publication/37165985_50_Div_in_Normandy_a_critical_analysis_of_the_British_50th_Northumbrian_Division_on_D-Day_and_in_the_Battle_of_Normandy)

Woodham Smith, C 1950 *Florence Nightingale*. Edinburgh: Constable

Zaloga, S J 2007 *Fortress 63: The Atlantic Wall (1) France*. Oxford: Osprey

Zdiarsky, J 2016 'Drop Tanks, USAAF'. *Info Eduard*, March 2016

## Websites

www.90thidpg.us/Research/90thDivision/History/AAR/june44.html

www.americanairmuseum.com

www.combinedops.com

www.fortgilkicker.co.uk/Dday.htm

www.ibiblio.org/hyperwar/ETO/Admin/ETO-AdmLog-6/ETO-AdmLog-6-1.html

www.ibiblio.org/hyperwar/USA/USA-E-Logistics1/USA-E-Logistics1-9.html#fn4

www.ibiblio.org/hyperwar/USN/Admin-Hist/147.5-ComNavEu/ComNavEu-9.html#page517

www.ibiblio.org/hyperwar/USN/Admin-Hist/USN-Admin-Guide/USN-Admin-Guide-1.html#use

https://maritimearchaeologytrust.org/embarkation-hards

www.nmrn.org.uk/news-events/nmrn-blog/future-sole-surviving-d-day-landing-craft-secure

www.pegasusarchive.org

www.piddlevalley.info/history/piddlehinton/sop/piddlehinton_chap10.php#ch-4

www.portsdown-tunnels.org.uk

www.skylighters.org/sausage

https://theddaystory.com

https://wartimes.ca

www.worcestershireregiment.com/bat_10_1939_1945.php

# Picture credits

T – top,  C – centre,  B – bottom
L – left,  R – right
ASM  Air Sea Media
IWM  Imperial War Museum
NARA  US National Archives and Record
   Administration

Cover  NARA
ii  NARA
iv–v  Historic England Archive
   (RAF photography) raf_3g_
   tud_uk_162_vp2_5095
vii  NARA
viii  Library of Congress, Prints &
   Photographs Division, FSA/
   OWI Collection, [LC-USW33-
   038043-C]
ix  Author's collection
x  © Historic England Archive
xii  NARA
1  NARA
2  Courtesy of St Paul's School,
   Lonsdale Road, London
3T  Historic England Archive
   (RAF photography) raf_
   ac371_uk1493_po_0013
3B  © Author
4T  NARA
4B  By C G P Grey (https://www.
   flickr.com/photos/cgpgrey/
   5023460502) CC BY 2.0
5  NARA
6  NARA
7 both  James Forty
8  NARA
9T  Historic England Archive
   (USAAF photography)
   us_7ph_gp_loc304_stbd_14038
9B both  © Author
10  NARA
11  Courtesy of St Paul's School,
   Lonsdale Road, London
12 both  Courtesy of St Paul's School,
   Lonsdale Road, London
13  Clifton College Archives
14T  Clifton College Archives
14B  NARA
15  © Historic England Archive
   DP104343
16  Ken Bell/Canada Dept of
   National Defence/Library and
   Archives Canada/PA-129122

17  © Historic England Archive
   based on Harrison 1951, map
   IV
18  Crown Copyright courtesy of
   Martin Warren
19T  Crown Copyright courtesy of
   Martin Warren
19B  By Alan Hunt (https://
   commons.wikimedia.org/
   wiki/File:Ramslade_House,_
   Bracknell.jpg) CC BY-SA 2.0
20 both  NARA
21 both  NARA
22T  By Malcolm Gould (https://
   commons.wikimedia.org/wiki/
   File:Aldermaston_Manor.jpg)
   CC BY-SA 3.0
22B  Author's collection
23  © IWM CH 15885
24  By Greenshed (https://
   commons.wikimedia.org/wiki/
   File:Statue_of_Sir_Arthur_
   Harris_outside_St_Clement_
   Danes.jpg)
25T  Crown Copyright courtesy of
   Martin Warren
25B  By Tony Crowe (https://
   commons.wikimedia.org/
   wiki/Category:RAF_High_
   Wycombe#/media/File:RAF_
   High_Wycombe_-_Tony_
   Crowe.jpg) CC BY-SA 2.0
26  Library of Congress, Prints &
   Photographs Division, FSA/
   OWI Collection, [LC-USW33-
   000983-ZC]
27T  NARA
27B  NARA via ASM
28T  Courtesy of Portsmouth News
28B  © ASM
29  Courtesy of Portsmouth News
30BL  © Author
30BR  © ASM
31  Adrian Dennis/AFP/Getty
   Images (495293507)
32L  Historic England Archive
   (USAAF photography)
   us_7ph_gp_loc302_fp_1040
32R  NARA
33T  Historic England Archive
   (USAAF photography)
   us_7ph_gp_loc302_fp_1018

34T  Education Images/UIG via
   Getty Images (630015476)
34B  By Antoine Taveneaux
   (https://commons.wikimedia.
   org/wiki/File:Bletchley_
   Park_23.jpg) CC BY-SA 3.0
35C  Bletchley Park Trust /SSPL/
   Getty Images (90737429)
35B  Bletchley Park Trust /SSPL/
   Getty Images (90737447)
36  © IWM H42527
37  © Historic England Archive,
   based on author's original
38  © Author
39T  © IWM MH 22716
39B  NARA via ASM
40  NARA
42T  © Author
42B  NARA
43  NARA
44T  By De Facto (https://
   commons.wikimedia.org/wiki/
   File:Commando_Memorial_
   at_Spean_Bridge.jpg) CC
   BY-SA 4.0
44B  NARA
45  NARA
46  © Historic England Archive,
   based on 'Training Map UK',
   www.combinedops.com
47T  © Historic Environment
   Scotland (RAF National
   Survey (Air Photographs),
   1944–1950 Collection) SC
   45870
47B  © IWM A 12060
48T  By dun_deagh (https://
   www.flickr.com/photos/
   dun_deagh/6180806522/) CC
   BY-SA 2.0
48B  Canada Department of
   National Defence/Library and
   Archives Canada/ecopy
50T  William Arthur/Alamy Stock
   Photo
50B  Courtesy of Tuck DB Postcards
51L  By Orionist (https://
   commons.wikimedia.org/wiki/
   File:British_Commandos_
   Patch.svg) CC BY-SA 3.0
51R  Crown Copyright courtesy of
   Martin Warren

| | |
|---|---|
| 52L | Airborne Assault Archives, Duxford |
| 52R | Crown Copyright courtesy of Martin Warren |
| 53L | Airborne Assault Archives, Duxford |
| 53R | Historic England Archive (RAF photography) raf_106g_uk_622_rp_3297 |
| 54 both | © ASM |
| 55T | © Author |
| 55C & B | Crown copyright via Battlefield Historian |
| 56 both | NARA |
| 57 | NARA |
| 58 | © IWM H 36593 |
| 59 | © David Sims |
| 60 | Historic England Archive (RAF photography) raf_hla_694_rs_4112 |
| 61 | © IWM H 35177 |
| 62 | NARA |
| 63 both | NARA |
| 64T | © Author |
| 64B | NARA |
| 65 both | NARA |
| 66 | NARA |
| 67T | © Historic England Archive, Shuttle Radar Topography Mission data courtesy of the CGIAR Consortium for Spatial Information |
| 67B | NARA |
| 68 | Historic England Archive (RAF photography) raf_106g_la_200_fp_1005 |
| 69TL | Historic England Archive (USAAF photography) us_30gr_loc11_v_0040 |
| 69TR | © Crown copyright. Historic England Archive nmr_74_6 (20 APR 1968, ST 9648/1) |
| 70 | © ASM |
| 71 | By Stevekraken (https://commons.wikimedia.org/wiki/File:Fort_Henry,_Studland.jpg) CC BY-SA 4.0 |
| 72T | © ASM |
| 72B | Extract of map: Headquarters Xix District, US Veterans History Project, and Collector American Folklife Center. *Area 'K': administrative map Operation Overlord South Western Zone, 15 April 1944.* Retrieved from the Library of Congress, (www.loc.gov/item/2011585266/) |
| 73T & C | NARA |
| 73B | © Author |
| 74T | NARA |
| 74C | © Author |
| 75 | © IWM H 38270 |
| 76 | © ASM |
| 77C | © IWM H 38244 |
| 77B | © Author |
| 78 | Tudor Barlow (Flickr) |
| 79 | NARA |
| 80 both | NARA |
| 81 | Lt Arthur L Cole/Canada. Department of National Defence/Library and Archives Canada/PA-183899 |
| 82 | Historic England Archive (RAF photography) raf_cpe_uk_1845_v_5021 |
| 83 both | NARA |
| 84 | NARA |
| 85T | © ASM |
| 85B | NARA |
| 86 | NARA |
| 87 | NARA |
| 88 | © ASM |
| 89T | © IWM A 25121 |
| 89B | © IWM A 24923 |
| 90T | Paul Richardson |
| 90B | © IWM T54 |
| 91T | © ASM |
| 91B | © Historic England Archive, based on David Ride sketch map via www.combinedops.com |
| 92L | © Richard Drew |
| 92R | NARA |
| 93 both | NARA |
| 94 | © Colin M Baxter |
| 95T | © Historic England Archive, based on David Moore |
| 95C | © IWM H 35554 |
| 95B | © Historic England Archive, based on David Moore |
| 96C | © Author |
| 96B | © ASM |
| 97 | © ASM |
| 98 | Wellcome Library, London. Wellcome Images images@wellcome.ac.uk http://wellcomeimages.org Aerial view of Netley Hospital. Royal Army Muniment Collection Netley Hospital. CC BY 4.0 |
| 99T | Wellcome Library, London. Wellcome Images images@wellcome.ac.uk http://wellcomeimages.org West Wing, Netley Hospital Photograph Memorabilia of the Royal Victoria Hospital, Netley. CC BY 4.0 |
| 99B | © ASM |
| 100T | © Author |
| 100B | © IWM A 21218 |
| 101 | © ASM |
| 102 | Historic England Archive (RAF photography) raf_cpe_uk_1893_rp_3152 |
| 103 both | NARA |
| 104 | US Army, Admin Order No 7, Operation Overload, South Western Zone, Annex 20 Administrative maps, 10 April 1944, Area L (Sheet 137+144 GSGS Series no 3907) |
| 105 | NARA |
| 106T | Barry at War Group |
| 106B | NARA |
| 108T | © Author |
| 108B | NARA |
| 109T | NARA |
| 109B | © ASM |
| 110BL | © ASM |
| 110BR | NARA |
| 111T | © ASM |
| 111B | © Author |
| 112 both | NARA |
| 113 | Historic England Archive (USAAF photography) us_7ph_gp_loc283_v_5045 |
| 114 | NARA |
| 115T | NARA |
| 115B | © Author |
| 116T | Historic England Archive (USAAF photography) us_7ph_gp_loc90_v_5017 |
| 116B | Author's collection |
| 117C | NARA |
| 117B | Historic England Archive (USAAF photography) us_7ph_gp_loc35_v_5038 |
| 118T | Historic England Archive (USAAF photography) us_7ph_gp_loc234_v_5020 |
| 118B | © IWM CH 12833 |
| 119T | Historic England Archive (USAAF photography) us_7ph_gp_loc97_v_5040 |
| 119B | © Richard Drew |
| 120 | © Adam Forty |
| 121T | Author's collection |
| 121B | © ASM |
| 122 | Historic England Archive (USAAF photography) us_7ph_gp_loc95_v_5025 |

| | |
|---|---|
| 123L | Historic England Archive (RAF photography) raf_cpe_uk_1974_fp_1366 |
| 123R | © ASM |
| 124 both | © Author |
| 125 | Historic England Archive (RAF photography) raf_cpe_uk_1934_rs_4079 |
| 126T | Historic England Archive (RAF photography) raf_cpe_uk_1890_rp_3165 |
| 126–7 | © Author |
| 127 both | © Author |
| 128 | © IWM H 37989 |
| 129T | Historic England Archive (RAF photography) raf_3g_tud_uk_156_v_5173 |
| 129B | © ASM |
| 130C | © ASM |
| 130B | © Robert Liddiard |
| 131 | Historic England Archive (RAF photography) raf_106g_la_23_rp_3003 |
| 132 | Reproduced by courtesy of the Essex Record Office C/W 3/4/9 |
| 133 | Historic England Archive (RAF photography) raf_106g_la_26_rp_3001 |
| 135 both | © Author |
| 136T | © Author |
| 136B | © IWM H 39000 |
| 137 | Historic England Archive (RAF photography) raf_106g_uk_491_v_5064 |
| 138T | NARA |
| 138B | © ASM |
| 139T | © Author |
| 139B | © ASM |
| 140 | © ASM |
| 141T | NARA |
| 141C | © ASM |
| 142 both | NARA |
| 143T | © ASM |
| 143T inset | © Author |
| 143B | NARA |
| 144T | © Jonathan Forty |
| 144C | NARA |
| 144B | © Author |
| 145 | © ASM |
| 146–7 | © ASM |
| 147CL | US Coast Guard |
| 147CR | © Author |
| 147B | © ASM |
| 148 both | © Author |
| 149T | NARA |
| 149B | © Author |
| 150T | Extract of map: Headquarters |

| | |
|---|---|
| | XIX District, US Veterans History Project, and Collector American Folklife Center. *Area 'K': administrative map Operation Overlord South Western Zone, 15 April 1944.* Retrieved from the Library of Congress (www.loc.gov/item/2011585266/) |
| 150B | © ASM |
| 151T | NARA |
| 151B | © ASM |
| 152 | NARA |
| 153 | © ASM |
| 154 both | NARA |
| 155 | NARA |
| 156 | Historic England Archive (RAF photography) raf_106g_uk_1274_v_5073.tif |
| 157T & C | NARA |
| 157B | © Author |
| 158 | NARA |
| 159T & BR | NARA |
| 159BL | US Army, Admin Order No 7, Operation Overload, South Western Zone, Annex 20 Administrative maps, 10 April 1944, extract from Area O (Sheet 143+146 GSGS Series no 3907) |
| 160 | NARA |
| 161 | NARA |
| 162 | Crown Copyright courtesy of Martin Warren |
| 163 | From Center for Air Force History (US) 1992 *Sunday Punch in Normandy* |
| 164 both | NARA |
| 165 | Historic England Archive (USAAF photography) US_7ph_gp_loc209_v_5045 |
| 166 | NARA via ASM |
| 167 both | NARA via ASM |
| 168L | © Author |
| 168R | NARA |
| 169 | NARA via ASM |
| 170 | NARA via ASM |
| 171 | NARA |
| 172 | © IWM FRE 10097 |
| 173T | © Jonathan Forty |
| 173BL | Historic England Archive (RAF photography) raf_cpe_uk_2018_rs_4019 |
| 173BR | © ASM |
| 174T | By Nilfanion (https://commons.wikimedia.org/wiki/File:Memorial_at_RAF_Manston_3.jpg) CC BY-SA 4.0 |

| | |
|---|---|
| 174B | © IWM CH 9822 |
| 175C | NARA via ASM |
| 175B | Historic England Archvie (RAF photography) raf_cpe_uk_2102_rs_4285/4286 |
| 176 | Historic England Archive (USAAF photography) us_7ph_gp_loc178_v_5021 |
| 177 both | © Author |
| 178 | © IWM CH 12255 |
| 179T | Department of National Defence/Library and Archives Canada/PL-30827 |
| 179B | © ASM |
| 180–1 all | © Author |
| 182 | US Navy/US National Archives |
| 183T | © IWM A 20180 |
| 183B | © ASM |
| 184 | NARA |
| 185T | © ASM |
| 185B | NARA via ASM |
| 186T | By Talskiddy at en.wikipedia (https://commons.wikimedia.org/wiki/File:St_eval_memorial.jpg) CC BY 3.0 |
| 186B | © IWM CH 12373 |
| 187 | Historic England Archive (RAF photography) raf_ct_89_541_rs_4020 |
| 188 | NARA via ASM |
| 190 | Crown Copyright courtesy of Martin Warren |
| 191T | © IWM A 27071 |
| 191B | © ASM |
| 192 | © IWM CH 13663 |
| 193 | NARA |
| 194 | © ASM |
| 195T | Historic England Archive (RAF photography) raf_106g_uk_1104_rv_6038 |
| 195B | By Les Chatfield (https://www.flickr.com/photos/61132483@N00/3147524517) CC BY 2.0 |
| 196 | Adrian Muttitt/Alamy Stock Photo |
| 197 | © IWM FL 292 |
| 198 | © ASM |
| 199 | Historic England Archive (RAF photography) raf_106g_uk_1104_rv_6036 |
| 200 | Earth from Space NASA/NSSDCA |
| 201 | © ASM |
| Endpapers | © Historic England Archive |

# Index